ONE LAW FOR ALL?

ONE LAW FOR ALL?

Aboriginal people and criminal law in early South Australia

Alan Pope

Aboriginal Studies Press

First published in 2011
by Aboriginal Studies Press

© Alan Pope 2011

All rights reserved. No part of this book may be reproduced or transmitted in any form or by any means, electronic or mechanical, including photocopying, recording or by any information storage and retrieval system, without prior permission in writing from the publisher. The Australian *Copyright Act 1968* (the Act) allows a maximum of one chapter or 10 per cent of this book, whichever is the greater, to be photocopied by any educational institution for its education purposes provided that the educational institution (or body that administers it) has given a remuneration notice to Copyright Agency Limited (CAL) under the Act.

Aboriginal Studies Press
is the publishing arm of the
Australian Institute of Aboriginal
and Torres Strait Islander Studies.
GPO Box 553, Canberra, ACT 2601
Phone: (61 2) 6246 1183
Fax: (61 2) 6261 4288
Email: asp@aiatsis.gov.au
Web: www.aiatsis.gov.au/asp/welcome.html

National Library of Australia
Cataloguing-In-Publication data:

Author: Pope, Alan (Alan Richard)

Title: One law for all? : Aboriginal people and criminal law in early South Australia / Alan Pope.

ISBN: 9780855757489 (pbk.)

Notes: Includes bibliographical references and index.

Subjects: Criminal law — South Australia. Indigenous peoples — South Australia. Equality before the law — South Australia

Dewey Number: 345.942305

Printed in Australia by Opus Print Group

Map by Brenda Thornley

Cover: 'Wiltjas', 2010, 600x750mm, Acrylic on canvas, © Joyce Walkabout, Iwantja Arts & Crafts

CONTENTS

List of Tables		vi
Preface		vii
Map		x
Chapter 1	*Introduction*	1
Chapter 2	*Legal policy and early practice*	9
Chapter 3	*Amenability and Jurisdiction*	26
Chapter 4	*Admitting Aboriginal evidence*	41
Chapter 5	*Language problems*	56
Chapter 6	*Inter se jurisdiction*	70
Chapter 7	*Murder and manslaughter*	88
Chapter 8	*Assault and Robbery*	105
Chapter 9	*Property offences*	119
Chapter 10	*Protected by the law?*	135
Chapter 11	*Conclusions and observations*	157
Appendix	*Cases involving Aboriginal people*	174
	1836-1862	174
Notes		192
Bibliography		234
Index		243

TABLES

Table 1: Aboriginal people charged with murder of Europeans 1836–1862 — 175

Table 2: Europeans charged with assault against Aboriginal people 1836–1862 — 178

Table 3: *Inter se* murder cases 1836–1862 — 179

Table 4: *Inter se* manslaughter cases 1836–1862 — 182

Table 5: Aboriginal people charged with assault against Europeans 1836–1862 — 182

Table 6: Aboriginal people charged with assault against other Aboriginal people 1846–1860 — 184

Table 7: Aboriginal people charged with theft 1836–1862 — 185

Table 8: Aboriginal people charged with stock theft 1836–1862 — 187

Table 9: Aboriginal people charged with robbery and hut breaking 1836–1862 — 189

Table 10: Aboriginal people charged with stock killing offences 1836–1862 — 191

PREFACE

This book has had a long and somewhat serendipitous gestation. My interest in contact history began when I was a teacher at Port Lincoln High School in the 1980s, teaching History to junior secondary classes which included some Indigenous students. I started researching local archives, and later the Mortlock Library, for information that could enliven and localise my Australian History lessons. Having studied only European and Asian History in an era when Australian History was seen as decidedly 'second class' at Adelaide University, the richness and relevance of this local history was a new discovery to me. My students responded well to the local narratives, especially when linked to fun excursions to nearby sites such as Boston Island. However, it was not until a colleague organised a three-day excursion into central and eastern Eyre Peninsula that the reality of the frontier experience came home to me and to at least some of my students. We visited the ruins of isolated shepherds' huts, scrambled over granite outcrops, walked along dry watercourses below farm dams — and started to get a feel for the fundamental clash over the land and its resources that was inevitably involved in the settlement/invasion of this countryside in the mid nineteenth century.

One experience from that excursion was particularly poignant and prompted me to learn more about the frontier contact experience. It was on a farm near Cleve, where a fifth-generation farmer had agreed to talk to our students about his family's early experiences. He was well educated and had clearly thought about how his inheritance and lifestyle was built at least partly on the dispossession, or worse, of the local Pangkala people. Standing by a small spring-fed waterhole, he attempted to explain the situation and choices that had faced both his ancestor and the Aboriginal people living on this land when all other water sources dried up. This was competition for scarce resources at its most basic — should the waterhole be fenced off and the Aboriginal people driven away so that stock could be watered through the long dry, or did humanity prevail and stock perish as more Aboriginal people came to get water from the diminishing source? Or worse, when Pangkala men started to steal his sheep to provide food for their families would the settler succumb to a more brutal survival instinct and take even more extreme measures against the Aboriginal population in order to avoid bankruptcy? West Coast farmers do not cry but this one's voice wavered with emotion (and the students became quiet) as he explained his ancestor's dilemma. He liked to think that his forebear had not shot or poisoned Aboriginal people, but his family history did record a drought year in which some hard decisions must have been taken to save the farm.

Years later, after I had written *Resistance and Retaliation*, another chance encounter focussed my interest further. I met Rob Foster from Adelaide University and when I said I was interested in looking more closely at the cases where Aboriginal people were brought before the courts, he told me of the existence of the early Supreme Courts records. This rich historical lode was buried in the basement of a city building, with access only available with the permission of the Sheriff of the Supreme Court. Naively, I approached this court official seeking access, beginning a long and unsuccessful correspondence. No doubt fully occupied with his extensive duties, the Sheriff of the day always fobbed me off with some reason why I could not be granted access to the stored records, and every time I suggested how the problem (e.g. inadequate lighting, no desk, Occupational Health and Safety concerns) could be overcome, he would come up with another. To cut a long story short, it was four years before I got access and that was only because, coincidentally, the Supreme Court Library decided to house all of the historical records within its main collection. I was then able to readily gain access to the Criminal Records and the early Judges' Notebooks, simply by explaining my purpose to the Librarian.

I was a part-time researcher and for years I spent my Saturdays in the wonderful old world of the Mortlock Library (this was before some bright bureaucrat thought of raising revenue by stripping it of books and hiring it out for functions). Mortlock staff members were always helpful, knowledgeable and supportive — I thank them all. Some indexing of relevant sources had been done but often it was just a matter of reading every newspaper edition. My problem was not the tedium but the endless distractions and digressions into irrelevant but interesting stories. Thursday evenings were spent in the State Records' Netley

Reading Room, where the archivists were also exceptionally helpful, not to mention patient.

By then I had been accepted by Deakin University as a doctoral candidate, again partly as a result of a chance meeting. I had bumped into the late Alby Jones, a former mentor who had completed his doctoral thesis at seventy-four years of age. He admonished me for never completing a doctorate and made the observation that I should only embark on a PhD in a field about which I was passionate — anything else was a waste of effort. On reflection, I abandoned my education studies and went back to History. This book is based on the research and thesis associated with that study and I gratefully acknowledge the support and encouragement I received over several years from Deakin's David Walker and Jan Critchett. Based in Geelong and Warrnambool respectively, we would meet for lunches at pubs in places like Colac — an unconventional approach to supervision but one that served me well.

I thank Rhonda Black and the staff of Aboriginal Studies Press for their more recent encouragement and support in bringing this book to print. In particular, I thank my editor, Margaret McDonell, who persevered to correct errors and omissions in my manuscript — any remaining are solely down to me.

CHAPTER 1
INTRODUCTION

When South Australia was established in 1836 it was British government policy that Aboriginal people within the colony's boundaries were to be considered as British subjects.[1] This meant that Aboriginal people were to be both subject to English law and entitled to its protection — there was to be 'one law for all' for inhabitants within the new colony. On arriving at Holdfast Bay in December 1836, Governor John Hindmarsh's first proclamation reinforced this policy, stating that Aboriginal people and settlers alike would be held accountable to British law and that settlers would be punished for violent or unjust acts committed against Aboriginal people.[2] This book examines this policy and its implementation, especially how and why it failed to be translated into practice within a colony expected to be more enlightened in its treatment of Aboriginal people than other Australian colonies. The approach adopted here is to provide, in this initial chapter, some contextual background before examining, in chapter 2, the 'one law for all' policy itself in some detail. Rather than describe the events and criminal cases involving Aboriginal people in chronological order, a thematic approach is used to provide the structure of this book. The themes are derived from the issues involved (e.g. admissibility of evidence, interpretation) and also the categories of crime (e.g. murder, property offences). Largely because these various themes and issues are played out by the early 1860s, the scope of this book is restricted to the first twenty-five years of settlement.

By the early 1830s the British colonies of New South Wales and Van Diemen's Land were well established and planning was underway for new colonial ventures. In London, Edward Wakefield and Robert Gouger were publicising their theories of systematic colonisation and lobbying for government approval and private support to put them into practice.[3] When news of Sturt's discovery that the River Murray reached the sea near St Vincent's Gulf arrived in London, the location of this new venture was determined. Not so, however, the nature of the proposed colony. Initially the proposers of this new venture argued for a private colony, but when the Colonial Office's legal adviser, James Stephen, declared their proposal to be 'wild and impractical' they moved to form the South Australian Association and submitted a revised proposal, this time for a chartered colony.[4] However, during the early negotiations between the proposers and the Colonial Office, the promoters were forced to accept that South Australia would need to be established as a Crown colony.[5]

South Australia was meant to be different.[6] It was to have no convicts and to adopt a controlled land distribution system which would avoid the dispersion of settlement, economic stagnation and the evils of land-grant favouritism that had caused problems elsewhere. All land in the colony was to be sold at a fixed minimum price, with most of the funds raised earmarked to ensure a steady supply of willing migrant labourers. South Australia was also to be self-supporting, meeting its establishment costs through land sales. Its promoters hoped that this financial independence would guarantee that it would be more independent than other British colonies, and largely trusted by the Home Government to run its own affairs. To these planned differences was soon to be added another, neither planned for nor welcomed by the entrepreneurs promoting the South Australian venture in the early 1830s. For while they lobbied for approval for a new colony based upon the theory of systematic colonisation, another reform movement also looked towards the colonies — humanitarianism. This movement was to influence the policy on the treatment of Aboriginal people in all Australian colonies in the late 1830s, but particularly so within South Australia. Because it was being deliberately planned as a colony with important differences from other colonies in Australia, South Australia provided an opportunity for those humanitarians who came to positions of power in London in the 1830s to implement their views on the treatment of Aboriginal peoples. Lord Glenelg's appointment to the Colonial Office in early 1835 came just at the time when negotiations were underway regarding the arrangements for the new colony. The fact that the colonial planners and investors needed to gain Crown approval for their venture, and that they were eager to quickly overcome any obstacles, gave Glenelg an opportunity to modify their plans to fit in with humanitarian beliefs.

While the colonial planners and investors might have privately sneered at humanitarian attitudes towards Aboriginal people, they had no choice but to deal with a Colonial Office dominated by officials of a humanitarian bent. Believing that Glenelg's proposals were likely to impede their personal hopes for land speculation on a large scale, the South Australian Commissioners resisted them.[7] In July 1835, the Colonial Office made it clear that the issue of Aboriginal rights must be resolved before the colony could proceed, but it was not until later in the year that the Colonial Office announced the means by which they expected this to be achieved. In the meantime the Commissioners stonewalled, hoping that they could find a way around these demands. But Glenelg persisted, determined to try out a new model for relations with an Aboriginal people faced with British settlement of their territories.[8] He reaffirmed to the Commissioners the then official view on the issue of Aboriginal land rights, arguing that settlement would be confined to 'those limits within which they can show, by some sufficient evidence, that the land is unoccupied and that no earlier and preferable title exists'.[9] The colony would not proceed until assurances were given that Aboriginal land rights would be respected, land would be purchased from Aboriginal people, and that a Protector of Aborigines would oversee Aboriginal interests and all land transactions.[10] The *Letters Patent*, establishing the new colony, would also establish the rights of Aboriginal people,[11] while the Protector of Aborigines would ensure that the requirements of the Colonial Office would be met by both colonial administrators and private settlers. The Colonization Commissioners were unimpressed by these restrictions and set out to minimise the extent to which they would be implemented once the colony was established.

Land was central to the South Australian venture and the threatened appointment of a Protector of Aborigines, with power to control and restrict land sales, was resisted vehemently. Glenelg held firm, however, insisting that the settlement be delayed until it was clear that Aboriginal rights would be protected, placing his hopes for the practical achievement of this in the appointment of the Protector and government control of land settlement. By that stage the planners had little choice but to meet the Colonial Office conditions, given how advanced were their plans for establishing the new colony. If these plans were not to be abandoned the Commissioners would have to at least appear to meet Glenelg's demands. So it was that the Commissioners agreed to avoid selling land clearly occupied by Aboriginal people, to provide them with educational opportunities and to reserve twenty per cent of land in the colony for the benefit of Aboriginal people.[12] Historians generally agree that the Commissioners probably had little or no intention of honouring these promises once the settlers were in South Australia.[13] They soon moved to ensure that all land in the colony would be open for public sale, and to deprive the Protector of any authority over land sales.

Another policy, amalgamation, was also intended to be implemented in South Australia. The view underlying this policy was that clashes between the two separate cultures within the new colony could be avoided by minimising their separateness in the first place. There should be an amalgamation of the two cultures — Aboriginal people were to be assimilated into South Australian society through the agencies of education and conversion. It was recognised that this would be a slow process bound to encounter considerable difficulties. Even so, South Australia was considered an ideal place to implement such a policy, particularly as it was not to be 'tainted' by convicts or ticket-of-leavers.

However, even settlers who accepted the amalgamationist approach would find it difficult to implement and sustain in practice once in the colony. Difficulties abounded: relatively few Aboriginal people were contacted initially, those who were had only selected interest in the newly transplanted culture, very few were interested in abandoning their own beliefs and customs, schools and missionaries reported difficulties and failure in educating Aboriginal young people, and close contact seemed often to lead to a breakdown of friendly relations. Nevertheless, the amalgamation policy underpinned a number of approaches that were given either theoretical support or practical trial in the colony's early years, including creating Aboriginal reserves within or near each town, allocating land from each survey for Aboriginal use, setting aside a percentage of land sales for Aboriginal benefit,[14] establishing schools for young Aboriginal people,[15] and encouraging the employment of Aboriginal people by settlers.[16]

Perhaps the policy with the greatest potential to change the way Aboriginal people and settlers interacted with British law in South Australia was that related to land.[17] The intention of the Colonial Office, enshrined in the *Letters Patent*[18] and accepted by the Commissioners, was that Aboriginal tenure would be recognised through settlers paying for the land.[19] The requirements of this policy were to be met, the Commissioners determined in 1836, through reserving sixteen acres in each eighty acre subdivision for the use and benefit of Aboriginal people. Eventually, they suggested, '20 per cent of all settled land would be held on their behalf, providing both land and income for their support'.[20] Unfortunately, land was also the path to personal fortune for leading colonists and once the colony was established the Commissioners retreated to the protection of the 1834 *South Australia Act*, which admitted no Aboriginal rights in the land.[21]

Some of the colonial planners in the 1830s were of the view that many of the problems encountered in the Australian colonies were associated with uncontrolled expansion of settlement. To avoid problems associated with an unplanned and dispersed frontier, settlement of new areas should be regulated to keep it in step with the growth of the population.[22] Accordingly, a fundamental approach adopted in South Australia was that of concentrating settlement by formally restricting its expansion. Not surprisingly, this was not a popular concept among those intending to emigrate (or indeed to speculate on land). The idea that colonists would have to ignore opportunities outside a prescribed area and that the best land would not be available to those who found it first did not make for an attractive proposition to potential colonists. While the colonial planners had some initial success in moderating this concentration principle, it was one which appealed to key humanitarians in the Colonial Office and so it was retained, with a limit of eight miles from Adelaide set as the boundary of settlement. However, it came under challenge within weeks of the actual landing in the colony.[23] With Light's surveying staff overworked, some land purchasers could not see why they should not simply 'squat' on a favourable site and have the survey catch up with their choice later. This pressure continued when settlers began to make their own private explorations of the territories outside the official limit of settlement. Those whose interests lay more in land speculation than establishing themselves in agricultural enterprise pushed even more forcefully for the restrictions to be dropped.

The concentration principle had considerable implications for colonial Aboriginal policy. If it had been adhered to strictly, it might have meant that most Aboriginal people outside the area of settlement could have continued their traditional lives largely unmolested for several more years than was the case. For those people within the decreed settlement zone, private and government resources might have been more effectively brought to bear to mediate when difficulties arose between settlers and the Aboriginal people. As the settlement expanded later, these resources could have been freed progressively to address the education of Aboriginal people further afield, including about the law and its implications for them. Yet, what was seen by officials as a legitimate tool of a planned colony was regarded merely as a restriction to land-interested colonists — concentration implied congestion and limitation of profits to the latter group. Its abandonment, particularly so early in the life of the colony, was a major factor in the failure of overall Aboriginal policy, including 'one law for all'. With the dispersal of settlement there was a serious loss of official control over race relations, the need to spread limited resources more widely, an increase of frontier contact outside of the view of the law, less likelihood of settlers and Aboriginal people learning each other's language, and a greater incidence of settlers deciding to take the law into their own hands.

Despite South Australia being hailed as a planned colony, very little provision was made for the establishment and operation of a legal system before the settlers actually arrived.[24] John Jeffcott, formerly Chief Justice of Sierra Leone, was appointed to oversee the administration of justice in the colony but delayed his departure until September 1836, and even then found time to break his journey in Hobart, before eventually arriving in April 1837. No magistrate accompanied the settlers and Hindmarsh swore in several colonists as magistrates soon after arriving at Glenelg. The assumption was that English law, its principles and procedures would operate in the colony. When Jeffcott eventually arrived in the colony the Supreme Court had not yet been established and in May 1837 he had to be granted a Special Commission of Gaol Delivery to enable him to try the cases outstanding. At the first sitting of the Grand Jury in May 1837 Jeffcott quickly confirmed that the forms and processes of English law would prevail in the new colony: grand juries were to be the structure used to legitimate prosecutions, all accused would have the right to counsel, and the use of juries would not be bypassed in his court.[25] Before the next sitting of the Court, the *Supreme Court Act*[26] formalised the court structures and defined its powers, which essentially concentrated legal functions into a single colonial court.[27] This Act also established an appeals system, through a Court of Appeals made up of the Council of Government (excluding any legal officials who might have a conflict of interest in matters before it). The intention was that a three-tiered system of justice be established but this soon proved too complex for the requirements of the small colony. Accordingly, the Supreme Court and the Resident Magistrate

Courts took on the bulk of the responsibility, with assistance from rural Justices of the Peace.

South Australian law as it would relate to Aboriginal people was also influenced by precedents and events in the other Australian colonies and so it is worthwhile briefly looking at the situation there. In the early years of New South Wales it was by no means certain that British subjectship was automatic for Aboriginal people and so there were doubts as to whether they were afforded protection under the law.[28] However, with the wider acceptance of New South Wales as a settled colony, Aboriginal people came to be more firmly considered as British subjects and thus amenable to British law.[29] As contact between colonists and Aboriginal people took place, with its attendant violent clashes, the pressures on the policy regarding their legal status acted to restrict the law's application to Aboriginal people. In 1805 Richard Atkins, the New South Wales Deputy Judge Advocate, advised Governor King that he did not believe Aboriginal people could be called on to plead before a court, despite their being 'within the pale of Her Majesty's protection'.[30] Not being amenable to such proceedings, Atkins argued, left only a resort to summary justice when Aboriginal people offended against the law. This remained the situation through Macquarie's administration, notwithstanding his proclamation of May 1816.[31] In 1825 London issued instructions that Aboriginal people should be protected in the enjoyment of their possessions and from violence and injustice.[32] Nevertheless, ambiguity remained and colonial governors had considerable room to interpret what such an instruction meant in practice.

In 1829 a well-known Sydney Aboriginal man was killed by other Aboriginal men in the Domain.[33] One of his alleged killers was arrested and the authorities were faced with the issue of extending British law to cover serious crimes among the Aboriginal people themselves. The Attorney General pondered the jurisdiction issue, referring the case to the Supreme Court for advice. Justices Forbes and Dowling advised that it would be unjust to apply British law in this circumstance.[34] So, despite the official view that Aboriginal people were subject to British law, there were clearly situations in which even the Supreme Court believed this not to be the case. The uncertainties which this apparent conflict caused did not again come to the fore in New South Wales until May 1836, at the same time as the first South Australian colonists were sailing to the new colony. In a trial of two Aboriginal men accused of murdering two other Aboriginal men,[35] in what became known as the

Murrell case, defence counsel questioned the court's jurisdiction over his clients, arguing that the presumption of citizenship could not be made in this case.[36] The Judges over-ruled this objection, stating that in New South Wales Aboriginal people were indeed 'amenable to the laws of the Colony for offences committed within it'.[37]

Despite the strength of this decision, not all of the judiciary agreed with it. When Bonjon came before Justice Willis in Melbourne on September 1841, charged with murder of a fellow Aboriginal man, the issue of jurisdiction once again was queried. Early in the proceedings, Willis stated his view that there was 'no express law which makes the aborigines subject to our Colonial Code'.[38] Perhaps realising that he had little chance of success given the Judge's views, the prosecutor decided not to proceed with the case,[39] thus avoiding a judicial decision contrary to the accepted view. The official position was that the Murrell decision held, but Willis' view struck a chord of agreement among many colonists. To many it hardly seemed practical, wise or expedient to push the influence of British law beyond the boundaries of relations between the two races into the largely unknown territory of Aboriginal customary law. The result was that, in practical terms within all the Australian colonies in the early 1840s, there was a reluctance to involve the courts and the police in dealings between Aboriginal people themselves. The policy might be clear but

> [it] was tempered by practices of non-involvement by law enforcement agencies in disputes between Aborigines, and ways were sought to reduce the impact of non-recognition through non-prosecution and mitigation of sentences.[40]

CHAPTER 2
LEGAL POLICY AND EARLY PRACTICE

The policy regarding the legal status of Aboriginal people at the time of the establishment of South Australia in 1836 is blurred somewhat by the colony's special nature. The 1834 *South Australia Act* enshrined the compromise between the colonial promoters and the Colonial Office,[1] which was determined to play a part in any new colonial venture. After substantial amendment the *South Australia Act* was passed, establishing a colony with a dual power structure. The Governor, responsible to the Colonial Office, would represent the Crown while a Resident Commissioner would act for the Colonization Commission. Accordingly, when looking at the policy regarding the legal status of Aboriginal people within the colony, it is necessary to consider both parties within this colonial power structure.

The Colonization Commission and their Resident Commissioner were concerned with land, labour and profit — humanitarian ideals were of little interest to them. The Commissioners' views on other aspects of the colony, including its legal arrangements, were determined by these three central concerns. When the Commissioners published a pamphlet in December 1835, outlining aspects of the proposed colony,[2] the only mention of Aboriginal people was under the heading of 'Protection of the Colony', meaning protecting the settlers' interests.[3] Their first report, drafted in June 1836 before the arrival of the colonists, included a section entitled 'Treatment of the Aborigines'.[4] This consisted mainly of commentary on a letter from Governor Grey to the Colonization Commissioners, outlining the Home Government's views.[5] The Commissioners put forward their own views on the Aboriginal inhabitants, point by point. First, regarding the requirement that Aboriginal people be protected, the Commissioners argued that the imminent arrival of the colonists would indeed be a benefit to them, as the colonists would displace the 'lawless squatters, the abandoned sailors, the runaway convicts...that now infest the coasts and islands'.[6] Second, regarding the vital requirement that Aboriginal rights to the land be protected, the Commissioners put up no contrary argument. No doubt they preferred to ignore this issue, being well aware that the precedence of the *South Australia Act* would be enough to ensure that it could be ignored once the new colony was settled.[7] Third, concerning the requirement that the Aboriginal people within the colony be introduced to European civilization, the Commissioners accepted some measure of responsibility for the physical and moral care of dispossessed Aboriginal people, by proposing that those in the settled areas would be 'permanently supplied with subsistence, and with moral and religious instruction'.[8] In essence then, the Commissioners' policy regarding the legal status of Aboriginal people was a pragmatic acceptance of the government's direction that they would be British subjects from the outset, subject to and protected by British law. The difference was more a matter of intention, since subsequent events suggest that the Colonization Commissioners had little or no intention of carrying out the spirit of the humanitarian-based aspects of the new colonial venture.

Although the boundaries of the respective authority of the Governor and the Resident Commissioner were to cause problems,[9] in the legal arena they were relatively clear. It was the former's role to 'establish all such Laws...as may be necessary'[10] within the colony, while the latter controlled the sale of lands and the employment of the resulting funds towards emigration.[11] The *Letters Patent*, although drafted by the Colonization Commissioners rather than the Law Officers of the Crown, nevertheless reflected the humanitarian concerns towards the indigenous people which had been insisted upon by the Colonial Office. The final paragraph of the brief document acknowledged the land rights of the Aboriginal people within the new colony:

> PROVIDED ALWAYS that nothing in those our Letters Patent contained shall affect or be construed to affect the rights of any Aboriginal Natives of the said province to the actual occupation or enjoyment in their own persons or in the Persons of their Descendants of any lands therein now actually occupied or enjoyed by such Natives.[12]

This statement would prove to be easily circumvented by reference to the 1834 *South Australia Act* itself, which made no mention of

2. Legal policy and early practice

Aboriginal people at all. Historians have concluded that the statement within the *Letters Patent* was mere window dressing by the Colonization Commissioners, intended to placate the humanitarians rather than be translated into practice.[13]

There was no mention of the law and its proposed operation within the *Letters Patent*, as this aspect of the authority for the colony was left for the resulting Order in Council, issued a few days later.[14] This Order granted colonial officials the power to make laws, appoint officials, constitute courts and impose rates and duties. However, the limitations to this authority were substantial. First, all laws would have to be 'transmitted to His Majesty for His approbation or disallowance, through one of his principal Secretaries of State'. Second, none could be 'contrary or repugnant to any of the provisions' of the *South Australia Act*. Third, all laws, institutions or ordinances would first have to be 'proposed by the said Governor or Officer Administering the Government'. Finally, the Governor and the senior colonial officials must 'conform to all such instructions as His Majesty shall from time to time be pleased to issue'. While this order clearly established the British Government's control over the new colony it also provided the Colonization Commission with a way around the dilemma of the rights to land affirmed within the *Letters Patent* by so strongly stating the supremacy of the 1834 Act.

How British justice would cope with reconciling the interests of an Aboriginal people whose culture was based upon occupation of particular territories, with one whose predominant interest was the acquisition and exploitation of that very land, was not considered in any detail before the colonists set foot in South Australia. One view was that the most practical judicial course for the new colony would be a form of legal separatism, allowing traditional Aboriginal law to coexist with that introduced from England, at least for some time. However, despite its commonsense appeal, such a proposal was doomed in the face of humanitarian influence in the Colonial Office. Once the general policy of amalgamation was accepted, then the legal system could hardly be predicated on separation.

Governor Hindmarsh was at pains to make this policy clear to the colonists before they had any significant contact with the Aboriginal people. Rather than his statement to the assembled colonists on 28 December 1836 being simply a proclamation of the colony, it was but the first in a series of statements of public policy.[15] The Governor confirmed the assumption of British citizenship for Aboriginal people:

> It is also, at this time, especially my duty to apprize the colonists of my resolution, to take every lawful means for extending the same protection to the Native Population as to the rest of His Majesty's Subjects...who are to be considered as much under the safeguard of the law as the Colonists themselves, and equally entitled to the privileges of British subjects.[16]

Colonists' behaviour towards Aboriginal people should reflect this, through the 'exercise of moderation and forbearance by all classes, in their intercourse...'[17] with them. Of course, Hindmarsh's decision to make the legal status of Aboriginal people the subject of his first public pronouncement within the colony may not have been simply based upon a belief that it was of prime importance to the colonial government. Rather, it may have been drafted and delivered more in recognition of the need to reinforce his authority, or even with its subsequent Colonial Office readership in mind. George Fife Angas had expressed much the same sentiment when he spoke at Hindmarsh's farewell dinner in London, giving a speech certainly made with its official audience in mind. He declared that, in South Australia, Aboriginal people would be 'fellow-subjects; under the protection of the same laws; entitled to the same privileges'.[18] Whatever Hindmarsh's motive in making the legal status of Aboriginal people the subject of this first proclamation, it publicly made clear that the official policy from the time that the first settlers were in the colony was to be, as Angas had stated, 'one law for all',[19] with British law taking precedence over the traditional laws of the Aboriginal people.

Although this policy sounded reasonable, it was to face considerable difficulties in implementation, none of which the government seemed to have considered in advance. In reality, Aboriginal people within the colony already had their own systems of laws and would continue to apply them. Additionally, while the Kaurna would quickly come into contact with the colonists, most Aboriginal groups would have little contact with the newcomers for several years at least. And even then, that contact would likely be on the frontier of settlement, inevitably involving clashes between settlers and Aboriginal people who could not be expected to know of the precedence of British law.

The first occasion upon which the Court could make a pronouncement as to the applicability of the law to the Aboriginal population did not involve an Aboriginal person as the accused. Rather, it took place in a case where two colonists appeared, at the very first sitting of the Supreme Court in May 1837, charged with the theft of several spears and waddies from a Kaurna camp. Although the men were acquitted, Judge Jeffcott took the opportunity to make a pronouncement from the Bench:

> They [the Aboriginal people] have been declared British subjects. As such they are entitled to the full protection of British law, and that protection, while I have the honour of filling the situation which His Majesty has been pleased to confer upon me, shall be fully and effectually afforded them. I will go further, and say that any aggression upon the natives, or any infringement of their rights, shall be visited with greater severity of punishment than would similar offences committed upon white men.[20]

In July that year it looked as if the court would have to deal with its first Aboriginal accused, when a settler was killed, allegedly by an Aboriginal person. This first post-settlement[21] killing of an European by an Aboriginal person took place not in Adelaide but at Encounter Bay, but word soon reached the capital that whaler John Driscoll had been murdered.[22] The alleged culprit, Reppindjeri, was arrested by another whaler, and Protector of Aborigines Dr William Wyatt went south to investigate the killing.[23] The Advocate General, Charles Mann, accepted that difficulties would arise over the need to rely upon evidence by Aboriginal people, but nevertheless thought it possible that Reppindjeri may have to face the 'infliction of the highest punishment of the law'[24] if the settlers were to be protected. The report of Wyatt's investigation, completed in September, revealed that Reppindjeri had considerable grounds to plead provocation as Driscoll had apparently molested Reppindjeri's wife.[25] Reppindjeri finally solved the legal problem by escaping from custody in December 1837, never to be seen by settlers again. The problems raised by the case were thus postponed rather than addressed.

The next killing of a settler, namely Enoch Pegler in March 1838, raised greater fears in the Adelaide community. Committed one night by the River Torrens, this crime was initially widely considered to be an unprovoked attack against an innocent colonist. The story soon circulating around town was that Pegler was sleeping off a drinking session on the riverbank when a group of Aboriginal men stabbed him to death. Even those who suspected that Pegler may have done something to provoke them trivialised that provocation by suggesting that he was murdered 'because he had killed some of their dogs'.[26] In fact, his actions had been more severely provocative as it was soon revealed that Pegler had drunkenly intruded into a traditional ceremony that night and, despite being told to leave, 'the deceased wanted to sit down among the natives between a man and a woman'.[27] Whatever the reason, the result was that a group of men surrounded Pegler and one plunged a reed-thin sharpened kangaroo bone twice into his heart. The next day rumour had it that the culprits were travelling north and some colonists wanted to ride after them, armed and ready for revenge. However, the mood calmed when the government interpreter, James Cronk, was told of Pegler's persistent offensive behaviour. Governor Hindmarsh issued a proclamation in an attempt to calm the settlers and warn them against hasty retaliation.[28] No-one was ever charged over Pegler's death.

April 1839 was a major turning point in relations between Aboriginal people and the European settlers. Dwindling traditional food supplies on the plains were taxed beyond their limit as land clearing and stock took their toll. Even so, the Kaurna did not immediately turn to sheep flocks as an alternative food source. Rather, in the autumn of 1839 they approached local shepherds, seeking small supplies of meat, flour or potatoes. Most shepherds were keen to establish close relations with local Aboriginal people, for their own safety and for companionship or sex. One of Osmond Gilles' shepherds, William Duffield, encouraged Kaurna men to walk with him while he tended his flock, both for company and to learn their language. On 21 April 1839 some of the men asked for rations again, but this time they were not willing to accept a refusal. When Duffield denied the men's request for food he was struck down from behind. The elderly shepherd awoke some minutes later to find himself pinned to the ground by two men while another inserted a long sliver of bone upwards beneath his ribs. Duffield lived for several days, remaining conscious long enough to describe the men who had attacked him. The main distinguishing feature in his description was neither their size nor facial features but rather that the three men 'had two dogs with them, one a red dog with a white tip to his tail, the other was a smaller one and black'.[29] With little more than this to go on, a party led by the Deputy Storekeeper Williams and Police Inspector Inman set out after the killers. Anger and fear again came to the surface in Adelaide and there was much talk of revenge against the men responsible for the murder. Meetings and informal gatherings were held about the town in the days after Duffield's death. Fears were held that this was the beginning of an organised campaign of resistance against the white invaders. There were calls for swift action against the Kaurna and some Adelaide residents plotted their own unofficial retaliation for this crime.[30]

One of the circulating rumours turned out to be true when it became known that a shepherd on John Hallett's property, James Thompson, had been killed in the last week of April. This crime was not reported until the Inman–Williams party, in pursuit of Duffield's killers, reached the area. Near the Para River they encountered a small group of Aboriginal people and engaged them in conversation via the Aboriginal interpreters accompanying the party. Among this group were Picha Cud Nacha, Wang Nucha and Tippa Warricha, whom Inman suspected were Thompson's killers. After dark, Inman and Williams returned to the riverside camp and arrested the three men.[31] News of Thompson's murder further fuelled 'excitement among all classes of the settlers',[32] and there was much talk of forming vigilante parties to take summary revenge on any Aboriginal people found near the scene of the crimes. But cooler heads prevailed and a more peaceful form of tension release was adopted — the issue was debated at length at several public meetings. Scapegoats for what was then the obvious decline in race relations were sought and publicly castigated — Dr Wyatt in particular was criticised for his handling of the Protector's portfolio. Acting Governor Stephen attempted to defend the Protector but his opponents were so many that his speech 'was rendered inaudible by hissing, groaning, cries of "question", and great laughter by the meeting'.[33] Governor Gawler later attempted to defuse the tense situation, arguing for a more rational view: 'Every town in England has its desperate and worthless characters; why should we expect less from native tribes in South Australia?'[34] The early arrest of several men for both the Duffield and Thompson murders forestalled any planned retaliatory actions by settlers.

There was no doubt that English law would be applied to the Aboriginal people involved, since Gawler had only recently reaffirmed the official policy that they were to be considered under British law, through an instruction to the Chief Justice:

> The Aborigines have been brought under British laws. To the utmost of my power, when they are guilty of crimes, I will not, from any mistaken sympathy towards them, suffer those laws to be evaded.[35]

This approach was widely considered to be not only correct in policy but also the best practical course for the colony. Bringing Aboriginal offenders before the courts was, as the *Southern Australian* argued, in their own long-term interests:

> the surest way to protect them, is to instil into their minds the knowledge of right and wrong, and thereby prevent the commission of acts which, if persisted in, will inevitably produce retaliation the most deadly and calamitous.[36]

The two trials were held late in May 1839 with that of Yerricha, Monichi and Parlobooka for the murder of Duffield coming up first. Addressing the assembled members of the Grand Jury, Chief Justice Cooper reminded them that the accused were subject to British law and would be tried 'by the principles of strict justice — without, I hope, prejudice or partiality'.[37] The local press had already all but condemned the six men facing trial, with the editor of the *Southern Australian* even going so far as to express the hope that 'no silly flaws in the indictments, or other legal objections'[38] would interfere with a swift conviction. Cooper was then confronted with the realities of Aboriginal people appearing before him. Being unable to take the oath, the accused were to be denied the right to give evidence even if there was an adequate interpreter available.

It soon became clear that the evidence against the three accused of Duffield's murder was 'almost all circumstantial'.[39] There were three problems with this evidence, raising doubts which could not be easily dismissed. First, there was the matter of the identification of those involved. Duffield, who had been able to give a deposition during his week-long ordeal, died before the accused could be brought before him. Therefore, under British law no positive identification had been made. At that point, Duffield's description of the dogs accompanying the killers became vital evidence in the case, but it was clearly evidence which would have been given little credence in an English court. Charles Mann, defending the accused men at the committal hearing, 'contended that the whole evidence against Yerricha was the circumstance of the dogs: and yet these dogs did not correspond with the description given of them'.[40] Second, Mann pointed out that Yerricha had only one eye, a particularly noticeable identifying feature 'which would be instantly observed, but no notice of any man having only one eye is taken in Duffel's [sic] declaration'.[41] Third, there was the weapon itself, a thin sliver of bone. It was confidently exhibited in court by the prosecutor, who conveniently played upon European notions that such a secretive killing method was treacherous and uncivilised. In fact, the exhibit was merely one that suited the wound, probably originally tendered only to illustrate the method of death. There was considerable doubt that it had ever been in the hands of the accused and Mann quickly seized upon this point, noting that it was found 'in the wallet of another native altogether'.[42] Indeed, it had been taken from a woman some miles from the scene of the crime and had no connection to the accused. Nevertheless, the defence was unable to overcome the obstacle of Yerricha's admission that he was present when Duffield was struck down. Many colonists were convinced that this made him at the very least an accomplice to the crime and they felt that this was enough to justify his conviction. It was widely argued that this was no time for the niceties of British justice, especially for Aboriginal people involved in violence against settlers. Chief Justice Cooper saw the evidence somewhat differently. Yerricha's admission only placed him at the scene of the killing and Cooper noted that, while being present alone was not enough to convict, 'so many corroborative circumstances occurred as satisfactorily to establish the prisoner's guilt'.[43] Found guilty, Yerricha was sentenced to death while Monichi and Parlobooka were acquitted.

The trial of the men accused of Thompson's murder took place the following day and also took little time to be decided. This trial was less complex and there were fewer obvious inconsistencies in the evidence, although the accused once again seemed to have little idea of the real nature of the proceedings. Picha and Tippa were acquitted but Wang Nacha was found guilty and sentenced to be hanged. Cooper attempted to communicate effectively with the accused but found the task difficult.[44] He was not able to adequately explain to the two discharged men just why they were being set free while their companion was taken back to gaol. Indeed, Cooper was bothered by the defendants' apparent lack of understanding of the process used within both the trials. During his sentencing remarks Cooper also voiced his concern that Aboriginal people were ignorant of the laws that they were at that time required to obey. It was necessary, he argued, 'that every one in the province, both the white men and the black men, should know the rules of the law'[45] and was clear that the responsibility for this education was with the Protector of Aborigines.[46] On 31 May 1839, Yerricha and Wang Nucha were brought from the cells in a cart to where a 'scaffold had been erected in front of the iron stores on the Park Land, North Adelaide'.[47]

Aboriginal people living in and around the town had been told of the event and encouraged to attend, the Governor being determined to gain the maximum deterrent effect from this first execution of Aboriginal offenders.

The 'one law for all' policy was again tested in the following year, when the brig *Maria* struck a reef off the south-east coast. The passengers and crew reached the shore safely and soon met up with members of the Milmenrura clan. Promising payment to their guides, the shipwrecked party set off on the long walk to Adelaide. However, something went horribly wrong and all twenty-six crew and passengers were killed by their guides, with their bodies being dismembered and strewn about the beach.[48] When news of this massacre reached Adelaide, Captain Pullen was sent to investigate. His report was considered by the Council of Government, who took legal advice from Chief Justice Cooper and Advocate General Hanson. Acting on their advice that the killings had taken place 'beyond the reach of British law',[49] Governor Gawler instructed the Police Commissioner, O'Halloran, to 'apprehend and bring to summary justice, the ringleaders in the murder, or any of the murderers (in all not to exceed three)'.[50] Two Milmenrura men incautious enough to run from O'Halloran's troopers were shot and left to die and two others, Mongarawata and Moorcangua, were summarily tried and crudely hanged on a Coorong beach.[51] As the Police Commissioner later reported:

> Having formally and deliberately investigated into every particular relative to the murders, in the presence of those of my own party off duty, the Encounter Bay blacks and the prisoners; and finding that neither of the culprits denied, though they would not actually confess their guilt, I proceeded to pass sentence of death upon them, by virtue of the authority and instructions received from your Excellency, for the guilt of these men was fully and clearly established by the united testimony of their tribe present.[52]

The decision to mount a military-style expedition to exact summary justice rather than deal with the ringleaders through due process of the law was not taken lightly. The Council of Government met on 12 August 1840 and the Chief Justice was asked to provide advice and a legal opinion.[53] Cooper's reply that day was a vital one: it would influence how he would deal with many of the Aboriginal offenders who would appear before him during the coming years.[54] For, instead of standing firm on his earlier view that all Aboriginal people were to be treated as British subjects, he offered a way out for the officials facing angry public demands for decisive action against the Milmenrura:

> I beg to state my opinion that the law cannot be brought to take effect at all under the circumstance referred to. I feel it impossible to try according to the forms of English Law people of a wild and savage tribe whose country, although within the limits of the Province of South Australia, have never been occupied by Settlers, who have never submitted themselves to our dominion, and between whom and the Colonists, there has been no social intercourse.[55]

The action against the Milmenrura was a military one and it can be argued that it was legal under martial law,[56] but what is of more concern here is the extent to which the policy regarding the legal status of Aboriginal people was modified by this martial action, regardless of whether it was conveniently deemed to be of a military nature against a 'hostile tribe'.[57] In taking the decision to act against the perpetrators of an admittedly horrific crime, the Council of Government did not foresee the criticism and difficulties that their decision would provoke. They probably even expected widespread support for their decisive action and felt that they would be able to exempt this incident from the more general policy relating to the legal status of Aboriginal people.

However, personal and political rivalries, along with continuing humanitarian views among some influential settlers, soon ensured otherwise. George Stevenson, editor of the *Register* and no friend to Gawler and his administration, mounted a campaign against the martial action. He demanded an explanation of the resort to summary justice and queried whether the better course would have been to have 'exhibited our own respect for human life, and only taken that of the murderers after a solemn trial, and after solemn conviction?'[58] Despite his confidence that public opinion was with him in this matter, Gawler was forced on to the defensive. He made the mistake of taking on the press, directing that the *Government Gazette* enter the debate.[59] This served only to fuel the fire of criticism emanating from the *Register* and *Chronicle*. The *Register* editorialised:

> The natives have been condemned and executed, not merely by an unauthorised, illegal, and unconstitutional tribunal, but upon evidence, which in a court either civil or military would not be sufficient to hang a dog.[60]

The administration did receive considerable public and some editorial support in this affair, the latter principally being from the *Southern Australian*.[61] While many colonists, including some of substantial influence within the colony, supported Gawler's contention that he was merely applying an 'energetic' approach designed to keep 'the administration of justice...in the hands of the government',[62] he alienated important allies and provided substantial ammunition for his enemies.[63] Gawler's arguments in defence of the summary action were detailed at a meeting of the Council of Government in mid September.[64] Smillie, the Advocate General, had been instructed to prepare a legal argument in support of the action and at this meeting he forcefully presented his interpretation of events and related policy.

These arguments, while they failed to quieten the critics, are important as they served to further define the policy as to the legal status of Aboriginal people within the colony.[65] The first strand of this argument centred on the issue of subjectship and its corollary, Aboriginal amenability to the law. The Governor pointed out that, at its meeting on 12 August, the Council of Government had found that the Milmenrura were in fact beyond 'the reach of ordinary British law'.[66] This being so, Gawler argued, he was entitled to consider 'the district in question as in a disturbed state, and of proceeding on the principles of martial law'.[67] Indeed, the Advocate General added, the threat had been substantial and more in the nature of an external threat than that of individuals flouting the law. It was more a matter of 'a whole hostile tribe, that is of a *nation at enmity with her Majesty's Subjects*'.[68] Second, it was argued that there was a limitation implicit within the established policy, namely that it applied only to those Aboriginal people living within the settled districts. Although this view was related to Cooper's notion of limited jurisdiction, it went further than that.[69] Smillie's view was that British subjectship, and its attendant rights under the law, did not apply to Aboriginal peoples in distant, unsettled parts of the colony. The government's view of the policy regarding the legal status of Aboriginal people was, he argued, more restricted than had been hitherto commonly thought. It could not

> be received without modification...it would be assuming too much, to hold that the same maxims and principles must be applied without modification to distant tribes, inhabiting a territory beyond the limits of our settlements, with whom we

have never communicated under friendly circumstances, whose language is equally unknown to us as ours is to them, and who betray, in all their intercourse with Europeans, the most savage and brutal hostility — who have never acknowledged subjection to any power.[70]

Third, it was also argued by the Advocate General that in practical terms the court could not have adequately dealt with the charges against the Milmenrura offenders.[71] The only surviving witnesses to the mass murder were Aboriginal people, none of whom were eligible to give evidence to a court as they could not take the oath.[72] Many colonists, including the Protector of Aborigines, agreed that in practical terms the courts could not have dealt with alleged offenders.[73] The Advocate General stated that, while he was convinced they were morally guilty, the circumstances and evidence were 'not of a nature which was capable of trial by jury, or which could have led to a conviction'.[74] Fourth, although the Governor himself did not go this far, there was the argument that the Milmenrura simply had to be taught a lesson in power. As Smillie bluntly put it: 'measures summary and severe were adopted to terrify the whole tribe by a sense of our power and determination to punish'.[75] This lesson, he argued, could have legally gone much further than it did, even to the extent of inflicting 'an indiscriminate slaughter among the tribe'.[76]

In the press, two clear views then emerged. The *Register* maintained the view that Aboriginal people were all declared British subjects through the proclamation of 28 December 1836.[77] Its editor, Stevenson, was in a position to know the intent of that proclamation since, as the Governor's Private Secretary at the time, he was instrumental in its drafting. However, the *Southern Australian* followed the Advocate General's line of argument, suggesting that the intention was not to declare all Aboriginal people within the boundaries of the new colony immediately to be subjects, but rather that this right was to be earned, as Aboriginal groups 'came into contact with the settlers and showed, by their friendly disposition, their implied agreement to be bound by British laws'.[78] Having defended his actions in taking the path of martial law, Governor Gawler reaffirmed his intention to bring both Aboriginal and European offenders to 'formal and condign punishment'.[79] When public criticism of his actions continued, despite the publication of his and the Advocate General's justificatory arguments, Gawler decided to call the bluff of his critics. At the end of September, again at a meeting of the Council of Government, he defiantly and somewhat petulantly declared:

> If it really be the fact, which I believe it is not, that the great mass of respectable and intelligent colonists are desirous that in cases of ferocious aggression the native tribes located beyond the limits of our settled districts should be treated as possessing the rights and privileges of British subjects, I may think it desirable to let the colony reap the fruits of such a system, whatever they may be.[80]

Nevertheless, the criticism of Gawler and Police Commissioner O'Halloran continued. While Gawler's recall in May 1841 was mainly attributed to his management of the colony's finances, there can be little doubt that the action against the Milmenrura had also served to undermine his reputation in London.[81]

There, the Colonial Office had sought a legal opinion on the Council of Government's reaction to the killing of the *Maria* survivors. The Law Officers of the Crown were in no doubt about the legal status of Aboriginal people within the colony or the jurisdiction of the colony's courts, and they advised that the proper practice was to bring the captured offenders to trial and that 'the summary execution of the supposed murderers was contrary to law; that the legal character of the Act, was murder'.[82] Accordingly, they further advised, O'Halloran and Gawler may have needed to be indemnified against any resulting prosecution, although it was later decided not to proceed to indemnify them until and unless a prosecution was mounted against any of the officials involved.[83] Given the considerable support within the colony for Governor Gawler's handling of the affair and the fact that it was grounded in advice from the Chief Justice, this was most unlikely. Few colonists believed that the law could have effectively dealt with the offenders, had they been arrested and brought before the court. Some, such as Tolmer, took a stronger line of argument, suggesting that the summary trial and execution of Mongarawata and Moorcangua was a pointer to the most effective way of dealing with Aboriginal opposition or violence within the colony.[84]

During 1841, clans along the Murray and Darling Rivers took action to impede the progress of overlanders moving stock from New South Wales into the new colony.[85] In April that year a party of overlanders, led by Inman and Field, was attacked on the Murrumbidgee and, several days later, defeated by a large Aboriginal force at the Rufus River crossing. When news of the attack reached Adelaide several graziers lobbied the Governor to take immediate action to protect this and other parties moving down the Murray.[86] However, by then cautious after the experiences of 1840, Gawler was not sure that protection of overlanding parties was a government responsibility. O'Halloran was sent to offer limited police assistance,[87] but before he and his party reached the scene Gawler ordered their return, apparently not wanting the police to clash with the Aboriginal people when 'the rescue of the sheep was the only object to be gained'.[88] Meanwhile, Field had organised a private party to recover the lost sheep. On 12 May this party encountered several hundred Aboriginal people and another clash took place, in which Field was wounded and two horses killed.[89] Pressure on the government to intervene increased but by then Gawler had been recalled. His successor, Grey, was called on to take 'prompt measures to protect the parties'[90] on the overland trail. Although also cautious about intervening, Governor Grey reluctantly agreed to send out a joint civilian–police party. Caught between maintaining the support of powerful land-holders in the colony and protecting his reputation at the Colonial Office, Grey recorded his reluctance at the Council of Government meeting of 10 July:

> The Aborigines of this country, as well as the settlers, are subjects of the Queen…It is therefore my duty, as well as that of the Council, to do our utmost to protect the Aborigines as well as the Settlers, and we should allow no circumstances whatever, to excite in our breasts a desire for revenge. We must, acting in the position in which we are placed, be dead to such feelings.
>
> I can, therefore, never sanction any mode of punishment which may involve alike the innocent and the guilty, men, women, and children in its consequences, and as I cannot in the present position of affairs see what might be the result of placing arms and ammunition in the hands of 18 persons, with whose disposition, degree of discipline, and feeling towards the natives, I am utterly unacquainted, I entertain a decided objection to pursuing this course.[91]

Nevertheless, he was persuaded to approve the expedition but was careful to protect himself by sending frequent reports to London detailing his proposed actions[92] and assuring the Colonial Office, in a reference to the *Maria* incident, that the policy being adopted was 'extremely different from that which has, on another occasion, been pursued in this province'.[93]

When it arrived in the area, this party found the sheep 'slaughtered… their carcases and bones thrown about in vast heaps'.[94] On 22 June 1841 the expedition came across an overdue party led by Langhorne, by then 'in the most wretched and deplorable state imaginable'[95] as they had lost four men, with several wounded, in a recent attack. O'Halloran and Tolmer searched for the culprits but were soon forced to retire to Adelaide, having managed to capture only a few women and children. On the last day of July 1841 Sub-Inspector Shaw, Protector Moorhouse, fifteen police and twelve civilians left Adelaide for the Murray.[96] Grey was determined to provide this party with instructions clear enough to avoid a repeat of the *Maria* reprisals, and so directed that 'the Aborigines are subject to the Queen, and that belligerent rights cannot be exercised against them'.[97] At the Rufus River, this party met up with another overlanding group, just as they were about to confront the resisting clans. In the resulting clash, superior firepower soon claimed fifteen victims, five fatally. Caught in crossfire, the Aboriginal people fled, some into the scrub and 'about fifty into the water, with the intention of concealing themselves in the reeds'.[98] For about fifteen minutes, the police and civilians sought out the hidden warriors, shooting them as they were discovered amongst the reeds. This action, led to the 'death of nearly thirty, about ten wounded'.[99]

To liberal-minded colonists this was little more than another massacre, given the stated policy regarding the status of Aboriginal people within the law. The subsequent public criticism (and perhaps his own doubts and desire to cover his own back) led Governor Grey to appoint an Enquiry of Magistrates to investigate the events on the Rufus River. The *Register*, describing the final encounter as a 'butchery of the blacks on the Rufus',[100] fell just short of demanding Moorhouse's resignation but argued that morally he had forfeited the right to be called 'Protector'.[101] Once again, editorial opinion split into two camps as the *Southern Australian* came to Moorhouse's defence, along with the *Adelaide Examiner*, which went so far as to portray the events as a 'gallant affair…in which a band of brave men'[102] had overcome great odds. The official inquiry into the incident accepted the Protector's explanations, concluding that the 'conduct of Mr Moorhouse and his party was justifiable, indeed unavoidable under the circumstances they were placed in'.[103]

2. Legal policy and early practice

The two summary actions against Aboriginal people, at the Rufus and on the Coorong, are significant events in the general history of race relations in South Australia, and even more so in the more specific history of the interaction between Aboriginal people and the law. The *Maria* aftermath and the final Rufus clash had much in common: both are cases where the policy that Aboriginal people were equal before the law was circumvented; both occurred in an atmosphere of passion aroused by prior killing and mutilation of Europeans by Aboriginal people; both involved participants and officials in justifications of their actions; and both had a profound effect on the government officials involved, including the Chief Justice and the Protector of Aborigines. These two quasi-military actions, within five years of settlement, threatened to subvert the policy of Aboriginal people being equal before the law. Ironically, however, these two events also strengthened the determination of two key officials to make that same policy work in practice. Cooper's strict approach to the issue of his court's jurisdiction over Aboriginal people (see chapter 3) can be traced to his role in the 1840 *Maria* executions. Similarly, Moorhouse's determined efforts in the 1840s and 1850s to bring Europeans who killed Aboriginal people to justice (see chapter 10) may be linked to his feelings of remorse and guilt over his failure to intervene to stop the slaughter of the Aboriginal people at Rufus River in August 1841.

CHAPTER 3

AMENABILITY AND JURISDICTION

Despite clear policy directions to the contrary, Chief Justice Cooper was not convinced that all Aboriginal people in the colony had automatically come within the jurisdiction of British law on settlement. In Cooper's opinion there were several factors which needed to be considered in cases involving Aboriginal people. First, were the accused aware of the fact that they had now came under British laws? If so, then they were clearly subject to them but, if not, Cooper found it difficult to accept that he had jurisdiction over them. In practice, this awareness criterion for eligibility was determined by Cooper's own test, initially based on whether the group to which the accused belonged had been in contact with Europeans for a reasonable time prior to the alleged offence. Second, despite a clear precedent being set by the New South Wales Supreme Court in 1836 in the Murrell case,[1] Cooper still had doubts about the application of British law in cases involving offences committed by Aboriginal people upon other Aboriginal people (i.e. *inter se*, between themselves). Third, Cooper did not believe that a person could be called upon to give evidence if he or she did not understand the nature of the oath. Fourth, there were problems associated with cases where a person had insufficient knowledge of English to be able to understand the court processes and no competent interpreter was available. It is the first of these issues, revolving around the issue of amenability to British justice and the consequent jurisdiction of the courts, that is considered in this chapter, with the other three issues being addressed in the following chapters.

Cooper's interpretation of the jurisdiction issue was not unreasonable or without logic. Certainly, in 1837 the House of Commons Select Committee on Aborigines had reiterated the view that Aboriginal people within the colonies had the same legal rights as colonists,[2] and Lord Glenelg had reinforced this in a directive to NSW Governor Bourke:

3. Amenability and jurisdiction

> Your commission as Governor of New South Wales asserts Her Majesty's sovereignty over every part of the continent of New Holland, which is not embraced in the colonies of western or southern Australia. Hence I conceive it follows that all the natives inhabiting these territories must be considered as subjects of the Queen.[3]

Even so, some ambiguity remained, particularly in the absence of a similar specific directive to the South Australian Governor. Were all Aboriginal people within South Australia amenable to, and protected by, British law at all times, from the very commencement of the colony? Or were there certain exceptional circumstances which could serve to modify this general policy as it was translated into practice? The 1837 Select Committee acknowledged that the situation was often not clear-cut, noting that even within a colony's declared boundaries problems could arise. In the frontier districts Aboriginal people could find themselves subject to laws of which they were not only ignorant but 'the whole spirit and principles of which are foreign to their modes of thought and action'.[4]

The Chief Justice's continuing doubts about his court's jurisdiction over Aboriginal people should not be seen as those of a maverick, out of touch with widely accepted legal and public opinion. Indeed, he was in good company in his interpretation of how British justice should be applied to Aboriginal people in the reality of the colony. At Port Phillip, when Bonjon came before Justice Willis in 1841, that judge argued that there was 'no express law which makes the aborigines subject to our Colonial Code'.[5] In Western Australia Governor Hutt had similar reservations about the applicability of British law to all Aboriginal people.[6] And there were, well into the 1850s, many supporters of the view that British law should ignore any transgressions among Aboriginal people, particularly if they were committed out of sight of sensitive colonial eyes. After the *Maria* debacle even Grey[7] moderated his earlier support of a strict policy of applying British law in all cases, latterly arguing in the Council of Government that the policy that Aboriginal people were always to be treated as British subjects could not 'be received without modification'.[8] British citizenship and its attendant amenability to British law should only be, Grey then argued, 'conferred on the natives as a boon and not as a right, in the rate and degree to which they would be beneficial to the natives...and not all at once'.[9]

Within a matter of months of making this statement, Grey succeeded Gawler and was installed as Governor; he was then able to better influence the implementation of the official policy.[10] Although Grey and Cooper were not completely in accord on the question of jurisdiction over Aboriginal people, their differences were relatively minor. The Chief Justice, rather than being persuaded to bring his view more closely into line with official policy, was probably encouraged in his flexible interpretation regarding amenability when the governorship changed hands in May 1841. From the time of his arrival, and particularly after his advice to the Council of Government on the proposed action against the Milmenrura clan in 1840, Cooper attempted to maintain a consistent line on the issue of jurisdiction over Aboriginal people, namely that 'only of the native population as have in some degree acquiesced in our dominion can be considered subject to our laws'.[11] Having declared the Milmenrura, so obviously living within the boundaries of the colony, to be outside of the reach of normal legal processes, the only logical line for Cooper to take was that other Aboriginal people within the colony could also be declared to be outside of his court's jurisdiction. The fact that the 1840 exclusion was made to support the use of martial law against Aboriginal people, while any later exclusions would be made in the interests of the Aboriginal people, did not present a difficulty for Cooper's position on jurisdiction.

Cooper did not believe that Aboriginal people would stay outside the jurisdiction of the courts in the longer term. Rather, as settlement advanced and Europeans and their institutions became established within a district, so amenability to British law would follow automatically for the district's Aboriginal inhabitants. To Cooper the process through which Aboriginal people would become fully amenable to British law was education. When sentencing Yerricha and Wang Nucha to death in May 1839, he placed the responsibility for such education at the feet of the Protector of Aborigines, expressing his hope that the Protector would 'make known to the other natives the cause of this unfortunate man's death, that it may be a warning to all of them'.[12] In the 1840s Moorhouse conscientiously attempted to do this but with limited success. Returning from a visit to the Mid-North district in 1842, he reported that Aboriginal people in the district '...fully understand when they are doing wrong, tendering themselves subject to our laws [and]... are conscious that they deserve punishment for attacks'.[13] Grey ordered that Moorhouse's report be published, noting on the docket that: 'it

3. Amenability and jurisdiction

establishes a fact very important just now, that the natives to the north, do not ignorantly violate the law — they will I think learn to restrain their longings'.[14]

The problem was, of course, that the Protector needed to perform this task over and again as the frontiers of the colony expanded, a process which continued into the 1860s. During the 1850s, in more outlying areas, this process was to be repeated many times, although by then the task was delegated to local officials who were assigned responsibilities as the local Sub-Protector of Aborigines. For example, in 1854 Sub-Protector Murray made it his theme at a ration issue on the west coast:

> I made it my care to impress upon their minds, and upon the minds of those present at the full moon distribution of flour, that not only was stealing a crime punishable by law, but receiving what was stolen was equally so: of the former they were fully aware, but had a very indistinct conception of the latter.[15]

The difficulty was one of resources: the Protector and his subordinates could not hope to meet this demanding educational role in pace with the advance of the settlers once the policy of containment was abandoned. Despite their efforts, many Aboriginal people in the colony were left to learn about European law through the lessons of bitter experience.

Lawyers appointed to represent Aboriginal people in court proceedings[16] needed little encouragement to raise the issue of jurisdiction, particular as they were well aware of Cooper's views. Although ignorance was no defence under British law these lawyers argued for Aboriginal people to be made exceptions, especially where they could produce evidence that their clients had little or no prior contact with Europeans. It soon became accepted practice that the courts would be less strict in their application of the law in minor cases involving Aboriginal people whose contact with Europeans had been minimal at the time of the offence. In cases involving more serious charges a conviction was likely to be recorded but often Cooper would recommend 'leniency after conviction where an offender had not known that the British law had effect'.[17] However, the test to ascertain this state of knowledge remained fairly strict. In 1842, for example, when Katamio was charged with stealing a calf from a newly established property north of Adelaide it was argued unsuccessfully in his defence that he did not understand the concept of theft, such was his limited contact with Europeans.[18] This case served to make clear what was meant by 'prior contact', as the argument of Katamio's counsel was rejected on the grounds that Europeans had been in the district for some months. By 1842, it was clear that Cooper considered that Aboriginal offences could be mitigated by ignorance only in the initial weeks of contact. In this case, Katamio was convicted of theft and sentenced to be transported for ten years.[19]

In November 1846 Cooper presided over the first *inter se* case,[20] involving a charge of murder against an Aboriginal male known only as 'Larry', who was indicted for the killing of another Aboriginal man, Rallooloolyoo.[21] Defence counsel Bartley argued that his client knew nothing of British laws and therefore owed no allegiance to them. Accordingly, he argued, 'Larry' could not be held to account for an apparent transgression against those laws. The case was complicated by the fact that no-one had yet managed to communicate effectively with 'Larry', including his lawyer. When asked to plead on behalf of his client, Bartley, knowing that Cooper was in the midst of a debate with government officials on the jurisdiction issue, submitted

> that the prisoner owed no allegiance to British laws. That we had only set ourselves down in this country. His offence might be punishable or might not by the laws of his own people, and were we to try him, he might be subject to a second trial by them. This was not a conquered country, nor was there any law, by which we, coming into it, could, without the consent of the natives, try offences among them.[22]

But the Chief Justice was one logical step ahead of the defence counsel. He prevented Bartley from expanding on this point by ruling that counsel was attempting to argue the case before a plea had been made. Bartley then proceeded to submit a 'not guilty' plea but again the judge refused to hear him. He was not, Cooper then stated, about to hear a plea put by a lawyer who had obviously been unable to receive instructions from his client. Whatever Bartley had to say it could not be, the Chief Justice bluntly pointed out, 'considered the pleas of the prisoner, who cannot even communicate with you. If I could receive a plea, I could try him'.[23] 'Larry' was at that point, technically at least, unrepresented before the court, a situation which the Chief Justice was not about to allow. Accordingly he remanded 'Larry' to the next sessions, recording in his notebook that 'the Plea cannot be rcd. — there is no person legally representing him'.[24] When no-one was able to communicate with 'Larry' when he appeared again in March 1847, Cooper dismissed the case.[25]

3. Amenability and jurisdiction

Official attempts to dissuade Cooper from ruling any further Aboriginal people to be outside of his court's jurisdiction had been neatly sidestepped by a determined Chief Justice unwilling to abandon a principle he had maintained since his arrival in the colony.

Aboriginal people's lack of knowledge about British law and its operation manifested itself in various ways. For the courts, it was not just a matter of determining whether an Aboriginal person understood the primacy of British law but also whether he or she understood processes associated with and based upon the common law of England, such as arrest. Without a reasonable period of prior contact with Europeans, could Aboriginal people be held legally accountable for actions which would otherwise clearly amount to resisting arrest? Some colonists believed that such legal distinctions should be abandoned in the name of pragmatism: in their view Aboriginal people could not be exempt from a law simply because they could not comprehend the processes involved. A more liberal interpretation, as Police Commissioner Finniss argued, would 'deprive settlers in new Colonies, and in the remote districts, of the protection of the law'.[26]

In 1846 a clash took place in the Adelaide Hills between a joint police–civilian party and two Aboriginal men. One of the latter, Mantyeuldi, having seen his companion struck down by a fatal sword blow, resisted when Corporal Rose attempted to arrest him. After thrusting a spear into the constable's arm Mantyeuldi fled, but was captured soon after and charged with malicious wounding. Brought before Cooper in early June, Mantyeuldi was released without penalty after the Chief Justice determined his actions to be reasonable in the circumstances.[27] The question was, Cooper instructed the Grand Jury, not just whether Mantyeuldi understood that Rose and Mulharan were police officers but whether he knew enough about European ways to comprehend that he was being arrested. It was, Cooper pointed out:

> one of those cases where it was difficult to apply English law to untutored natives. Should the difficulty prove to be in favor of the native, he ought to have the favor; as the natives are amenable to our laws, so they were entitled to any benefit arising from them.[28]

The Chief Justice stated that he felt bound not to proceed in this case once he was convinced that Mantyeuldi had little prior contact with settlers and that he could not have known the import of Rose's arrest. The length of prior contact with Europeans was a factor that Cooper was to routinely consider in his sentencing, even in cases involving serious crimes. Taking this factor into account, while not always appreciated by officials when applied to direction of juries and sentencing, was generally regarded as being reasonable when it came to appeals for clemency. For example, after Ngarbi was sentenced to death for one of the 1842 Port Lincoln murders[29] and the Executive Council reviewed the execution order, the length of time that the convicted person had been in contact with Europeans was given serious consideration. However, since Ngarbi had lived for many months adjacent to the woman he murdered and had established a friendly relationship with her, he had little chance of having his sentence commuted on these grounds. The commutation request was denied, largely because, as Grey later noted, he was satisfied that not only had Ngarbi 'been well acquainted with Europeans [but] that he had experienced various acts of humanity and kindness at the hands of the very persons he had murdered'.[30]

In 1846–47, the jurisdiction issue came to a head. Early in 1846, two shepherds were murdered by Aboriginal people and in May of that year the police arrested three men for the killings: Meiya Murkata, Nakundah Biddeah and Wodla Murkata.[31] Communicating with the three men was difficult despite the best efforts of 'Charley', a Kaurna man, and Protector Moorhouse. After several remands, during which time the Protector hoped to learn enough of their language to be competent to interpret,[32] the three men came to trial before Cooper in the Supreme Court.[33] The Chief Justice was again reluctant to try Aboriginal people with so little contact with Europeans prior to the offence in question. This was, he declared, an 'exceptional case',[34] since they 'belonged to a tribe who had previously had no intercourse with Europeans [and were]...altogether ignorant of our Laws and customs'.[35] At the hearing comment was made that the shepherds were venturing into unsettled territory when they were attacked and Cooper was tempted to dismiss the case on this ground. However, well aware that such an action would meet with criticism in government circles, the Chief Justice took the more cautious path of taking advice on the options open to him. Accordingly, the three men were again remanded while Cooper sought a determination from the Advocate General as to their fitness to plead. In doing so, as he recorded in his notes, he 'stated very strongly my doubts of their being fit subjects for the jurisdiction of the Court and [asked]...whether they should be put on their trial at all for an offence arising with the first Europeans ever entering their territory'.[36] Advocate General Smillie subsequently sought a direction on this from Governor Robe, readily admitting that the three men did not meet the Chief Justice's criteria for falling within his jurisdiction. Smillie advised Robe that the trial should go ahead even though he thought it unlikely that Cooper would proceed.[37]

Robe eventually agreed but did the Chief Justice the courtesy of sending a copy of the Attorney General's letter to him for reaction, thus providing Cooper with another opportunity to put forward his views on the jurisdiction issue.[38] Cooper replied a few days later, in a tone suggesting something of a decline in relations between the Chief Justice and the Advocate General:

> The learned Advocate has expressed himself somewhat obscurely in speaking of his hesitation to abandon proceedings which have by previous authoritative sanction been declared to be the only legal mode of retribution against the Aborigines and I do not entirely understand the point wherein he seeks for directions, and I can therefore only say that if it be admitted that the above mentioned Aborigines came for the first time into contact with Europeans when the offence with which they are charged was committed, I do not think them fit subjects for trial in our Criminal Court. They appear to me to be in the same situation with respect to us as the natives in the neighbourhood of Glenelg were when Gov Hindmarsh raised the British Standard in 1836.[39]

In so replying, Cooper limited his view on jurisdiction even further than he had previously been willing to, by restricting his denial of jurisdiction to cases where the accused encountered 'for the first time' the Europeans 'at the time of the offence',[40] rather than extending for some weeks. It seemed that, by this time, the Chief Justice was restricting any exceptional treatment to cases where there was absolutely no prior contact.[41] Of course Cooper would have been well aware, given the size of the Adelaide community at the time, of the trend of legal and official opinion on this issue and perhaps this refinement was an attempt to accommodate those views without abandoning the essential principle of his earlier opinion. One interpretation of Cooper's motivation in so strongly defending his position on jurisdiction is that he was determined to stick with the principles he had outlined to the Government in Council in 1840. Given that his advice at that time played a major part in determining events which led to the summary executions of the Milmenrura leaders and their political aftermath, Cooper's reluctance to modify his views is understandable. Having given advice which proved flawed, Cooper may well have been unwilling to admit his mistake, despite the result being that this locked him into a position which was increasingly out of step with government policy and community attitudes.

Nonetheless, at this point the Governor determined that it was time to bring an end to Cooper's independence in the matter of Aboriginal amenability to the law. Through Colonial Secretary Mundy he let the Advocate General know that he remained unconvinced by the Chief Justice's arguments. On the same day the Colonial Secretary instructed the Protector of Aborigines to 'use every endeavour to find means of communicating intelligibly with the Natives now lying in Her Majesty's Gaol'.[42] Robe pointed out that in the case of Murkata et al. there had been contact between settlers and Aboriginal people in the area of the attack prior to its occurrence. The Governor could not, of course, know whether Meiya, Nakundah and Wodla had been involved in this prior contact but by then he was determined to take a hard line, whatever had been their prior actual experience of settlers. Robe advised that he was:

> neither prepared to admit, unless proved in evidence, that the Natives charged with the murder came for the first time into contact with Europeans on that occasion; nor that they are beyond the jurisdiction of our Courts, even if their previous non-intercourse with Europeans be proved.[43]

Accordingly, Cooper was to be directed to proceed with the trial even though it was well known that other factors might well abort it. In addition, the Advocate General was instructed that it should be made clear to the Chief Justice that he should no longer apply his 'prior contact' criterion for Aboriginal amenability to the laws, as it 'would lead shepherds in charge of remote flocks to adopt the law of the savage, namely that of retaliation'.[44] Cooper then had little choice but to proceed with the case, but soon took the opportunity to show who held the decisive legal power in the colony. As Smillie had predicted, the Chief Justice then found other difficulties in the case to be insurmountable. When the three men finally appeared before him in March 1847, Cooper discharged them on the grounds that the court could not communicate effectively with the accused, and had no future likelihood of being able to do so.[45]

Governor Robe also had directed that the 1841 Opinion of the Law Officers of the Crown be transmitted once again to the Chief Justice.

3. Amenability and jurisdiction

Cooper's reply to the subsequent letter from the Advocate General throws some light on the earlier proceedings regarding the amenability issue, particularly the earlier willingness of both Gawler and Grey to accept his interpretation in the matter. Cooper, in returning his opinion, replied that he had seen it before and that Grey had 'expressed his entire acquiescence in my opinion but whether he made it known to His Majesty's Secretary of State I do not know'.[46] A few days later the persistent Cooper sent another letter to Robe, outlining once again his objections to applying the law to all Aboriginal people:

> Another difficulty occasionally arises from meeting with native prisoners whose language is not only unknown, but who themselves as far as can be ascertained have never become known to Europeans until the occasion out of which the charge against them has arisen. In cases of this kind I think it improper to try the accused according to the forms of English law.
>
> My opinion rests on the ground that wild and savage people whose country although within the limits of the Colony has never been occupied by settlers; people between whom and the settlers there has been no intercourse, and who, until the moment of the commission of their alleged offence, have never been known, cannot reasonably be deemed cognizant of our assumed dominion over their country or themselves. They appear to me to be in the same situation with regard to us now as the whole native population were to Governor Hindmarsh and the first settlers immediately after they had raised the British standard on their first landing at Glenelg.[47]

Even so, Cooper was willing to make a further compromise on his often stated principle, suggesting that he would turn something of a blind eye to the problem in future cases, by no longer enquiring 'into the degree of knowledge of our law which aborigines brought to trial before me may possess, unless my attention is called to this question in any particular case'.[48] Of course, the latter observation can be read as an invitation to defence counsel to raise just that question when defending an Aboriginal client.

However, Robe was determined to finalise the issue and he decided to refer it once again to London. Two despatches were drafted within three days.[49] In the first, he summarised Cooper's objections to trying Aboriginal people[50] while in the second he explained that Cooper had already 'discharged or remanded, on account of the difficulties in the way of trial'[51] several Aboriginal accused and included a copy of Cooper's most recent correspondence. The Governor plainly put his case for a reaffirmation of the official policy, arguing that there was but one course open, 'namely to consider all persons dwelling within the limits prescribed by the Act of Parliament, whether British or foreign, or Aboriginal, as amenable to British Law, and under its protection'.[52] Robe argued that Cooper should proceed to try Aboriginal people and leave considerations such as lack of prior contact to be considered by Executive Council if and when it reviewed the sentence.[53] Probably Robe hoped to receive a reply which would strengthen his hand in making such a direction to the judiciary. Nevertheless, the Colonial Office did not consider the issue to be particularly urgent and did not reply for over a year, perhaps because its officials believed that the issue had been settled some years before in New South Wales.[54] While awaiting this reply from London, Robe maintained his position that the Chief Justice was wrong in his interpretation of the law regarding Aboriginal people. When, in 1848, Cooper found himself with little choice but to try an Aboriginal person for the murder of his wife,[55] Robe was able to apply his preferred process. Cooper sentenced Melaitpa to death, giving the Executive Council the opportunity to review the sentence. Governor Robe considered this to be the correct forum for consideration of the factors restricting Cooper, and the Executive Council commuted the sentence to life imprisonment.

By the time London replied to his earlier despatch Robe had been replaced by Sir Henry Young.[56] In this reply Secretary of State Earl Grey agreed that Cooper's attitude presented 'considerable difficulties' but could give little new advice, being content to add merely a rider to Robe's conclusion, namely that an Aboriginal person was 'in no wise injured by the assumed legal jurisdiction over him, but on the contrary, enjoys additional protection'.[57] Earl Grey sought to downplay the problem, noting that it had only involved 'a few cases of difficulty'[58] and that time would overcome the difficulty. Once again, however, there was a strong statement that the policy of applying British law to all Aboriginal people should continue. Acknowledging that this policy presented the judiciary with some difficulties, Grey affirmed that 'still greater difficulties would be occasioned by departing from uniformity of rule'.[59]

Despite the unequivocal reiteration of London's view as to the amenability of Aboriginal people to British law, the issue of jurisdiction still occasionally surfaced in the Supreme Court of South Australia. London and its representatives in Adelaide might be certain as to the policy but many settlers, particularly those with any knowledge of frontier life, believed that reality required a somewhat more flexible approach. There were colonists, of course, who took this flexibility to mean that they should simply operate outside the law, meting out rough frontier justice via the whip or gun. However, many took the view that justice, or perhaps more importantly the longer term economic interests of the new landowners, was not served by the strict application of British law in all situations involving Aboriginal people. Thus, while Cooper's tendency towards leniency in situations where Aboriginal people had little prior contact with settlers may have been out of step with the official policy, many settlers agreed with his interpretation. Petitions calling for clemency for (or early release of) convicted Aboriginal offenders were not uncommon and attracted large numbers of signatures.[60] Admittedly these petitions most often related to *inter se* cases but they were also made in some cases where the victims were Europeans.[61] During the late 1840s and throughout the 1850s, despite instances of brutality and retaliation, the sympathy of a significant number of colonists was still with the Aboriginal people who were being dispossessed. The view that the frontiers of the colony were being pushed forward too rapidly was accepted by some colonists, particularly those already established in the 'settled districts'. It was also accepted among some colonists that incautious and ruthless settlers often brought Aboriginal wrath down upon themselves. Even a policeman with considerable experience in frontier stations could find fault with the settlers pushing north on Eyre Peninsula, reporting that, in regard to an increase in sheep thefts in 1848: 'the settlers themselves are in many ways to blame, and have in many instances, brought upon themselves the aggressions of the natives'.[62]

For example, when James Baird was killed by Kokatha clansmen in November 1850, few colonists in Adelaide or Port Lincoln had much sympathy for him once the details of the incident came to light. Despite being warned against taking his flock of 2,000 sheep north of Streaky Bay to establish a new run, Baird pushed ahead with his plans, accompanied only by two employees and his female Aboriginal companion. When contact was made with several Kokatha clan members, the woman argued with Baird and left the camp.[63] Soon after, while attempting to retrieve sheep stolen from his flock, Baird was killed and his companions retreated south. Pulgulta was arrested for the murder but when he appeared before Cooper, the Chief Justice once again expressed reservations about trying a man so clearly lacking experience of Europeans.[64] But Cooper did not need to force this issue since it was soon agreed that it 'would require two years for Mr. Shearman [sic] to make himself sufficiently acquainted with their language to act as interpreter'.[65] Eventually the indictments against Pulgulta were abandoned on the grounds that no-one was able, or likely to be able, to communicate with him.

In June 1855 Peter Brown, a shepherd on the McKechnies'[66] station near Franklin Harbour, was murdered when he interrupted a raid on his flock. Eleven Pangkala men were arrested and brought to Adelaide, with four of their number eventually being found guilty and sentenced to be hanged.[67] The jury recommended leniency and many settlers, including the McKechnie brothers themselves, believed the sentence of death to be too harsh a punishment for Aboriginal people with almost no prior contact with Europeans. A petition for executive clemency was arranged and signed by 270 settlers, many of whom believed the condemned men 'not being in equal degree amenable to the laws of our nation with those who have derived the advantages of its institutions'.[68] The Protector of Aborigines and the Advocate General were consulted and the latter strongly advised against commutation, backing up his opinion with the argument that punishment of convicted Aboriginal offenders served to protect other Aboriginal people from extra-legal European retaliation:

> for unless they are punished in the same degree for offences against whites as the whites are for offences against each other, or against them, they must be placed beyond the pale of the law and exposed to the unchecked retribution of whom they injure.[69]

Smillie made a notation on the docket of his opinion that a pardon 'would endanger the lives of those who have a right to look for protection to our laws'.[70] The Executive Council could do little else but reject the petition for clemency, since its argument was based mainly on the proposition that Aboriginal people in remote areas were 'not equally amenable to the laws of this country as those who derive advantages from its institutions'.[71] George Beresford, the Governor's Private Secretary, wrote to the petitioners explaining this rejection:

> To change the existing law, and abolish the punishment of death altogether, may be a fair subject of discussion, but is a question beyond the province of the Executive. So long as the present

law exists the Governor feels he would be shrinking from a painful duty without adequate justification if he were to modify the sentence of the prisoners in the absence of all mitigating circumstances.[72]

The four men (Eelulta, Palingulta, Weenpulta and Watniltie) were executed at Franklin Harbour on 14 January 1856, in the presence of forty of their clanspeople.[73]

Defence counsel continued to raise the issue of jurisdiction throughout the 1850s, although by then usually only in *inter se* cases. Their intention was probably to introduce the issue more with a view to encouraging leniency in sentencing than in genuine hope of dismissal of the charges against their clients. For example, in December 1853 Bailey argued that the court should decline to hear charges of murder against Tinkanor, Woringena, Ngallabammu and Tunkanayman on the grounds that the court 'did not have jurisdiction'[74] over them. His submission was denied and all four men were found guilty of manslaughter and sentenced to three years' imprisonment.[75] In an 1858 case, when Piulta, Moniah and Warreah appeared in the Supreme Court charged with the murder of Beerea the year before, their defence counsel argued that different standards of provocation applied in the two cultures. Introducing evidence that the victim had killed several of Piulta's clansmen, he argued that under traditional law the three accused had little choice but to act as they did. The jury was unconvinced in Piulta's case and he was convicted and sentenced to death.[76] In 1859, when defending Wooloobully against a charge of murder,[77] Fisher argued that their motives and 'acts should not be judged in the same manner' as those of a 'white man'.[78] Apparently the deceased, Baldanant, had fired a gun at Wooloobully, prompting him to retaliate with a fatal spear thrust. He immediately showed remorse, witnesses testified, offering his spear to the wounded man to take instant revenge.[79] Judge Gwynne, in his summing up, noted that it was 'extremely difficult…to apply the laws made for a civilized nation to the customs and habits of the natives of this colony'.[80] Nevertheless, he had little choice but to direct that Wooloobully be found guilty of manslaughter. However, the jury, perhaps impressed by the accused's display of remorse, chose to acquit.

When in February 1858 it seemed that Piulta would go to the gallows for murder,[81] the issue of Aboriginal amenability to British law again surfaced in the public arena. The *Register* ran an editorial article calling for commutation of Piulta's sentence and the *Observer* reprinted this later the same week. Execution was too harsh a punishment, the editorial argued, since 'only notorious murderers are ordinarily hung'[82] and Piulta had 'not committed a crime which his race regard as atrocious'.[83] Late in February, it was announced that the Executive Council had decided to commute Piulta's sentence although the extent to which they agreed with the views publicised through the newspapers was not revealed.[84] The doubts lingered in some minds, even if they were not founded on good law. For example, in February 1860 the *Register* noted that the forthcoming March Supreme Court sessions had its 'usual quota of natives to be tried'[85] by a court enforcing a system of 'imposed' laws 'but which it were a stretch of presumption altogether unwarrantable to suppose they are able to appreciate'.[86] The issue may have been long settled officially and accepted by the judiciary but many settlers still could not fully accept that British law should without exception apply to the Aboriginal inhabitants of the colony.

It is probably true to say that the further one went from Adelaide the fewer supporters of such tolerant (albeit often patronising) views could be found.[87] Nevertheless, doubts about the amenability of Aboriginal people to British law were raised throughout much of the period under study here, both within the legal profession and the wider community. For most colonists, however, this tolerance suffered a major blow on 11 March 1861. At Hamilton, near Kapunda, Mary Rainbird and her two young children were murdered by a group of Aboriginal men.[88] Even more chilling to the European populace than the brutality of the rape and murders was the fact that the perpetrators were well known in the district — indeed, all but one had been born and raised after European settlement of the area. Following the Rainbird murders, discussion turned from issues of jurisdiction, education and civilisation to questions of how to control Aboriginal people by placing restrictions on their location, behaviour and freedoms.[89]

CHAPTER 4
ADMITTING ABORIGINAL EVIDENCE

Even before Chief Justice Cooper expressed doubts about the Supreme Court's jurisdiction over Aboriginal people within South Australia, officials had encountered legal problems of a more practical nature. When Reppindjeri was arrested in 1837[1] the problem of receiving Aboriginal evidence came to the attention of officials. Being British subjects, Aboriginal people were not explicitly banned from testifying but longstanding requirements relating to the admissibility of evidence in English (and therefore colonial) courts effectively prevented them from so doing. The essential question was whether an Aboriginal witness could take the oath, an act which implied both an understanding of the English language and an acceptance of the Christian faith. Given that the two potential witnesses in any case against Reppindjeri were Aboriginal women who neither understood English nor the basic tenets of Christianity, the difficulties seemed insurmountable. As for Reppindjeri himself, legal practice of the day denied him an opportunity to testify since accused persons were not entitled to give evidence on oath,[2] even if he had been otherwise able to do so. So, despite many colonists wishing to bring Reppindjeri before the court and, indeed, a general view that he was guilty of murder, the rules of evidence discouraged any action against him.

By the early 1840s officials and legal practitioners in South Australia were well aware of moves for reform relating to Aboriginal evidence in the eastern colonies[3] and Western Australia.[4] However, convictions had been secured in the 1839 trials for the murders of Duffield and Thompson without the need to address the issue of Aboriginal evidence and it was not until after the hanging of Moorcangua and Mongawarata that the issue gained any momentum. Defending his actions over the *Maria* killings, Gawler denied that the admissibility of Aboriginal evidence would have made any difference to his decision to declare martial law.⁵ He did, however, agree in principle that all British subjects should be able to give evidence in court. In practice though, his view was that instituting such a right for Aboriginal people would involve 'most formidable difficulties'.⁶ Perhaps more in the hope of deflecting criticism than of reforming the system, Gawler put forward a bill similar to those proposed in Western Australia and New South Wales. Introduced in late September 1840, the bill was passed but could not be acted upon until royal assent was received.⁷ Assent was not forthcoming and so this half-hearted attempt to address the issue of Aboriginal evidence lapsed. The issue was revived by Grey when he assumed the office of Governor but even then it was not to be a priority of his administration. It was not until August 1844 that any steps were taken to allow Aboriginal people to give evidence in South Australian courts, although even then only in a limited way.⁸

Before considering these moves towards reform, however, it is worthwhile looking at relevant events in the 1840s. As early as 1840 Grey had pointed out that the 'greatest obstacle' to the application of British law to Aboriginal people was that they were 'unable to give testimony in a court of justice'.⁹ Grey's suggestions regarding Aboriginal policy generally, and their relationship to British law specifically, were widely distributed and discussed within the colony. However, it was not until September 1841 that the absolute necessity of allowing Aboriginal evidence was brought home to Adelaide officials, when William Roach was placed on trial for the murder of an Aboriginal man, Worta Kudnaitya.¹⁰ Roach, a stockkeeper on a Mid-North station, eventually admitted that he had killed Worta accidentally during an argument which began when Roach accused the deceased man of stealing sheep. Worta's daughter, Katta Murtana, was present and accused Roach of deliberate murder but her evidence could not be accepted. The Protector urged the Crown Solicitor to offer a reward to entice one of Roach's colleagues to give evidence against him, noting that this evidence would be needed to secure a conviction.¹¹ No reward was provided and no action was taken to change the rules relating to Aboriginal testimony. Two witnesses, Wilson and Cross, did give evidence for the prosecution but under cross examination their accounts tended to throw doubt on Roach's guilt rather than confirm it.¹² To a mixed reaction among colonists, Roach was acquitted in March 1842.¹³

Meanwhile, one of the responses to the 1841 clashes on the Murray was to establish a government station at Moorundie. Edward John Eyre, granted magisterial powers, took charge of the station and it was not long before he saw the difficulties faced by Aboriginal people unable to use legal processes. He raised the issue of the admissibility of Aboriginal evidence in several of his reports, such as in 1842.[14] Eyre, stressing 'the importance of bringing the subject before the Council at an early date',[15] supported his argument with instances from his recent experience — the rape of a Murray woman by a group of Aboriginal men, several *inter se* allegations and two cases of alleged wrongdoing by settlers had been dropped because only Aboriginal evidence was available. From these instances, Eyre pointed out, Aboriginal people in his district 'naturally deduce an inference unfavorable to the justice of the white man'.[16] The Governor, although sympathetic to Eyre's arguments, did not move to put forward a new bill, contenting himself with a note on the correspondence file that Eyre be reminded that the current law allowed Aboriginal evidence from 'any native acquainted with the nature of the Oath'.[17] In practice, of course, this was no help.

From late 1843 to mid 1844, after word arrived in the colony of the enabling Act mentioned above, debate intensified on the worth of reforms to enable Aboriginal people to give evidence. Many colonists opposed the reforms[18] but there were some who agreed with the views of one correspondent to *The Observer*:

> If they break their oppressor's laws they are punished by the lash and the gallows; but if they suffer injury from their oppressors the black man's evidence is unavailing — violation, spoliation or murder may be perpetrated before their eyes, and yet, for want of white man's evidence, the guilty may walk at large.[19]

In early 1844 Eyre once again urged action, writing to the Colonial Secretary and Police Commissioner on the issue. He pointed out that he remained restricted in his actions by the 'existing state of our law of evidence'.[20] Traditional tribal structures and relationships were breaking down rapidly under pressure of European settlement, Eyre noted, with violence and intimidation becoming a frequent occurrence among the groups assembled in and around Moorundie. Eyre persisted in his call for legislation, writing again in May 1844 to point out:

the difficulties that are in the way of administering justice between the Aborigines and Europeans in cases where no other evidence than that of the Natives themselves can be adduced; a position equally injurious to both the European and the Native and which can only be remedied by the passing of a Colonial Act upon the subject; (under authority of a recent act of Parliament enabling the Governors of Colonies with the consent of the Legislative Councils, to legalise the evidence of the Aborigines) — should His Excellency upon further consideration deem such a measure necessary.[21]

The cautious Grey finally was prepared to act and he noted on this letter that he was 'preparing the draft of an Act, which will in some degree remedy the evils complained of by Mr. Eyre'.[22]

The *Aboriginal Evidence Ordinance Bill*[23] was introduced in early August 1844 and met with little opposition within the Legislative Council.[24] Not so, however, in the press. Prominent pastoralists opposed the reforms and enlisted the support of the *Register*, by then under a new editor. Claiming that ninety per cent of colonists were opposed to the Act's provisions, the latter mounted a campaign against the bill from July to August 1844, detailing what were claimed to be 'insuperable objections'[25] to the measures. Capitalising on the growing colonial desires for greater independence, the *Register* accused the legislation's supporters of operating 'under the sanction of express instructions from home'.[26] First, it was argued that Aboriginal people could not be relied upon as witnesses: they found it near impossible to adopt an objective stance and when it came to telling the truth, their 'habits of lying…are notorious'.[27] This argument received a boost a few years later when the Protector let it be known that even he had doubts about the reliability of Aboriginal evidence.[28] Other perceived problems affecting the reliability of their evidence were Aboriginal people's lack of confidence and certainty when being questioned closely and their apparent eagerness to please the person conducting the interview. Second, it was suggested that admitting Aboriginal evidence was a pointless exercise, since so few Aboriginal people could make themselves understood. Initially, when dealing mainly with the Kaurna, officials had kept pace with learning the language of the Aboriginal people with whom they had contact.[29] However, as settlement spread rapidly after the abandonment of the containment policy, the colonists encountered Aboriginal clans whose language was spoken neither by government officials nor Aboriginal interpreters from neighbouring groups. Third, the opponents of the legislation argued that one proviso within the bill rendered Aboriginal evidence meaningless — namely that 'the degree of weight and credibility to be attached to any such evidence'[30] would be at the discretion of the court. The assumption behind this argument was that European juries would give little credibility to Aboriginal evidence, particularly as it usually would have to be given through an interpreter. While this third argument was hardly a valid one for not proceeding with the evidentiary reforms, its underlying assumption proved in practice to be all too true (see chapter 6).

If legal practice was to be brought closer to the policy that Aboriginal people were British subjects with equal rights before the law then the main provisions of the 1844 Act were vital, even if they were limited in scope. The preamble noted the common exclusion of Aboriginal evidence and argued that 'much failure of justice may ensue, and many serious offences and crimes…may pass unpunished'[31] if this situation was not remedied. There were four major provisions of the 1844 Act. First, Justices of the Peace would be able to take 'informations of complaint' from Aboriginal people upon an 'affirmation or declaration to tell the truth, the whole truth, and nothing but the truth, without administering the usual form of oath'.[32] Second, Aboriginal written declarations and examinations could be admitted 'as evidence upon the trial of any cause, civil or criminal in this Province'.[33] Third, the judgement as to 'the degree of weight and credibility to be attached to any such evidence' was placed within the discretion of the Judge or Justices of the Peace.[34] Fourth, the former requirement that Aboriginal evidence be corroborated by the evidence of Europeans was removed.[35]

However, this Act was just a first step towards remedying the legal difficulties experienced by Aboriginal people in South Australia's courts.[36] Major limitations on Aboriginal evidence remained even after its successful passage, particularly because it included two provisos: first, that no-one could be convicted 'upon the sole testimony'[37] of an Aboriginal person and second, any facts affirmed by Aboriginal witnesses needed to be 'corroborated by other evidence'.[38] The political and economic realities of the day, particularly on the frontier, probably explain why these two provisos were included. Major instances of Aboriginal opposition to settlement had been experienced in the previous two years.[39] Settlers in various districts newly opened to settlement had been forced into taking expensive countermeasures against repeated attacks on stock and employees, with bankruptcy not being an uncommon result.[40] Several police and military expeditions had been mounted against resisters and in the more recently settled districts relations between colonists and Aboriginal people remained strained in 1844. In such a climate, the colonial government was under pressure to take strong action against Aboriginal offenders. At the same time, it was fearful of settlers taking the law into their own hands. Given the delicacy of the situation on the frontiers of settlement in 1844, the politically astute course was to include the above provisos in the legislation. Not to do so might well have accelerated the trend towards illegal retaliatory measures being adopted by more ruthless settlers. The government was walking a fine line and not all colonists were impressed by the compromise expressed in the 1844 legislation. Some settlers felt that the reforms had not gone far enough (for example, its failure to deal with the problem of interpretation) while others objected to the corroboration proviso, including Eyre, who believed that in practice it would neutralise the advantage it was intended to grant. As he pointed out by way of example, 'if a native were ill-treated or shot by an European, and the whole tribe able to bear witness to the fact, no conviction and no punishment could ensue'.[41]

The issue remained academic, since Governor Grey, quite understandably given the earlier history of similar reforms in other colonies, took the cautious course of not implementing the 1844 Act until formal assent was received from London. Soon after it was passed by the Legislative Council, the Police Commissioner sought advice from the Advocate General as to whether the Act should be applied in current cases: in particular could Aboriginal evidence be admitted in situations where the incident took place before the passing of the legislation but the matter remained to be tried?[42] His question was answered when Grey's determination to await royal assent was made known. Thus it was not until 1846 that Aboriginal evidence was in fact admissible in South Australian courts.

However, it was not long before the worth of the reform was shown when Tentipurran was able to lay an information of assault against a settler, George Lawson, in August 1846. The attacker was found guilty and fined, in what Moorhouse described as the 'first case of a Native preferring a charge successfully since the Ordinance, allowing the Natives to give evidence without the sanction of an oath, came into operation'.[43] The following year saw the first European, Donelly, convicted of murdering an Aboriginal person and, although Aboriginal evidence played only a minor part in the proceedings, it did receive some attention in newspaper reports of the trial. A ten-year-old Aboriginal boy, identified only as 'Jemmy', was called to give evidence against Donelly.[44] Despite the reforms, Chief Justice Cooper was cautious about receiving this evidence (perhaps mainly because of the age of the witness) but he decided to proceed when he satisfied himself that 'he understood that he was not to say anything that was false'.[45]

By this time, however, the issue of Aboriginal evidence had been considered again and an amending bill placed before the Legislative Council. The corroboration proviso in the 1844 Act was then widely seen as problematic, since its effect in practice was to place most *inter se* crimes, and indeed those of ruthless settlers acting alone, outside the scope of the law. The 1844 Mt Bryan case,[46] along with that against Donelly, made it impossible to deny that there were indeed brutal men capable of cold-blooded murder within South Australia. Doubts also remained as to the weight to be attached to Aboriginal evidence, a matter which the Protector of Aborigines formally raised in July 1846.[47] Moorhouse was still disturbed about the reliability of that evidence, especially in cases where an Aboriginal witness was called to 'give evidence in matters affecting unfriendly tribes, [as] he would not hesitate to disregard truth, in order that he might injure them'.[48] In cases where Aboriginal people were called upon to give evidence against Europeans, Moorhouse was more confident of the truthfulness of their accounts, since in such cases 'they have no tribal jealousies to influence them'.[49] However, his experience was that Aboriginal evidence was at its most reliable when given as a 'simple narrative'. Aboriginal witnesses, Moorhouse argued, had considerable difficulty understanding the process of, or the reasoning behind, cross examination. Under cross examination, the Protector pointed out that an Aboriginal witness was likely to 'assent or dissent, just as he thinks the Counsel wishes him'.[50] An amending bill to the Aboriginal Evidence Act was passed by the Legislative Council in late July 1846, in which section five was repealed and replaced with a new proviso intended to restrict the role of uncorroborated unsworn Aboriginal evidence in cases involving transportation or death.

Still unaddressed was the issue of unsworn Aboriginal interpreters being used to assist the courts. This was once again brought to the attention of the authorities early in 1847, when the Government Resident at Guichen Bay reported on a case that had come before him recently. An Aboriginal man and his wife had been arrested for assault, on the information of one James McKenzie. However, the suspicions of the Government Resident, Butler, were aroused and when he investigated he found that the accused man had suffered a gunshot wound, apparently at the hands of McKenzie. The stock owner and his companions were unwilling to provide any details of the incident but Butler found an Aboriginal witness who was willing to give evidence that contradicted McKenzie's allegations. The problem was that this witness could not speak English and so needed his evidence translated by another Aboriginal person, whose interpretation would also be unsworn. Butler decided to allow the interpreted evidence and subsequently discharged the two accused Aboriginal people.

Local settlers expressed concern over his action and the Government Resident sought the advice of the Advocate General on the admissibility, in future cases, of evidence interpreted by an unsworn interpreter.[51] The Advocate General agreed that this was a problem area because, 'where evidence is given through the interpretation of another, the interpreter must be sworn'.[52] His suggested solution was to defer proceedings until an interpreter who could take the oath could learn the language or the prospective witness could be taught enough English to be able to give testimony without the aid of an interpreter. These were hardly practical solutions, as even Advocate General Smillie admitted they would involve 'considerable time and difficulty'[53] and Butler was unimpressed by Smillie's answer. He addressed the issue in his next report, arguing that '[h]umanity and justice to the natives as well as justice and protection to the settlers render it very desirable'[54] that interpreters be found. Governor Robe was by then well aware of the problem and was close to being persuaded by the Advocate General's view that the law should be amended to extend the oath dispensation to cover the interpretation of evidence.[55] In the meantime, however, his only advice to Butler was that he either find a European capable of interpreting or learn the local language himself.[56]

The Chief Justice was even more aware of the problem and in March 1847 he advised the Governor to consider further amendment of the legislation covering Aboriginal evidence 'to authorize the use of an unsworn Interpreter in any case where no Interpreter can be found to whom it may be proper to administer an oath'.[57] In subsequent despatches to London the Governor raised this issue for consideration but he did not receive a reply while he was still in office.[58] He did act on

4. Admitting Aboriginal evidence

Cooper's advice in 1848, instructing the Advocate General to draw up an amending bill to 'facilitate the admission of unsworn testimony of the Aborigines'.[59] The resulting legislation, passed on 21 July 1848, replaced the 1844 and 1846 Acts.[60] It provided for testimony without the taking of the oath, for complaints and evidence to be presented as written statements, and allowed for the acceptance of unsworn interpretation of evidence. However, the earlier proviso that no person could be convicted of a capital offence on the sole testimony of an Aboriginal person or people still remained.

The following year, another case highlighted the remaining difficulties, particularly those relating to the weight and credibility to be attached to Aboriginal evidence. James Brown, a prominent settler in the South-East of the colony, was tried in June 1849 for the murder of several Aboriginal people (see chapter 10). In summing up, Acting Judge Mann reminded the jury of the 1848 provisos and advised that the witness Lindaw's evidence did 'not appear to have that degree of confirmation upon which a charge so serious can be supported'.[61] That same year, another related Act was passed by the Legislative Council.[62] Finally, the two problematic provisos introduced five years before were repealed, to be replaced with a section that gave the Judge or Justices of the Peace the responsibility of assessing the 'weight and credibility' of 'evidence given without the sanction of oath'.[63] There was virtually no opposition to the reforms within the Legislative Council and the bill passed on 24 July 1849 after minimal debate.[64] It was only then, almost thirteen years after settlement of the colony, that a settler could be convicted of an offence by the sole uncorroborated testimony of an Aboriginal person.

Within weeks of the passing of the last of the series of Aboriginal Evidence Acts, its provisions were put to the test in the Supreme Court. Clashes between settlers and Aboriginal people had reached a peak on both Yorke and Eyre Peninsulas during 1849 and feelings among settlers (and indeed Aboriginal people) were running high.[65] Several Aboriginal people had been poisoned on Mortlock's station;[66] brutal attacks had led to the death of several settlers on the west coast;[67] rumour had it that a large group of Aboriginal people had been driven over a cliff at Elliston;[68] and five Europeans were before the court on charges of murdering Aboriginal people.[69] The September Supreme Court sessions presented the chance for British justice to be shown to be capable of operating impartially, particularly as by then the formal obstacles relating to Aboriginal evidence, jurisdiction and interpretation had been largely removed. Nevertheless, that September — despite the evidentiary reforms — British justice was still found wanting, as the two cases below show.

The first case involved two Yorke Peninsula settlers, Harry Jones and Thomas Morris, charged with the murder of an Aboriginal person named Melaityappa.[70] An eyewitness, Piaria, gave convincing evidence that the shooting was unprovoked but his evidence was interpreted by another Aboriginal person and the strength of his account, as previously given to Moorhouse, was lost in the translation.[71] The jury found that there was reasonable doubt as to intent and acquitted both the accused. A similar case, also much reliant upon Aboriginal evidence, came before the Police Court early in September 1849. On Yorke Peninsula in August of that year, sheep had been stolen from Penton's station and a party led by the overseer, George Field, set out in pursuit. Two Aboriginal people were members of this party: Murra (a shepherd in Penton's employ) and Kokunea, who had been recruited to track the sheep stealers. At the coast the posse caught up with a group of Aboriginal people who had some of the sheep with them. The Europeans opened fire, reportedly into the air. Taking to the water to escape, the Aboriginal people were soon out of effective range but Nantariltarra returned to the beach to rescue a child who had been left behind in the panic. A shot, apparently fired by Field, struck Nantariltarra in the head and he and the child slipped beneath the surface. Their bodies were recovered and buried by the European party and the matter may well have rested there. However, the investigating police officer, Sergeant McCullough, interviewed Murra and Kokunea and was impressed by their statements that Field had deliberately shot to kill the unarmed and fleeing Nantariltarra. At the committal hearing, with Jimcrack acting as interpreter, Kokunea testified that 'the black man came to her, and that man (pointing to the prisoner) shot him'.[72] Defence Counsel Smith argued that 'the corroboration of unsworn testimony required by the Act was not produced'[73] and it became clear that there was little chance of securing a conviction — the evidence of the two Aboriginal people could not sustain the charge against a wall of silence among the Europeans who witnessed the incident.

This failure of Aboriginal evidence to convict Jones, Morris and Field was in itself not especially surprising given the circumstances put to the jury. However, when in the same Supreme Court sessions Aboriginal people were found guilty almost exclusively on the evidence of other

4. Admitting Aboriginal evidence

Aboriginal people, the hypocrisy surrounding the weighing of Aboriginal evidence was exposed. Aboriginal people could at that time certainly give evidence but that evidence was considered, where colonists were in the dock, as being inferior in weight and credibility to that of European witnesses. Two such cases, heard only days after the acquittal of Jones and Morris, involved Aboriginal men facing charges of murder. The first case related to the murder of an Eyre Peninsula settler, Charles Beevor, who had been killed in April of that year. Four men (Kulgulta, Nintalta, Malgalta and Mingulta) and one woman (Yabmanna) were arrested and charged with his murder. It was clear that Aboriginal evidence would be crucial in their trial and the *Register* expressed the hope that this evidence would contribute not only to their conviction but that it would be 'found sufficient to justify capital infliction' upon them.[74] At their trial the main evidence against the five was indeed given by other Aboriginal people and although some obvious conflicts and inconsistencies emerged, the four men were found guilty (Yabmanna was acquitted).[75] Moorhouse acknowledged that:

> had they been Europeans, the Juries would not, from the evidence produced, have brought them in guilty...the chief evidence against them was given by Natives, a kind of evidence which a few days before had been rejected as dangerous, and unsatisfactory, when given against Europeans.[76]

Other leading Adelaide residents, notably the Bishop of Adelaide, agreed with the Protector. A petition for clemency was drawn up and forwarded to the Governor, who referred it for comment to Charles Mann, the Acting Judge in the case. In his response Mann suggested that one of the four, Nintalta, had not been directly involved in the murder and that he may have been acting under duress. As to the other three men, Mann had 'no doubt' of the guilt.[77] The Executive Council commuted the sentences of Nintalta and Malgalta but ordered that the execution of the other two men proceed[78] — Kulgulta and Mingulta were executed 'upon the spot where the murder was committed'[79] on 9 November 1849.[80]

The second significant case heard in the September 1849 sessions was that against Mingalta and Malgalta (not the same man in the case above) who were accused of the murder of John Hamp, a hutkeeper on Pinkerton's station at Lake Newland. The main evidence against the two men turned upon statements from other Aboriginal people (especially Winnulu), their possession of pannikins and knives, and Sergeant Geharty's claims to have matched Mingalta's footprints to those at the

51

crime scene.[81] Despite Winnulu's testimony casting more doubt than certainty, the jury returned a verdict of guilty. However, public doubts about the case and its conduct led to a petition for clemency and the two men were later reprieved.[82]

The events of 1849 made it clear that, despite the reforms regarding the admissibility of Aboriginal evidence, judges and juries alike would continue to make full use of their right to make their own assessments as to its weight and relevance, and to do so with prejudice. Where Aboriginal people were in the dock on serious charges they were generally received, as the Protector conceded, with 'little sympathy or compassion before tribunals composed entirely of white men'.[83] Although the official view was that courts should exercise 'some extra degree of care...when the proof mainly rested upon native evidence',[84] Aboriginal people rarely received the benefit of this caution — rather they could expect any evidence given by their peers to count heavily against them. In cases involving Europeans, however, Aboriginal evidence was treated very cautiously, often to the point of dismissal. Even where the offence of the European accused was minor, Aboriginal evidence was given little credence. For example, in March 1849 a young Aboriginal girl, Mary, was called to give evidence against a European woman, Maria Hinch, on trial in the Supreme Court for picking pockets. Not surprisingly, given that the girl was the only eyewitness to the alleged offence, defence counsel Stephen objected to her being called. He argued that it was 'improper that she be put on oath'[85] but Cooper disagreed, quickly establishing that Mary 'believed there was a God, and that she would be sent to hell if she told a lie'.[86] He accepted her unsworn statement [87] but Stephen then took another tack, attempting to argue that his client should not be convicted on the unsupported evidence of an Aboriginal witness. But Cooper was not about to countenance this argument and cut Stephen off bluntly, directing that the case was 'sufficiently supported'[88] to allow it to go to the jury. However, the jurors were less impressed with Mary's eyewitness account and acquitted Maria Hinch.[89]

Defence counsels may not have had the sympathetic ear of the Chief Justice on this point but they realised that they could successfully play upon the doubts about Aboriginal evidence which commonly remained in many jurors' minds. These doubts did not only operate in the interests of Europeans, although this was usually their effect. In 1849, for example, Fisher raised the issue during his defence of Nammoingyu, who was charged with attempted murder of an Aboriginal woman.[90]

4. Admitting Aboriginal evidence

He cautioned the jury 'against convicting the prisoner, as the only proof of his guilt rested upon native evidence' and Nammoingyu was acquitted.[91] A few years later, when Marielare (known to settlers as 'Jemmy Rankin') was charged with the murder of an Aboriginal shepherd, Loorumumpoo, even the prosecution warned the jury that the case rested on Aboriginal evidence and that 'consequently their statements were to be taken with great caution'.[92] In this case, defence counsel Hartley based his argument on the issue of intent but in the end it was the doubt attached to Aboriginal evidence which swayed the jury to acquit. The eyewitness accounts of Markerlembelan and Yawaman, as well as the evidence of the native policeman, Neterrie, apparently counted for little.[93] As late as 1860 a Supreme Court Judge would make it clear that Aboriginal evidence was to be given less weight than that of Europeans even when given consistently by three separate witnesses, one of whom was described as being 'remarkable [sic] intelligent'.[94]

During the 1850s, by which time the more formal barriers to the admissibility of Aboriginal evidence had been removed, other obstacles either emerged or were deliberately put in its way. First, there were difficulties associated with obtaining Aboriginal evidence even where it was considered relevant to do so. Identifying and locating Aboriginal witnesses consumed considerable time and resources. Police officers were not able, or at times were unwilling, to track down Aboriginal witnesses. Especially in cases involving Europeans, Justices of the Peace were not always willing to delay proceedings to allow Aboriginal witnesses to be found. However, displaying the double standards which persisted despite the evidentiary reforms, they were more than willing to use their 'power to remand'[95] Aboriginal prisoners for long periods to allow an investigation, arrange for an interpreter or to suit the convenience of European witnesses. In cases of serious delay in bringing a matter before a court, the Protector was largely powerless to intervene to bring on the matter, except for his right to formally 'apply for a habeas corpus'.[96] Even when Moorhouse considered the delay serious enough to undertake this time-consuming course, unsympathetic rural court officials could frustrate his efforts.[97] Second, where Aboriginal witnesses were close at hand, Europeans soon found that they could be encouraged to move on for the duration of any trial, simply by offering a relatively small bribe. This was particularly so where an Aboriginal person was the informant against the accused European. For example, in Port Lincoln in March 1850 the local magistrate found no case to answer against James Young when he appeared on an assault charge preferred by Munarabidni. The informant, well known about the town, left the district just before the case was called and local intelligence suggested that he had been bribed by Young to do so. Charles Driver, the local Government Resident, noted that this practice was common, with few Aboriginal people prosecuting a matter 'when settling it out of Court is attended with such convincing arguments as food and clothing'.[98]

In the following year, when Yailgalta Wipapi laid a charge against local settlers whom he alleged had assaulted him at Koppio, he failed to appear at the hearing. In this case the local police had offered the complainant food and shelter but it seemed their offer had been trumped by the settlers involved in the clash — the 'charge, therefore, fell to the ground'.[99] Having ensured his non-appearance the settlers then took the opportunity to prefer a countercharge against Yailgalta, alleging that he had broken into a hut and stolen provisions prior to the clash which prompted the original charge — the countercharge did not proceed. Third, the disappearance of key Aboriginal witnesses suggested actions more serious than bribery and subornation. Government Resident Butler, for example, when asked to find two Aboriginal women to give evidence at the trial of Tatty Wamboureen in 1848[100] bluntly replied that it was too late to have the women attend, 'if indeed they could be found, as the practice is either to kill them or keep them out of the way'.[101] In another case, heard in January 1847, the Police Commissioner's Court was told by the Protector of Aborigines that Wambarno had suffered a 'threat of shooting' to discourage him from giving evidence against Peter McDuff.[102] Another documented case was that of Brown discussed earlier, in which Moorhouse made the mistake of not taking his key witness into protective custody (see chapter 10). Within days of making her statement, Leandernin had disappeared and it was assumed locally that she had been murdered or 'made away with'.[103]

During the period under study here Aboriginal people did eventually win the right to testify in the courts where — it had been claimed since 1836 — they would be treated equally as British subjects. Nevertheless this was achieved only after crucial delay, and even then with substantial and ongoing restricting provisos. Juries remained sceptical of Aboriginal evidence, particularly in cases where Europeans were in the dock. Some colonists found pragmatic ways to circumvent the admissibility of Aboriginal evidence, while the majority of settlers remained unable to come to terms with Aboriginal evidence having sufficient weight

4. Admitting Aboriginal evidence

to convict a colonist. In practice then, little changed in the courts despite the evidentiary reforms of 1844–49. Indeed, they made so little impact during the 1850s that the Sub-Protector of Aborigines at Wellington, at the close of the decade, justified his failure to prosecute whites for supplying alcohol to Aboriginal people by pointing out that such prosecutions would have relied upon Aboriginal evidence. The implication, backed by the experience of the previous decade, was that such prosecutions would be bound to fail.[104]

CHAPTER 5
LANGUAGE PROBLEMS

In the early years of the colony many settlers were confident that the difficulties of communicating with the Aboriginal inhabitants would soon be overcome. After all, the Protector of Aborigines was instructed specifically to learn the language of the indigenous people and a number of Kaurna people in Adelaide soon learned enough English to make themselves understood, at least in basic transactions. However, this early confidence was based on two assumptions, both of which proved false. First, that the Aboriginal people within South Australia were culturally homogeneous, speaking a number of dialects of essentially the one language. It was not until 1840 that it was officially recognised that the linguistic situation in the colony was far more complex than this, with Governor Gawler noting the 'diversity of their languages — dialects would seem to be too weak a term'.[1] Second, it was assumed that the settlers had time on their side, since the policy of containment meant that they would for some considerable time need only to communicate with Aboriginal people within a limited geographical area around Adelaide. Even when the diversity of Aboriginal languages in the colony became known, settlers and officials continued to expect that they would be able to use Kaurna interpreters in any interactions with Aboriginal people in more distant areas. Once the frontier advanced to the South-East, Mid-North and Eyre Peninsula districts, this became more difficult and, at times, impossible.

It was widely assumed that the Protector of Aborigines would rapidly become fluent in the Aboriginal language/s, but this soon proved not to be the case. George Stevenson, the initial interim Protector, had little time for the Protector's duties and no inclination to learn even the Kaurna language. Walter Bromley, his successor, had potential in this field, being a teacher who had written a book on the Canadian Indians.[2]

5. Language problems

Unfortunately, Bromley proved to be more a man of intentions than action and, although expressing his interest in studying the Aboriginal languages and to 'publish an extensive vocabulary',[3] he accomplished neither during his short term of office. Dr William Wyatt, appointed to the post in 1837, was given more detailed instructions than his predecessors, including one to quickly learn their language, so as to better 'enable them to appreciate our modes and habits, our moral and political laws, and our intentions towards themselves'.[4] Wyatt was not much interested in this task but as his instructions authorised him to engage an interpreter 'to facilitate intercourse between yourself and the Aborigines generally',[5] he found someone who was. James Cronk, a man of little formal education but considerable curiosity, took on the role as an official extension of his personal interest in the Aboriginal people and their way of life. Quickly developing a rapport with Aboriginal people in Adelaide, Cronk was soon reasonably fluent in the Kaurna language. Another minor official, Deputy Store-keeper Williams, also learned enough Kaurna to communicate with many of the Aboriginal people in and around the town. Indeed, in 1839 he wrote a pamphlet,[6] containing a limited vocabulary and sample phrases, which was widely distributed within Adelaide during 1839–40.[7] In the meantime, the two Lutheran missionaries Teichelmann and Schurmann were researching a detailed Kaurna grammar and vocabulary.[8] Both would have preferred to have spent more time on this task but were pressed to publish their book as soon as possible by 'some of the most intelligent individuals in the Colony',[9] who were no doubt aware that communication difficulties were becoming a problem in the relationships between colonists and Aboriginal people.

This was nowhere more so than in the courts, as was revealed in the 1837 Reppindjeri case discussed earlier. Although Kalinga was able to interpret between Reppindjeri and his captors, because she could not take the oath this was of little use in a court of law. As noted earlier, this case never came to trial; nevertheless, it foreshadowed the language-related problems the courts would face in attempting to deal with Aboriginal offenders. The Advocate General, Charles Mann, observed that 'our ignorance of the language of the natives is so great' that serious problems would arise in applying 'the strict rules of English Law'.[10] Despite the best efforts of European interpreters, by the time of the May 1839 murder trials Chief Justice Cooper had serious doubts as to whether the defendants even understood the proceedings, since any explanations could 'only be done through the medium of interpretation, in a broken language, of which the interpreters themselves only have a limited knowledge'.[11] During the period during which Aboriginal people could not give evidence they were also not allowed to act as interpreters of sworn evidence. This meant that until after the evidence reforms came into force in 1846, a colonist had to act as interpreter. In practice this role usually was undertaken by either the Protector of Aborigines, James Cronk or one of the Lutheran missionaries. Few other Adelaide-based settlers were knowledgeable enough, even of Kaurna, to attempt to interpret the subtleties of legal issues such as intent, provocation and malice. Once contact was made with Aboriginal people speaking languages other than Kaurna, the difficulties were compounded. While an official such as the local Government Resident or Sub-Protector could be delegated to learn the language of an alleged Aboriginal offender, this was often simply not a practical course when the defendants were awaiting trial.[12]

Usually, the best that the few European interpreters could do in these cases was to recruit a Kaurna man who could understand something of the language of the defendant/s. He then acted as an intermediary interpreter, translating the evidence into a blend of Kaurna and English for the European to interpret for the court. More often than not, the result was far from satisfactory. For example, when Piaria interpreted Aboriginal evidence in the Police Court in August 1849, his 'knowledge of English was very limited, and considerable delay occurred before a connected statement could be obtained'.[13] Not that the situation was always much improved by Europeans acting alone as interpreters: Cronk was not a man of sober habits; the Protector and Sub-Protectors were often distant from Adelaide; and frontiersmen who could speak local dialects were considered to be less than impartial. An example of the latter problem was seen in 1849, when Morris was charged with assaulting two women, Monarto and Yurnani.[14] The Judge had only two interpreters from which to choose: 'Jimcrack' (Monarto's husband) and a European named Christopher Christian, who turned out to be the lover of Yurnani.[15] Chief Justice Cooper opted for the former, partly because the European contender arrived at the Supreme Court decidedly drunk.[16]

Even when local officials were summonsed to interpret, their actual knowledge of the language of the Aboriginal people in their district often proved to be limited. For instance, when in 1846 Pilgalta was

5. Language problems

charged with wounding his wife Marinna, both Schurmann and Constable Geharty attempted to interpret.[17] The former deferred to the more northern-based policeman but Geharty soon got into difficulties. As the magistrate noted, after deciding that it was wiser to acquit Pilgalta, the policeman 'was quite unable to interpret much of the evidence, or to convey other than the very inadequate meaning of anything said either by the bench or by the witnesses'.[18] In the 1850s the situation was improved somewhat when members of the Native Constabulary became available as interpreters. However, even their interpretation rarely went smoothly either because the Aboriginal police officer only had minimal knowledge of the relevant dialect or the court had difficulty communicating effectively with the constable himself.[19] European police officers did have considerable contact with the clans along the frontier and it was at times suggested that their services be enlisted as interpreters in court proceedings. However, the conflict of interest in such situations, particularly in remote areas where only one or two constables were stationed, was obvious. The Supreme Court Judges remained cautious about police involvement in interpreting although local Justices of the Peace were less discerning. A typical example of this judicial caution was seen in 1860 at the trial of Padneltie and Popeltie for murder.[20] A key witness, 'Tommy', took the stand but 'considerable difficulty was experienced in obtaining from this witness an intelligible reply'.[21] Constable Bissett, in court as a prosecution witness, offered his services to interpret the evidence given by 'Tommy'. Defence counsel Stow objected at once and the Judge declined Bissett's offer.[22] Thus, the evidence from this Aboriginal witness was not completed and the two accused were found guilty.[23]

In both the Police Court and the Supreme Court, the prevailing view in the late 1840s and 1850s was that justice was best served by remanding any prisoners with whom the court could not effectively communicate, in the hope that some means of interpretation would be found before the case came up. This was not a situation with which Chief Justice Cooper was particularly comfortable but, given that he was no longer able to dismiss the charges on lack of jurisdiction grounds, he had little choice in the matter:

> This difficulty of interpretation has on several occasions made it impossible to try natives, and has caused me much embarrassment as to the disposal of the Prisoners. In cases where no other

difficulty than that of interpretation exists, and in which there is a probability that means of interpretation may be found within a reasonable time, I think it justifiable to remand Prisoners to afford an opportunity of obtaining this means.[24]

These remands were often renewed at the next sessions, resulting in, as Acting Judge Mann noted, 'the necessity of postponing the trial for periods of time unknown in practice under any other circumstances'.[25] Aboriginal prisoners could spend many months on remand in the Adelaide Gaol before their case came to trial. Of course, such lengthy remands also caused difficulties with the attendance of prosecution witnesses, many of whom had to travel considerable distances to appear. At times the delays and difficulties became too much for both officials and witnesses, especially when the expense and trouble seemed disproportionate to the crime. In 1845, for example, when an Aboriginal defendant known only as 'Charley' appeared in the Adelaide Police Court charged with sheep stealing, he was remanded in custody twice in May and eventually bound over until the September sessions.[26] At that point the prosecution, perhaps considering that 'Charley' had spent enough time in gaol even if he was guilty, declined to present any evidence since they still had no-one available who could speak his dialect.[27]

The situation was not greatly improved by the provisions of the 1844 *Aboriginal Evidence Act*, since that did not provide for an unsworn interpreter to translate evidence even where the person giving that testimony was by then able to be heard without taking the oath. As Advocate General Smillie noted in 1847, soon after the Act was implemented in the Supreme Court for the first time, the main difficulty remained, that of 'the impossibility of interpreting their evidence'.[28]

At this point Smillie recommended reforming the law to extend the oath dispensation to cover the translation of evidence as well as for original testimony.[29] The Governor took the point and indicated to London that the problem was particularly noticeable when dealing with Aboriginal people from distant areas, where 'the only means of communicating with the newly discovered tribes is by interpretation of natives adjacent to them, with whose dialects Europeans have become acquainted'.[30] As noted in the preceding chapter, the law was amended in 1849 to overcome this difficulty.

No doubt at times many colonists felt that the Bench was being too cautious in its insistence that Aboriginal people must be able to

5. Language problems

understand court processes, whether directly or through interpretation. However, in June 1846 there was a case which highlighted the importance of Aboriginal people being aware of the processes, their rights and of the proceedings themselves. When Mantyeuldi ran into trouble with the police south of Mt Barker that month, he found himself facing an assault with intent to maim charge.[31] His situation was grim but to his good fortune Mantyeuldi had some knowledge of both the English language and the basic workings of the introduced law. Reminding Moorhouse of the speeches he had made to Aboriginal people about putting their faith in British justice, Mantyeuldi received the Protector's support in challenging the account of the police officers who had arrested him. Mantyeuldi's brush with the law occurred on 12 May, two days after a shepherd's hut had been ransacked, when Corporal Rose and Constable Mulharan entered an Aboriginal encampment and become suspicious of the origin of European clothing in the possession of Mantyeuldi and a companion. Without any explanation the two officers attempted to arrest and handcuff the two Aboriginal people, both of whom resisted. When threatened with a spear, Rose fired a warning pistol shot in the air whereupon Mantyeuldi speared him, although not seriously. Despite Rose's wound the policemen gave chase to the now fleeing men. Mulharan charged with his sword drawn and Mantyeuldi's companion was struck down. The wounded man reacted by grabbing the horse's bridle and thrusting a spear into the constable's side. At that point the noise of the affray attracted some nearby shepherds, and Garratt, the station overseer, did not hesitate to shoot the anonymous Aboriginal man dead. Mantyeuldi received a sword wound in the affray and he was arrested and taken to Strathalbyn to be treated by the local doctor before being arraigned.[32]

However, Mantyeuldi was neither cowed nor unaware of his rights. At his trial before Chief Justice Cooper he showed he could speak English adequately, supporting his claim that during the affray he had repeatedly stated that he had done no wrong. Cooper agreed that the prosecution case turned on whether the two Aboriginal men were aware that Rose and Mulharan were in fact constables operating within the law. If the policemen had not made this clear before attempting the arrest then they were acting outside of the law and the Aboriginal people were entitled to resist. Personally Cooper was not convinced that they had done so, but left it up to the jury to decide 'whether the police constable was lawfully acting in the execution of his duty'.[33] The jury decided that

Corporal Rose had acted in haste and accordingly found Mantyeuldi to be not guilty.[34] Had Mantyeuldi not had the opportunity to learn English while in the employ of settlers, it seems unlikely that this would have been the result.

The language issue came up again in three cases in the March 1847 Supreme Court sessions when Chief Justice Cooper implemented his view that, in cases where there was little or no hope of effective communication with accused Aboriginal people, he should dismiss the charges against them. The first case, mentioned earlier (see chapter 3), involved three Aboriginal men (Meiya Murkata, Wodla Murkata and Nakundah Biddeah) arrested in 1846 for the murder of two shepherds (Whitney and Scott). It immediately became clear that considerable language difficulties would have to be overcome if the case was to be heard in the Supreme Court. At the committal hearings Moorhouse was assisted by 'Charley', made a native constable specifically to undertake this task,[35] but both interpreters had great difficulty making themselves understood to the defendants:

> Kudnutya, the native brought in with the prisoners, was examined through the joint interpretation of Charley and Mr. Moorhouse, the former, one of the Broughton tribe, translating from the Mt Arden language into his own, and the latter reducing it to English. It was about ten minutes before a single answer could be obtained, and then it was in the form of an inquiry: 'What they (the Commissioner and Mr. Moorhouse) had to do with it? and why he need tell them anything?'[36]

Several remands followed, in the hope that the Protector could learn something of the language spoken by the accused man and thus facilitate this process. When on 21 September 1846 the three appeared in the Supreme Court, Moorhouse was forced to admit that he could offer only a limited, second-hand interpretation by using 'Charley' as an intermediary.[37] Cooper, on the grounds that these men had no prior contact with Europeans, believed that he did not have jurisdiction over them anyway. However, by this time he was unwilling to make such a decision on his own and so referred this 'exceptional case'[38] to the Advocate General for him to make a determination as to their fitness to plead.[39] What was within his power, however, was the decision to grant bail and, in an unusual decision where Aboriginal people were concerned, Cooper remanded the prisoners on their own recognisance to appear at the March 1847 sessions.[40] In the meantime, Moorhouse was directed to 'use every endeavour to find means of communicating intelligibly'[41] with the men, including learning the language himself.[42]

Governor Robe, acting on advice of the Advocate General, directed that the case proceed.[43] His concern over the problem of interpretation led him to comment on the 'legal difficulty' and to enclose two relevant reports[44] in his next despatch to London, in which he promised to report further after the trial of the current cases.[45] When the three accused appeared in the Supreme Court on 17 March 1847 the Chief Justice did indeed make his judgement — all were discharged, since Cooper considered that 'there would have been no probability of convicting the prisoners'[46] even if the hurdles of communication could be overcome. An interesting later development showed that it was not only Europeans who could interfere with witnesses — one of the released men, Nakundah Biddeah, was charged with assault on the interpreter 'Charley', apparently in revenge for his role in the trial.[47]

The second case considered in the March 1847 sessions and relevant to this language issue involved an *inter se* murder charge against an Aboriginal man known only as 'Larry', mentioned earlier in relation to the amenability issue (see chapter 3). Charged in 1846 with the murder of Rallooloolyoo,[48] 'Larry' spoke no English and no-one could be found to 'interpret to him the proceedings of the Court'.[49] Accordingly, 'Larry' was remanded and when he next appeared Cooper felt compelled to discharge him for the want of the means to interpret proceedings to him since the Protector assured him that there was 'no probability of attaining this means within a reasonable time'.[50]

The third case also led to the accused Aboriginal man being discharged when no interpreter could be found. In the South-East of the colony, a shepherd called Richard Carney disappeared while travelling. A search party found first his gun and then his battered body, buried in a shallow grave. Investigations suggested that three Aboriginal men were involved in his death but only one, Tatty Wamboureen, was able to be questioned.[51] Some circumstantial evidence implicated Wamboureen and he was committed for trial at the December 1846 sessions. However, no witnesses arrived and he was remanded until the next sessions, giving the prosecution time to arrange for an interpreter.[52] At the March 1847 hearing, a supposed interpreter was introduced by the Protector but he soon proved unable to interpret sufficiently well to satisfy the Chief Justice, who was again bothered by the 'the absence of any interpreter who could communicate with him'.[53] When Tatty appeared again some months later, the Advocate General put forward another Aboriginal youth as interpreter, who had been 'for some months under instruction in the School...[and had] acquired a fair knowledge of English'.[54] However, the Judge was not convinced of the accuracy of the translation and declined to accept it.

Few colonists understood the difficulties involved and some expressed their frustration at the failure of 'these erudite gentlemen'[55] either to find Aboriginal people who could speak English and the Aboriginal dialect in question or to 'seize the opportunity to learn the language'[56] themselves. Governor Robe was also becoming impatient with this inability to cope with dialects spoken by Aboriginal people who were by that time well within the European-settled areas. Responding to the Guichen Bay Government Resident's report regarding Wamboureen, he tersely noted that Government Resident Butler or his clerk should learn the language themselves. It was not in fact until March 1848 that Wamboureen finally had his case heard.[57] By then a youth named Duncan Smith had been recruited to interpret the Boandik language and he was set the task of learning Wamboureen's related dialect.[58] His interpretation proved adequate but the delay in bringing on the case meant that vital European witnesses had left the colony and so the prosecution then had little choice but to abandon the case. After being in custody for fifteen months, Wamboureen was discharged.[59] The Government Resident at Guichen Bay was worried about the effect of this case not being addressed to the satisfaction of the settlers in the area. If the law was shown to be ineffective in a case where an Aboriginal person was suspected of involvement in an unprovoked killing then settlers were more likely to abandon legal means of redress in the future:

> Humanity and justice to the natives as well as justice and protection
> to the settlers render it very desirable that an interpreter of some
> description should be obtained.[60]

In April 1847 at Port Lincoln, Mingulta was arrested and charged with assault. However, in the 'absence of a competent interpreter the prisoner was remanded from time to time'[61] while local officials looked for someone to interpret. In June, theft was added to the charge and Magistrate Driver was obliged to transfer the case to the Supreme Court. When Mingulta appeared before Cooper at the September 1847 sessions, the assault charge was not proceeded with but it was hoped that Schurmann would be able to interpret proceedings relating to the theft. However, Schurmann told the court that 'he had no longer any confidence that he should be able effectually to interpret'.[62] Cooper then decided to dismiss the charge against Mingulta 'on the grounds of his protracted confinement being deemed by the court a sufficient punishment'.[63] He was not to know that Mingulta would appear before him again within two years on a charge of murdering Charles Beevor. Mingulta's 1847 release on what many Eyre Peninsula settlers considered dubious grounds was not lost, however, on those who attended his trial and execution in 1849.[64] In the meantime, three other men, 'Tommy' Kudnutya, 'Rosy Wine' and 'Frying Pan' had been released in June 1848 when the prosecution declined to proceed on the grounds that interpretation would not be possible.[65]

The task expected of interpreters such as Schurmann and Smith was at times simply too great as the frontier of settlement advanced faster than they could learn the languages of Aboriginal people encountered. For example, during the 1848 trial of Warrapoonen and Ngilmanin for theft from a station hut near Robe, Duncan Smith admitted defeat in interpreting their dialect.[66] Three years later, Schurmann was still having trouble with the upper Eyre Peninsula dialects, finding them simply too difficult to learn quickly. Pulgulta was discharged in 1851 when Schurmann declared that he would need two years 'to make himself sufficiently acquainted with their language to act as interpreter'.[67] When Bakilti and Puterpynter were acquitted of the murder of Mrs Easton in the same year,[68] Aboriginal evidence, interpreted through Ilgalta and Schurmann, suggested that the accused were merely opportunistic thieves who had only entered Easton's hut after others had committed the murder. An Aboriginal witness stated that at the time the murder was committed, 'Bakilta [sic] was outside the hut cutting grass, and that another…named Malpita, did the deed'.[69] In this case the anger of the murdered woman's husband was directed at the interpreters. James Easton questioned Schurmann's integrity, alleging that he was biased in his interpreting:

> During the trial of Pakilte [sic] for the murder of my wife, when told to give the usual warning to the witness, to tell the truth, the form of which he put it was, 'Be careful; of what you say, or the white men will be angry with you.', in consequence of which the old man became frightened and did not tell all he knew respecting the murder.[70]

This accusation illustrates a problem facing both interpreters and the courts which relied upon their services. Those able to interpret Aboriginal languages effectively were not perceived as being impartial — and there was some justification for this view, given the circumstances in which they acquired their linguistic knowledge. Interpreters fell into four categories: missionaries; officials with some responsibility for Aboriginal affairs (e.g. Sub-Protectors, Government Residents); settlers who developed an interest in Aboriginal society (e.g. Duncan Smith); and Aboriginal people from neighbouring districts. All had, almost by definition, close contact with Aboriginal people and so were more likely to develop an understanding and appreciation of their situation and customs. In many cases they probably felt at least some (and at times, considerable) sympathy with and compassion for the accused and, within the boundaries of their oath, were tempted to interpret sympathetically. Given that police officers were often ruled inappropriate to act as interpreters, it is understandable that at times interpreters would be accused of bias by court observers. No such criticisms were levelled at them by the judiciary, however, as no doubt those on the Bench understood the difficulty of the task.

In the 1850s the boundaries of settlement were pushing into the Flinders Ranges and beyond, where languages could often not be translated effectively even by Aboriginal people from neighbouring areas. In 1852, for example, a shepherd was killed on Hayward's station near Lake Torrens. As Moorhouse reported, there was 'considerable difficulty in prosecuting an inquiry amongst the tribes inhabiting the neighbourhood of Lake Torrens; they speak a dialect altogether different from any that I have been in contact with before'.[71] On the west coast of the Eyre Peninsula similar difficulties led, in 1852 and 1853, to further abandonment of proceedings against Aboriginal people charged with stealing or killing sheep.[72] In the 1853 case six men, all of whom had at some time worked as casual shepherds on Pinkerton's station near Mt Wedge, were charged with stock theft.[73] They were sent to Adelaide for trial, along with Kumbilti, a Nauo man who was to act as interpreter. Although these men had been able to communicate well enough with Pinkerton's men to provide shepherding assistance to them, the standard required within the Supreme Court proved to be of a higher order. The court was unimpressed by Kumbilti's interpretative skills and Moorhouse was asked whether another interpreter could be found. He advised that 'there was no European, to his knowledge, who could speak the prisoner's language'.[74] There being 'no person able to interpret the native language...the Judge directed the acquittal of the Prisoners'.[75] Even closer to Adelaide problems were sometimes still being encountered with interpretation, such as when two Aboriginal men appeared in the Kooringa Court indicted for the murder of John Richardson. The local magistrate experienced considerable difficulties with their language and reported that he hoped to find a competent interpreter before the case reached the Supreme Court.[76] These and other similar incidents led Tolmer, then Police Commissioner, to suggest 'speedy amendment' of the law.[77]

Despite such expressions of concern about interpretation of Aboriginal evidence from as early as 1845, little was done to address the problem. Indeed, beyond restricting the advance of settlement to a pace that would allow languages to be learned before wider contact, there was probably little that could have been done. Had the original policy of containment been adhered to, perhaps this could have been achieved. In practice, the courts, with the assistance of the Protector of Aborigines and his locally based Sub-Protectors, were left to cope with the problems of learning and understanding Aboriginal languages as best they could. To some extent officials simply hoped that the problem would be overcome when all of the colony's regions were populated by settlers. Unfortunately, as Cooper noted in 1847, this was only a longer term solution, since the rapid 'extension of the sheep runs had rather the effect of increasing' the contact with more Aboriginal groups, speaking quite different languages.[78] Certainly the problem continued until the frontier stabilised in the late 1850s, with language difficulties still at times threatening to be an insurmountable barrier throughout that decade.

For example, in 1855 Ninchulta was charged with the murder of a young Aboriginal woman, Maria Gonarto.[79] Magistrate Robinson was not convinced that the interpreters brought forward were up to the task and declined to have them continue. Sub-Protector Minchin offered his services but as he was also the informant, Robinson again declined, stating that it would be 'a very unusual course to allow a prosecutor to act as interpreter'.[80] With little prospect of the situation improving with time, the magistrate refused the prosecution request for a further remand and discharged the prisoner. The situation was similar when, in August 1859, Bungildo was tried for assault with intent to rape and indecent assault. Once again court officials had difficulty communicating with the accused. Just when it looked as though he might have to be discharged, Bungildo pleaded guilty to the lesser charge, apparently on the advice of Bartley, his defence counsel. Bungildo was gaoled for 18 months with hard labour after the Judge ruled that he understood the nature of his offence and the gist of the proceedings.[81] Another case that same year resulted from an attack at Fowler's Bay on a well-sinker named Thomas Shepherd, allegedly by a group of five Aboriginal people. Bashed, speared and left for dead, Shepherd nevertheless managed to get back to his camp. Three men, later given the names 'Billy', 'Georgy' and 'Jacky', were arrested and brought to Adelaide to stand trial. Inspector Holroyd foreshadowed interpretation problems, his 'own native guide not being able to speak or interpret their language'.[82] No interpreter was found but when the trial began it quickly proved that such assistance was not necessary. Shepherd declared that the three were not the men who had attacked him and accordingly they were discharged.[83]

When the cases outlined in this chapter are reviewed, once again the integrity of government officials and officers of the courts is clear. One is left with a clear impression of officials making considerable effort to see that Aboriginal people who ran foul of British law understood the charges and were aware of the course and meaning of proceedings against them. While Aboriginal people as a group within South Australia were not well served by the British criminal law during the first twenty-five years of the colony, the blame for this cannot be attached to court officials or defence lawyers. In eight of the thirty-two murder cases heard between 1836 and 1862, the conservative policy on interpretation led to the discharge or acquittal of the eleven Aboriginal defendants involved. Despite growing concern, particularly among rural-based colonists, government and legal officials held firm to the view that, having brought Aboriginal people within the scope of British law, they should be entitled to be discharged when no-one could be found to adequately and fairly interpret between them and the Court. On their own, the cases where difficulties in interpretation led to the discharge of the accused Aboriginal person could perhaps have been accepted by most colonists, perhaps even by many in the rural districts. However, few colonists distinguished between discharges on the basis of the criteria by which they came about. Rather, public opinion was shaped by the total number of alleged Aboriginal offenders who were discharged, whether resulting from difficulties in interpretation, jurisdictional problems regarding some Aboriginal groups, or evidential requirements. When all three legal impediments to successful prosecution of alleged Aboriginal offenders are considered together, the extent of their threat to the operation of the law (particularly from the pastoralists' perspective) is revealed. During the period 1836 to 1862, a total of sixty-eight individual Aboriginal people were so discharged (including nineteen on *inter se* charges) either prior to or during legal proceedings. The majority of these were released during the 1840s, the major period of frontier expansion. Few of these discharges were for minor infringements: indeed, eleven dischargees had been indicted for the murder of either settlers (nine) or another Aboriginal person (two). Included within this total are twenty-nine Aboriginal defendants discharged from hearings related to stock theft, robbery or stock killing. Given these figures, the concerns of some colonists that the legal system was failing to deal with Aboriginal offences against European life and property are understandable. If, from the pastoral perspective, the policy that Aboriginal people were to be subject to the law was intended primarily to protect European interests, then too many Aboriginal people appearing before the courts were being sent back to their homelands with only the 'punishment' of having been brought to Adelaide and remanded in custody until their court hearing. The perception of a significant number of settlers, including those with considerable influence within the colony, was that the adherence to strict legal and evidential procedures when Aboriginal people were in the dock was not in the settlers' (or even, some argued, the colony's) interest. Unfortunately, when the law and its agencies failed to adapt quickly enough to address such concerns, some settlers moved to take the matter into the own hands, as will be discussed in chapter 10.

CHAPTER 6
INTER SE JURISDICTION

Despite the policy that Aboriginal people were subject to British laws, the courts took several years to accept that this applied in situations where Aboriginal people had not been long in contact with settlers. Even once this general question of jurisdiction was resolved, a more specific doubt remained: should British law apply when the offences involved only Aboriginal people? When Aboriginal people committed acts against other Aboriginal people (i.e. *inter se*) were the police and courts entitled — or indeed obliged — to interfere? Or should there be some acceptance that Aboriginal people did have a system of customary law which was best left to operate unimpeded where Europeans were not immediately involved? These questions are significant when considering the implementation of the 'one law for all' policy, since the attitude taken towards such *inter se* crimes gives an indication of the level of commitment to the view that the law was intended to protect both European and Aboriginal interests. Having supplanted customary law with the British import, legal officials could be expected, if they were genuine in their stated view that all Aboriginal people were protected by this law, to intervene in cases where some Aboriginal people were making victims of others.

In law this *inter se* field had already been settled by the 1836 NSW *Congo Murrell* case.[1] There the Full Bench of the NSW Supreme Court had considered a defence counsel's objection to the law being applied where only Aboriginal people were involved and had ruled that Aboriginal people were entitled to the protection of the law, whatever the situation or whoever the participants. However, four years later Justice Willis' unsuccessful challenge to that decision[2] struck a chord of agreement among many Australian colonists. To them it hardly seemed practical, wise or expedient to push the influence of British law beyond the boundaries of relations between the two races into the largely unknown territory of Aboriginal customary law. The result was that, in practical terms within all the Australian colonies in the early 1840s, there was a reluctance to involve the courts and the police in dealings between Aboriginal people themselves.[3] Expediency and pragmatism were the watchwords of this practice. Very little was known of the legal customs of Aboriginal people, especially in newly settled South Australia. Adelaide-based officials placed their hopes in the policy of containment of settlement, which they believed would largely avoid the necessity for British law to become involved in traditional disputes.

George Grey visited Perth in 1838–39, soon after a major *inter se* case had been considered by Executive Council in that colony.[4] He spent several months there and no doubt discussed the *inter se* issue in his several meetings with Governor Stirling and Advocate General Moore. On his return to Adelaide, Grey drafted a report suggesting ways that Aboriginal people could be brought within European society, sending it to Lord Russell in London and Governor Gawler in Adelaide.[5] Grey had little time for Aboriginal customary law[6] and he strongly criticised existing Aboriginal policy, suggesting that the root cause of its failure was based on the erroneous principle that 'so long as they only exercised their own customs among themselves…they should be allowed to do so with impunity'.[7] Admitting the humanitarian motives underlying the current policy, Grey argued that it in fact condemned Aboriginal people within the colony to 'barbarous laws and customs'.[8] He concluded that all Aboriginal people within the colony should be immediately made 'amenable to the British laws, both as regards themselves and Europeans'[9] and that officials should abandon the policy of turning a blind eye to *inter se* offences, and 'be required to protect a native from the violence of his fellows, even though they be in the execution of their own laws'.[10]

When, later in 1840, an Aboriginal man was observed by several workers at the Encounter Bay whale fishery to murder his wife, the issue was raised by correspondent the *Register*: 'I trust…he will be brought to justice. Permit me to ask, are not the natives in this country amenable to British Law?'[11] Colonists with similar views may have expected the situation to change when Grey became Governor in May 1841. However, Grey's views proved more difficult to put into practice than to expound, and the expedient approach of leaving *inter se* offences to be settled through customary law continued. Throughout Grey's term of office no attempt was made to intervene legally in relations among

Aboriginal people themselves, even though several opportunities for such intervention occurred. Such a reform had to await other developments in the colony.

With the collapse of the containment of settlement policy, settlers were soon establishing themselves in relatively remote locations. By the mid 1840s the separation of the two races was no longer distinct: the frontier was fluid rather than rigid, with Aboriginal people moving to live and work in the European society while retaining links with traditional culture. The view that in country districts the two societies, and therefore the two laws, could be kept somehow separate was soon exposed as unrealistic and impractical. Chief Justice Cooper's early opinion that the murder of one Aboriginal person by another was not a crime against English law[12] was more difficult to uphold once Aboriginal people and settlers were living within a society which was moving, however slowly, towards integration. However, despite this all but a few incidents involving violence and revenge among Aboriginal people still took place beyond European eyes. Thus, until Aboriginal evidence became accepted in the mid 1840s, there was little that could be done through the courts to address *inter se* offences.[13]

It was not until 1846 that the courts faced the *inter se* issue directly. In November of that year a Grand Jury indicted 'Larry' for the murder of Rallooloolyoo.[14] However, this indictment was not so much a change in policy or judicial direction as a reflection of the fact that many Aboriginal people were by then operating within two cultures, blurring the lines of demarcation between the two colonial societies. Rallooloolyoo worked as a shepherd and his murder was more difficult to ignore or explain away than those reported to have taken place among more traditional Aboriginal groups. Having encouraged Aboriginal people to adopt a new way of life, the settlers could not easily escape the implied obligation to protect them when they did so. When 'Larry' appeared before the Chief Justice, Cooper made it clear that he saw no jurisdictional difficulties beyond his standard requirement that the accused must have been in contact with Europeans for a reasonable time before the alleged offence.[15] As he later explained:

> I feel it difficult to say that the Supreme Court has not the jurisdiction to try such a case if it be admitted that it has the jurisdiction to try a native for an offence against a settler; and such jurisdiction has been exercised in the latter case not only here but in the neighbouring Colonies.[16]

Even so, Cooper believed that it was not solely up to him to make this decision. It was, he suggested, a 'question of policy'[17] as to whether it was 'expedient that offences committed by the natives among themselves should be inquired into'.[18] If the Government believed that Aboriginal people should not be answerable to the courts for actions committed *inter se*, then he felt that 'a law should be passed to that effect'.[19] In the absence of such legislation the Chief Justice declared his intention to hear *inter se* cases. These views were expressed by Cooper in court, in response to the plea made by counsel defending 'Larry', Bartley.[20] As noted earlier (see chapter 3) Cooper stopped the proceedings because Bartley clearly could not effectively communicate with his client. 'Larry' was remanded until the March 1847 sessions but when he still could not be communicated with, Cooper discharged him.[21] This first *inter se* case was abandoned but the policy had been confirmed by the Government's acceptance of the Chief Justice's position that Aboriginal people were within his court's jurisdiction when they committed crimes against members of their own race. Over the next few years that policy would be developed and strengthened as the courts considered other *inter se* cases. However, in practice it would remain somewhat limited in application.

It was only a few months before a second Aboriginal man appeared in the Supreme Court charged with murdering another Aboriginal person, but this time the victim was a native constable. Nakundah Biddeah was one of three men charged with the murder of shepherds Scott and Whitney in 1846.[22] Language difficulties led to the three men being discharged but not before 'Charley', an Aboriginal constable, had incurred their enmity. On his release, Nakundah allegedly plotted to murder 'Charley'. Using a young woman to entice him beyond police protection, Nakundah allegedly speared and disembowelled the man who had assisted in his arrest and given evidence against him. However, even by the time Nakundah appeared in the Supreme Court in September 1847, no-one had managed to learn enough of his dialect to adequately interpret the proceedings to him and Cooper had no choice but to discharge him.[23] This decision was discussed widely within the community and contributed to the increase of public support for legal action against Aboriginal people who committed acts of violence against other members of their race. No longer did many colonists wish to turn a blind eye to violence among Aboriginal people. As one colonist wrote in December 1847: 'while much cant is used with reference to their being 'British subjects' and *protected*, &c., they are not *protected* from each other! but only from the whites'.[24]

It was not until 1848 that the Supreme Court recorded a conviction in an *inter se* case. Melaitpa, known to Europeans as 'Bobbo', lived and worked on a station near Burra and when he speared his wife 'Mary' in May 1848 his crime was quickly brought to the attention of the authorities. Arrested and indicted for murder, Melaitpa appeared in the Supreme Court in June 1848, with Bartley again conducting the defence.[25] Bartley's line of argument was familiar, beginning with a challenge to Cooper's right to hear this case on the grounds that there was no established principle that Aboriginal people could be tried for *inter se* offences and 'as there was no Act of the Imperial Legislature authorising such a procedure, it was not competent for the Court to interfere'.[26] However, Cooper replied in kind, using much the same argument as he had in *R v 'Larry'*. The Chief Justice pointed out that while Bartley might be making a 'protest' the court could not consider it to be a plea, since Cooper remained unconvinced that Bartley was acting on his client's instructions in making such an argument. The defence attempted to continue his argument, suggesting that Melaitpa would be adequately dealt with under traditional law, but the Chief Justice cut him short. Cooper then proceeded to explain the reasoning underlying his position on the court's jurisdiction in *inter se* cases:

> With respect to those persons who have lived with Europeans, many of them have been tried, and some have suffered death, for crimes perpetrated against the white population, and the Home Government has sanctioned the act…[there was] no reason, if the natives were liable to be punished for crimes against white people, and white people for crimes against them, why, as British subjects, they should not be liable to punishment for crimes against each other.[27]

The trial proceeded, with damning eyewitness evidence being given by 'Jackey', the twelve-year-old brother of the deceased. Melaitpa was convicted and sentenced to death but Cooper, 'having doubts upon the subject laid the matter before Colonel Robe'.[28] These doubts were not about the *inter se* jurisdiction issue but rather his ongoing difficulty with uncorroborated Aboriginal evidence.[29] When the Executive Council considered the issue, Moorhouse added to these doubts by advising that Melaitpa's tribe had not been informed of the superiority of British law nor that they were 'subject to trial before the British Courts for offences against each other'.[30] Although the Executive Council commuted Melaitpa's sentence to twelve months in prison with hard labour, Governor Robe backed the Chief Justice's decision to proceed with the trial, arguing in his report to London that denial of jurisdiction *inter se* 'would affirm the principle that the aboriginal native may slay his wife or child in our streets'.[31]

However, not everyone agreed with this view, including George Stevenson, who remained convinced of the value of customary law. Having drafted the original proclamation declaring Aboriginal people to be under the protection of the law, he took the not unreasonable view that he knew the real intention behind that declaration. It was not, he now editorialised, intended to apply where 'the offences…are purely native'.[32] To apply the law *inter se* was a 'dangerous interference with the laws and customs of the natives'.[33] The Melaitpa case was, in Stevenson's view:

> at the very best an indecent waste of time of our courts and juries — a sort of mock trial, followed by a mock sentence, which dare not, and cannot, and was never intended to be executed.[34]

He continued to protest at this extension of the law, referring to it derisively as a 'grand scheme for interfering by rules of English Law with tribes who never heard of England'.[35] Pointing out in 1849 that the settlers still had very little understanding of the operation of customary Aboriginal law, Stevenson declared it 'monstrous…to subject them to penalties for that which may…be not only no offence, but a legal and authorised act'[36] under their own customary law. However, the policy was by then firmly in place and Stevenson's protests, despite gaining some support among settlers who saw involvement in *inter se* cases as a waste of the colony's limited legal resources, had little practical effect.

During 1849 two more *inter se* cases came before the Supreme Court. In January, Kambalta was charged with the murder of his wife, Muliano, two years before.[37] Remanded in custody for several months, Kambalta denied that he had speared Muliano. Problems with evidence and lack of witnesses led the Advocate General to eventually decide not to proceed with the prosecution and accordingly Kambalta was released.[38] The second case, however, involved an incident witnessed by several Europeans. On 25 November 1849, in Rundle Street, Nammoingyu was seen to approach a young Aboriginal woman, Kurtainoggaka,[39] and deliberately stab her. Three Europeans chased the offender through the streets until Sergeant Eames intervened and arrested Nammoingyu. Remanded in custody on a charge of stabbing with intent to murder, he appeared in the Supreme Court on 4 December 1849. Evidence given by Kurtainoggaka and Nuntullum suggested that Nammoingyu was a rejected suitor.[40] Fisher strongly defended the accused but once it became clear that Nammoingyu had lived and worked in the town for more than four years and had a reasonable understanding of English, the Chief Justice had little sympathy with the defence arguments.

Nevertheless, the prosecution went to some length to refute the view that the 'actions of the Aborigines were beyond the jurisdiction of a British Court of Law',[41] reminding the jury that this proposition had been 'advanced and over-ruled'.[42] It was by then the case, the Advocate General pointed out, that 'policy as well as humanity renounced such a doctrine'.[43] In his summing up, Cooper also addressed the *inter se* issue directly. Referring to the Melaitpa case the year before, he explained that since defence counsel had objected to his assumption of jurisdiction he had raised the issue with the Governor in June 1848. Although Governor Robe had communicated with London on the *inter se* issue, Cooper's understanding was that 'No answer had been received, and he therefore had continued to act upon his own responsibility'.[44] Given that the wound inflicted was slight and that Kurtainoggaka had made a complete recovery, the Chief Justice recommended that Nammoingyu be found guilty of assault only. The jury agreed and he was gaoled for 12 months with hard labour.[45]

A few months later an Aboriginal man, Budlaroo, was killed near Clare. An Aboriginal youth, Kutromee,[46] was arrested and remanded to Adelaide for trial. The case came up in early February but was held over for two days while officials conferred. The Advocate General then informed the court that the prosecution had decided not to proceed, probably because of the lack of witnesses and interpreting difficulties, and Kutromee was released.[47]

In May 1851 two other cases came before the Chief Justice, sparking considerable public discussion and newspaper debate on the *inter se* issue. In the first, Tukkurm,[48] Nyalta Wikkanin and Kanga Worli were charged with killing Maltalta, who was travelling to Adelaide when he was attacked and fatally speared, apparently for trespassing on their territory. Tukkurm was acquitted while Nyalta Wikkanin and Kanga Worli were found guilty and sentenced to death.[49] The second case involved four men (Weepin, Ngaiere, Tarroti and Penchungya) who were all charged with the murder of an Aboriginal man, Mayponin. In this case, Cooper directed the jury to acquit on the grounds that there was insufficient evidence. This the jury did, although they made the point of requesting that the record noted that their decision was 'under his Honour's direction'.[50] Their decision met with the general 'approval of the community'[51] including most of the settlers in the district where the killing took place, apparently because they understood the four men to be ignorant of European law.[52] The Government Resident reported that the Aboriginal community, including the alleged offenders themselves, were surprised that the killing was of any interest to the authorities:

> they spoke openly to the settlers of what they had done, and when they were told the Police would eventually apprehend them, they said — 'Why will the Police come and take us; we have not killed a white fellow'.[53]

Right from the start, these two cases did not go smoothly. Chief Justice Cooper may have felt that the *inter se* issue was resolved but the Grand Jury remained unconvinced. While ultimately willing to convict 'in the two cases brought before them in which aboriginal natives were charged with the murder of other aboriginal natives',[54] the jurors were not particularly happy about doing so. AH Davis was jury foreman and he drafted a lengthy submission, which the other jurors all signed.[55] It pointed out that several of their number had

> done violence to their own natural feelings of equity and justice; since...the Grand Jurors conceive that if the subjugated tribes be uncivilized men, it is morally incumbent on the superior people, in the first instance, to confine their interference to the mutual protection of both races in their intercourse with each other, and not to meddle with laws or usages having the force of law among savages, in their conduct towards their own race.[56]

A majority of the jurors believed that, in the first of the two cases, Maltalta's killing was within the traditional law of trespass and that bringing the case before the court raised 'serious questions' of a similar kind of trespass on customary law 'by punishing that as a crime which, in the minds of the persons punished, was simply the enforcement of their own code of justice'.[57] As for the second case, the jurors believed this to involve actions based upon 'prevalent superstitions'[58] among the

Aboriginal people, rather than malice. The courts should tread carefully in the *inter se* field, they suggested, and judges should 'define the limits within which it shall be the province of British law to interfere between the aboriginal natives in their own social relations'.[59] The Grand Jury rejected the view that intercourse with Europeans automatically rendered Aboriginal people liable to British law when acting *inter se*, arguing that 'limited intercourse' should not 'justify us in breaking up all their own internal system for the punishment of offences to which all their previous traditions and habits give force and sanction'.[60]

Cooper was somewhat taken aback by this strong expression of views so contrary to current policy and his recent practice. However, he was not goaded into an abrupt response even though he quite forcefully rejected the Grand Jury's arguments.[61] Rather, in a lengthy reply, the Chief Justice reviewed the issue, pointing out that this was a matter which had 'occupied his most serious attention'[62] and on which he had publicly made his views known. He went on to remind the jurors that Aboriginal people were British subjects and of his condition that Aboriginal people must have been in contact with Europeans before he could assume jurisdiction over them. If that condition was met, however, he felt bound to say that if Aboriginal people were amenable for offences committed against colonists, then 'he could not point to any law by which they could escape the consequences of crime committed amongst themselves'.[63] Cooper could see no half-way jurisdiction over Aboriginal people — if the 'court had jurisdiction to try one offence, it had jurisdiction to try all offences'.[64] The trial proceeded and the concern expressed by Davis and the other jurors was rejected by Cooper in his summing up, during which he directed that the men in the dock were indeed 'subject to our laws' and that accordingly the jury must 'find as in an ordinary case between Europeans — according to the evidence'.[65] This they did, with two of the men (Kanga Worli and Nyalta Wikkanin) being found guilty and subsequently sentenced to be hanged.[66]

Even while these two trials were proceeding, the debate on *inter se* jurisdiction was being aired within the colony's newspapers. Once again, Stevenson was at the forefront, using his editorial columns to dissent from Cooper's arguments and rulings. On the same day that Cooper delivered his address to the jury, the *Gazette and Mining Journal* attacked Cooper's interpretation of the law in *inter se* cases, arguing that 'we are by no means so clear that we possess the right to punish natives for offences among themselves'.[67]

Stevenson concluded:

> There will be no end, in short, to the absurdities and inconveniences which this unnecessary meddling with "offences among themselves" must create; and it seems to us that the views of the Judge, as much as the doings of the Protector, deserve to meet special discouragement. We do not go so far as to maintain that his Honour is wrong in a legal sense...But we do maintain that in misdemeanours among the natives themselves it is physically impossible for our Courts to render justice.[68]

The *Register* joined the debate, commenting on both the Grand Jury's presentment and Stevenson's commentary upon it, in a feature article. This accepted the correctness of the policy that Aboriginal people should be held responsible for their *inter se* actions but denied that traditional law was involved in the recent murders. Such violence among Aboriginal people was more a matter of 'the wild spirit of native revenge...[and] their horrible superstitions'[69] than the operation of customary law. Nevertheless, the *Register* argued, Aboriginal people were entitled to the protection of the law when attacked by other Aboriginal people:

> It is not easy to understand on what basis of morality rests the reasoning which would hang a white man for taking the life of a blackfellow, because that of a British subject, and yet would refuse to prevent the most outrageous crimes among the natives themselves.[70]

Soon after, the Chief Justice drafted the first of two letters to the Governor relating to this case.[71] In this letter he once again aired the *inter se* issue, referring to the 1847 and 1848 cases and setting out the views expressed by the Grand Jury. He refrained, however, from suggesting that a pardon was appropriate in the case of Kanga Worli and Nyalta Wikkanin. It was not until two weeks later, after the issue had been well and truly aired in the press, that he wrote a second letter, this time suggesting that both men be pardoned on the grounds that they were following traditional custom in violently confronting the stranger crossing their territory.[72] Moorhouse had investigated this aspect of the case and had probably discussed his findings with Cooper in the period between the Chief Justice's first and second letter. The result was that the two defendants were reprieved in late May and pardoned two weeks later.[73]

For almost two years, the *inter se* issue receded into the background, perhaps because settlers once again turned a blind eye to crimes committed by Aboriginal people against other Aboriginal people. The only case to be prosecuted in this period was one that could hardly be ignored since it involved the murder of two South-East shepherds (Warrinyerrimu and Youngmonamen) in July 1852, allegedly by members of a clan from the Glenelg River area. Three of the attacking group were arrested and brought to trial in Adelaide in August 1852.[74] Perhaps because the slain men had clearly crossed the cultural frontier and were making their way, at least economically, within the settlers' world, there was no controversy over the trial of their attackers. 'Ballycrack', 'Crackingyounger' and 'Potpouch' were convicted and sentenced to death, although their sentences were quickly commuted to life imprisonment.[75]

The *inter se* issue was to be raised again several times between 1853 and 1855. In May 1853 a case involving the brutal murder of a woman by her husband at Port Adelaide came to the attention of the authorities. The woman, Watte Watte, was apparently well known and liked by settlers in both the town and the port.[76] This fact, allied to the crime having being committed within the settled area, made it unlikely that this case of domestic violence would be ignored as so many had before it. The inquest into the woman's death heard evidence that Kauadla (also known as 'Peter') had struck Watte Watte with a waddy several times in the course of an argument. Moorhouse suggested that Kauadla was a nasty character and that he 'had heard from the natives that he [Kauadla] killed a native woman with a spear five years ago'.[77] Kauadla was arrested and brought to trial in the Supreme Court in May 1853. Bartley was appointed as defence counsel and he took three lines of argument during the proceedings. First, he argued that Kauadla was acting traditionally in beating his wife, an act not recognised as a crime in customary law. Second, he denied any intent to kill, arguing that Kauadla had intended only to chastise Watte Watte. Third, he adduced evidence of provocation, calling a witness who testified that Watte Watte had 'been in the habit of going with a white man, and sometimes left her husband for a fortnight at a time'.[78] A curious jury member destroyed the first argument by asking whether the Aboriginal people themselves considered Kauadla's actions to be wrong. Defence witness Tainmunda was invited to reply but his answer operated against the accused: 'We call him a murderer. He was wrong. We consider him wrong and call him a murderer'.[79] The jury took no account of the second argument, which would have reduced the charge to manslaughter, and found Kauadla guilty of murder. However, in consideration of the third line of the defence's argument, they 'recommended him to mercy on the ground of the provocation he had received'.[80] Despite describing Kauadla as 'cruel and barbarous', when he sentenced him to death the Chief Justice gave notice of his intention to forward the recommendation for mercy to the Executive Council.[81] The result was that Kauadla's sentence was commuted to imprisonment for two years. Later that month the *Register* devoted considerable space to an editorial on the subject of this commutation.[82] While agreeing that few colonists wanted to see Kauadla executed, it argued:

> The law which made the aborigines of Australia British subjects was meant for their protection…the case is strangely altered when the law, instead of a shield, becomes a spear — an avenger, instead of a protector. When, as in the case of Kauadla, a native is charged with a crime of the nature of which he is ignorant, before a Court of whose jurisdiction he knew as little, the solemn forms and the legal paraphernalia of the trial look painfully like a farce, and the sentence, inevitable according to law, is preposterous according to common sense.[83]

However, the editorial could suggest no practical alternatives and was forced to concede that, given all the circumstances of the case the final sentence was 'as judicious as could have been chosen'.[84]

In December 1853, four men were charged with the murder of another Aboriginal shepherd, 'Billy', who was employed on Doughty's station in the South-East of the colony. It was alleged that Tinkanor, Woringena, Ngallabammu and Tunkanayman had murdered 'Billy' in June of that year. When the case came up in the Supreme Court, once again the defence counsel, Bailey, objected to the case being heard on the grounds that the Supreme Court did not have jurisdiction over these men in *inter se* matters. His objection was quickly overruled and the trial proceeded, with witnesses Newooman and Krupkrup Bonat giving an account of the disagreement. Their evidence raised doubts about malice and intent and Bailey was able to use it to call for a verdict of manslaughter. Justice Boothby summed up favourably to this view and the jury returned a manslaughter verdict.[85] All four men were sentenced to three years in prison with hard labour.[86]

In 1855 another three cases involving *inter se* crimes were tried in the Supreme Court. The first, in February, arose out of the killing of an Aboriginal male, known only as 'Alick', near Penola in the previous October. Monboit and Wrochoven were arrested in December 1854 but it soon became clear that neither was involved in the actual killing. However, it was alleged that they were present at the time and so both were charged with 'being present at, and aiding and abetting the murder'.[87] When the case came before the Supreme Court, the prosecution had little evidence that the pair were even present and none to suggest that they were involved in any substantive way. The police held little hope of capturing the actual killers and the Judge ordered that Monboit and Wrochoven be discharged.[88]

Meanwhile, two men had been arrested and charged with the murder of an Aboriginal shepherd named Loorumumpoo, who worked on McFarlane's property near Wellington. It was alleged that Marielare and Poowoolupe had killed the shepherd on or about 11 December 1854 by beating him to death with their waddies.[89] In March, Poowoolupe managed to escape from custody and a decision was taken to postpone Marielare's trial until the next sessions, in the hope that his compatriot would be recaptured.[90] This turned out to be the case and the two men eventually stood trial in August 1855. Defence counsel Hartley conceded that the men had killed Loorumumpoo but argued that Poowoolupe had instigated the attack, perhaps because he was aware that the Aboriginal witnesses would testify that greater blame lay with Marielare.[91] Much of the trial argument centred on the issues of malice and the Aboriginal custom of using violence to resolve differences, with Hartley making much of Marielare's lack of any intent to kill. With the prosecution case relying completely on Aboriginal witnesses, Hartley was no doubt buoyed by the prosecution's surprising expression of doubt as to their reliability: '[Aboriginal witnesses] were…exceedingly ignorant of their duty as witnesses, and consequently their statements were to be taken with great caution'.[92]

However, Justice Boothby was not impressed by Hartley's arguments. On the issue of malice, he commented in his summing up that it was 'not enough…for the accused to deny malice; the law assumes malice in life-taking'.[93] Regarding the customary law defence, the Judge made it clear that the two accused men, both of whom could speak English and had considerable previous contact with Europeans, were subject to British law. Boothby declared that he 'knew no standards whereby to fix the responsibilities of aboriginal natives with the regard to the taking of human life except that of the law'.[94] Perhaps the jury saw matters differently, for they voted to acquit both men.

The third case that year was a particularly interesting one. Two Boandik men, Warenboorimen and Parichboorinen, were accused of the murder of an Aboriginal woman, known as 'Mary', at Spring Station in the South-East of the colony.[95] 'Mary' was well known among the Europeans around Glencoe, where she was employed as a shepherd when the gold rushes caused a severe shortage of rural labour. At the trial in late November 1855, it soon became clear that this case involved Aboriginal customary beliefs if not traditional law. 'Mary' was apparently regarded by some Boandik people as having spiritual powers and when Warenboorimen's wife died, he held 'Mary' indirectly responsible for her death. Defence counsel Bartley seized upon this, arguing that the accused were obliged under traditional law to take revenge for the victim's 'bewitching' of Warenboorimen's wife and therefore ought to be acquitted.[96] However, the court interpreter, Duncan Smith, locally regarded as an expert on Boandik cultural customs and language, expressed the view that revenge killing was not an accepted custom among the Boandik clans. Justice Boothby, in his summing up, agreed that the jury should consider 'the effect native customs might have upon this case'[97] but reminded them 'that while the natives held the act to be perfectly right and justifiable, the English law regarded it as murder'.[98] Nevertheless, he did point out that they could apply 'the leniency which the law allowed (and) find the prisoners guilty of manslaughter'.[99] This the jury did and Boothby gaoled both men for three years with hard labour.

A similar case was that of *R v Langaryngarynga and Eroyngaree*, heard in the Supreme Court in August 1859. Charged with the murder of Pantwirri at Lake Albert in February of that year, the two men pleaded not guilty and were defended by Bartley. Aboriginal witnesses testified that Pantwirri was considered to be a magician or wizard and that the defendants believed (as apparently did other members of their clan) that the deceased had used his powers to kill Langaryngarynga's father.[100] In particular, Pultirri's evidence painted a picture of two men convinced that they were exacting rightful revenge and lawful punishment. Justice Boothby directed the jury that they should bring in a verdict of manslaughter if they attached credibility to Pultirri's evidence.[101] This they did and the two men were sentenced to a gaol term of six months.

Incidentally, Langaryngarynga escaped several weeks later while working in the Adelaide Gaol quarry and was never seen again by Europeans.[102]

In the following year, two other men were tried after taking part in what was apparently a killing accepted under customary law. Pinberri was a Pangkala man, living near Franklin Harbour on Eyre Peninsula. Allegedly, members of his clan decided that he must die although it was not clear in what ways he had offended them, other than being declared to be a 'maniac' or 'madman'.[103] Popeltie and Padneltie were delegated the task and accordingly killed Pinberri in September 1860. Both men were charged with murder and at their trial the court was told by witnesses that they were acting on behalf of the clan, although difficulties with language and interpretation meant that this issue was not able to be pursued at any depth.[104] Defending counsel Stow sought an outright acquittal but the Judge directed that a verdict of manslaughter was an option for the jury, if they considered the killing was 'in accordance with some superstitious practice. This would not constitute murder'.[105] However, the jury returned a verdict of not guilty and both men were freed.

As *inter se* cases came up more frequently before the courts, ways had to be found to deal with the problems they entailed. These included opting initially for a charge of manslaughter, the reduction of the murder charge to that of manslaughter after indictment, a direction from the bench for a conviction on the lesser charge, or for juries to take the latter course of their own accord. For example, in 1857 there were two separate murder cases which resulted in convictions for manslaughter. The first case involved Gootoognuyerie and Toorapennie, charged with the murder of Courkin (known to Europeans as 'Jemmy Adams') near Strathalbyn in June 1857.[106] Initially denying the charge, the two men confessed when brought to stand trial in Adelaide and the charge against them was then reduced to manslaughter. Fisher acted for their defence, arguing that the men had been intoxicated at the time of the killing. George Mason, called upon to interpret, agreed to give favourable character evidence for both men, a fact that seemed to impress Acting Judge Mann.[107] When the jury returned a guilty verdict, he sentenced both to gaol for six months with hard labour.[108] In the second case Beerdeah was charged with the murder of an Aboriginal man, 'Bullocky', at Tillowey also in June 1857.[109] In this instance it also seems that Beerdeah's willingness to cooperate with the police and to make a full confession led the Advocate General to reduce the charge to manslaughter.[110] Beerdeah was found guilty of manslaughter and sentenced to imprisonment with hard labour for six months.

In 1859–60, several *inter se* murder cases came before the Supreme Court. At the February sessions two Boandik men, Meenaltie and Mandeltie, were charged with the murder of an Aboriginal man near Mt Gambier. The deceased was a traveller, certainly a stranger to the area, and he was killed by several blows of a tomahawk to the head. However, there seemed to be no eyewitnesses and the case collapsed for want of evidence.[111] Within a week, the same result was reached in a case where the reverse situation had occurred — three Aboriginal people from the Flinders Ranges killed a local man while visiting Port Lincoln. In this case, heard in October 1858, Magulta, Minulta and Kaneguiltie were charged with the murder of Nulguiltie. The three men were brought by ship to Adelaide to stand trial but when they appeared the prosecution declared itself unable to proceed.[112] In another case in the same court in May 1859, Wooloobully was clearly remorseful about his slaying of Baldanant at Mt Burr earlier that year. The deceased, known to local Europeans as 'One Cold Morning', was a popular worker on one of Leake's stations. Apparently the two friends had a disagreement after a traditional ceremony and Baldanant fired a gun at Wooloobully. Unharmed but angry, Wooloobully fetched a spear and thrust it into Baldanant's stomach. Aboriginal witnesses recounted that he immediately expressed regret at what he had done, even to the point of offering his head to be beaten with a waddy by the wounded man. But Baldanant died that night and the local police constable arrested Wooloobully on a charge of murder. At the trial, defence counsel Fisher argued that there was neither motive for murder nor intent to kill. He warned the jury about making judgements based on their own experience, stating that when considering cases involving Aboriginal people 'their acts should not be judged in the same manner as a white man is'.[113] Justice Gwynne, in his summing up, was clearly sympathetic towards the accused and even suggested that it remained 'extremely difficult to apply the laws made for a civilized nation to the customs and habits of the natives of this colony'.[114] He directed the jury to either find Wooloobully guilty of manslaughter or to acquit him. Reportedly impressed by the remorse of the accused, the jury set him free.[115]

While the *inter se* cases detailed in this chapter show that the policy of Aboriginal people being entitled to the protection of British law even within relationships among themselves was put into practice from the late 1840s, a closer look at the circumstances of the cases suggests that the policy was only implemented in a very limited way. Given the disruptions to traditional life caused by the expansion of settlement within South Australia, the number of *inter se* cases seem relatively few. Of the forty-six Aboriginal people charged with the murder of another Aboriginal person during the twenty-five years under scrutiny here, only twenty-seven of these people had their cases heard in full. The other nineteen were either not prosecuted at all after their initial indictment or went before the court only to have the case abandoned during the trial — usually on the initiative of a frustrated prosecutor but also at times as a result of the Judge acting to dismiss the charges. Where the cases did run their course, ten of the accused men were acquitted and six found guilty of murder, while another nine were convicted on the reduced charge of manslaughter. None of those convicted of murdering another Aboriginal person were executed despite several death sentences being handed down. Once these sentences were commuted, the convicted men usually served out their sentence of between two and three years in prison before being released, although two men were pardoned soon after their reprieve. These figures suggest that even though the official policy evolved into considering *inter se* cases in the same light as those committed against Europeans, in practice such crimes were always seen as being of a lesser order — indeed, to many colonists including some within legal circles, not always to be considered as a crime at all.

The common thread running through most of these cases is that they took place 'under the noses' of the settlers, or more particularly, within the range of the authorities. They were situations which could not easily be ignored; first, because the victims were Aboriginal people who had made the choice to live largely within the settler community; second, because the crimes were a clear affront to the authority of local officials or police; and third, because they particularly offended European sensibilities. This argument is supported by there being only three cases of assault by Aboriginal people against other Aboriginal people recorded in the court and newspaper records examined during this study. While murder and manslaughter were considered crimes serious enough to warrant official intervention in Aboriginal society, lesser crimes were only very rarely so. Indeed, the three cases were the authorities did take legal action were of a severity that they could well have warranted attempted murder charges. Of course, it is true that the data available to this study is biased towards the more serious *inter se* cases in that assault charges would have been heard in the local Magistrates' Courts. However, even allowing for unreported rural assault cases it seems reasonable to conclude that the very limited number of such cases found suggest that they were overlooked by police rather than pursued. This reluctance can be partly attributed to practical reasons, such as the limited manpower in frontier police stations within the colony and the difficulties with Aboriginal evidence and interpretation detailed earlier. However, it also reflects a more fundamental reason, namely that many settlers and officials remained unconvinced that British law should intervene within *inter se* relations, or that it was in practice capable of effectively doing so.

At an 1860 Legislative Council Enquiry, some members still had enough reservations about the policy to address it when taking evidence. For example, the Reverend Farrell was asked whether he thought it advisable to treat Aboriginal people 'strictly according to the letter of the law'[116] in *inter se* dealings, to which he replied that it 'hardly meets the even course of justice'.[117] Even the former Protector of Aborigines, Moorhouse, could not bring himself to support the extension of the British law to cover *inter se* situations: 'Offences amongst themselves should be settled amongst themselves, but offences against Europeans should be settled by British law'.[118] This view probably reflected the majority settler opinion throughout the 1850s but there were those who would have preferred a more aggressive application of the policy to bring *inter se* relationships under British law. For example, when the Bishop of Adelaide travelled through the northern districts in 1857, he was shocked by the violence within Aboriginal communities he visited:

> I heard of one murdered by other natives at Saltia Creek while dragging wood, and another at Pekina. I saw and handled one whose head had received three chops with a tomahawk at Aquaba, he having previously killed an opponent who had challenged him to fight.[119]

While he believed that part of the fault for this situation lay with his own institution's failure to bring Christianity to the Aboriginal people, the Bishop also observed that the police were turning a blind eye to most *inter se* crimes. He called on the Government to remedy this situation, to which the Police Commissioner replied that the police could not interfere too far in matters of customary law: 'One man steals another man's lubra, and has, perhaps, lost his life for the offence. It is native law'.[120]

CHAPTER 7
MURDER AND MANSLAUGHTER

The murder cases in the first three years of the colony were considered in chapter 2 so this account begins at 1840, commencing with a closer look at events in and around Port Lincoln. Established in 1839, this Eyre Peninsula settlement soon became the most vulnerable European outpost in the colony. Initial relations between settlers and the Nauo–Battara clans were amicable but clashes became inevitable as settlers took over choice sites on the coast and moved inland in search of pastures for their stock. For example, in March 1840, on Hawson's station a few miles out from the town, the owner's young son was killed. When Frank Hawson refused food to a Battara group, they forced entry into a hut, leading to a confrontation during which the boy was fatally speared. Hawson's killers were not identified and no charges were ever laid.[1] Late in the summer of 1842, more Battara men took action to resist further encroachment on their lands. Sporadic raids on stations and flocks escalated to the point where they 'struck terror and dismay into the hearts'[2] of many settlers, forced most outpost families to take refuge in Port Lincoln[3] and threatened the very existence of the township.[4] At Brown's station, in March 1842, the proprietor and a shepherd named Lovelock were both killed in an attack. The settlers were better prepared when raiders struck again, this time at a neighbouring station owned by Charles Dutton. In a counterattack they 'succeeded in capturing the leader of the tribe, Nantes'.[5] Nantes admitted to leading the earlier raid on Brown's property and he was sent to stand trial in Adelaide for murder. The settlers hoped that a harsh example would be made of Nantes, but they were to be disappointed. European witnesses failed to appear when he came before the Supreme Court, apparently because the station owners would not pay to send their stockkeepers to Adelaide.

The Advocate General therefore dropped the murder charge, proceeding only with a charge of sheep stealing.[6]

Meanwhile the clashes around Port Lincoln intensified. On White's station George Baldock was killed in early 1842. Moorpar was tried in the Supreme Court in September 1842 for this crime, was found guilty and sentenced to death.[7] However, doubts about the evidence led to a commutation of this sentence and, in 1845, a pardon.[8] On 28 March, at Long Ponds near Port Lincoln, a large party of Aboriginal people attacked the huts on Biddle's station. The owner was killed, along with James Fastings and Elizabeth Stubbs.[9] The latter's husband survived the attack and was able to name the attackers. Nultia and Moullia were arrested and sent to Adelaide for trial on three counts of murder and one of attempted murder[10] while Ngarbi was indicted for the murder of Elizabeth Stubbs.[11] In March 1843 Nultia and Moullia were convicted and sentenced to death.[12] However, the Governor made it clear that Moullia's sentence would be commuted after the execution of Nultia, who was hanged on 4 April 1843. Moullia was imprisoned at Port Lincoln, despite Governor Grey's doubts about the value of his continued detention,[13] but he was pardoned in 1845. Ngarbi's case, heard in July 1843, was not helped by Stubbs' evidence that his wife had showed kindness to the accused only days before her death.[14] Ngarbi was convicted of being an accessory to murder but nevertheless was hanged in June 1843.

Meanwhile, in 1842, a murder with a different motivation had been committed to the south of Adelaide. McGrath, Pew and Chase were heading to Port Phillip along the Coorong route, guided by four Aboriginal men: Wira Maldira, Wekiweki, Koorykownimmi and Pantowyn. While camped in the sandhills at Moorundungah (now known as McGrath Flat) these four men decided to attack their employers. The motivation for their actions may have been a dispute over payment or the overlanders' alleged rape of a Ngarrindjeri woman earlier that day.[15] George McGrath died from his injuries and his companions fled into the scrub. Wira Maldira and Wekiweki were eventually arrested and charged with murder in 1845, with the former being found guilty when damning evidence was given against him by his compatriots, Koorykownimmi and Pantowyn.[16] Sentenced to death, Maldira was hanged on 29 March 1845.[17] Wekiweki was convicted in June 1845 on the lesser charge of assisting in the murder and also sentenced to death but this sentence was commuted to life imprisonment.[18]

While most colonists had little sympathy for the plight of Wira Maldira, this was not the case when another Aboriginal man was charged with murder in the following year. Richard Carney disappeared in the South-East in November 1846 and a search soon discovered his body in a shallow grave. The inquest revealed that several blows to the head were the cause of death and police enquiries implicated Tatty Wamboureen in the killing. He was arrested, taken to Robe and there remanded for trial in Adelaide.[19] Two difficulties soon emerged: an inability to interpret Tatty's evidence[20] and the failure to find three witnesses.[21] Duncan Smith learned enough of Tatty Wamboureen's dialect to determine that Carney had been involved sexually with Wamboureen's wife — one account even suggests that the couple were having intercourse when Carney was killed.[22] Chief Justice Cooper had doubts about the ability of his court to try Wamboureen, given the lack of progress in interpreting his language.[23] Eventually, in March 1848, when even the European witnesses failed to appear, the prosecution abandoned the case and he was discharged, having spent fifteen months in custody.[24]

By the mid 1840s, the area around Port Lincoln was well settled and pioneers moved northwards along both coasts of the Eyre Peninsula, establishing sheep runs in two broad coastal bands. Clashes over land and water resources developed within a season or two of European settlement. In early 1846 two shepherds, Scott and Whitney, disappeared from Tennant's station. Meiya Murkata, Wodla Murkata and Nakundah Biddeah were charged with their murder but there was little evidence against the three,[25] with Chief Justice Cooper noting that there was 'no probability of convicting the prisoners even if the means of interpretation could be found'.[26] After several remands, the prosecution abandoned the case and the three men were released.[27]

Aboriginal resistance activities on the peninsula reached a peak in 1848–9 when the Protector noted that 'collisions have occurred, attended with loss of life, amongst the Europeans as well as the Natives'.[28] Many of these Aboriginal deaths went unrecorded but those of the settlers became well known throughout the colony. The first of these was a result of an incident which took place in mid June 1848, when an isolated hut on Pinkerton's station at Lake Newland was attacked. John Hamp was killed and his body mutilated by sawing his head 'into two pieces with a hand-saw'.[29] When a police party arrived a few days after

7. Murder and manslaughter

the discovery of Hamp's body, the trail was cold and the police admitted that there was 'little probability of the offender being identified and brought to justice'.[30] However, a local man, Mingalta, had been observed behaving suspiciously a few days before Hamp's body was found. The following January, when Venus Bay police encountered Mingalta they found that he and a companion, Malgalta, had in their possession a pannikin and knives thought to have belonged to Hamp. Sergeant Geharty interrogated the two men and they confessed to a killing of a man known to them as 'Tommy',[31] thought to be their nickname for Hamp. The two men were charged with murder and the evidence against them seemed substantial, including evidence of Mingalta being at the scene, the possession of the utensils, their vague confessions, and the statement of an Aboriginal eyewitness, Winnulu.

However, the prosecution was not to have the smooth ride it expected. When the case came before the Supreme Court, Chief Justice Cooper was ill and Charles Mann was acting on the Bench. Defence counsel Bartley cross-examined Sergeant Geharty, hoping to show that the confessions were made under duress but instead revealed the opposite — although the defendants had been 'cautioned to say nothing',[32] the men had made their statements in casual conversations during the journey to Port Lincoln. Accordingly, Acting Judge Mann ruled them inadmissible, later suggesting that it was 'obvious that Geharty had transmitted a mere inference of his own mind into an absolute admission of guilt'.[33] Even so, things looked bad for the two accused when Winnulu gave evidence that he had been present at the attack on Hamp's hut. He stated that Malgalta had thrown the first spear but that one thrown by Mingalta had delivered the fatal blow. The others present had then all speared 'Tommy', mutilating his body and leaving it in a waterhole. Bartley seized upon Winnulu's evidence, arguing that there was considerable confusion over the location of the killing being described and suggesting that this account related to an altogether separate killing. He argued that this would also explain the confessions, which may have referred to an earlier killing of an unknown frontiersman or even another Aboriginal person. As to the use of a saw to cut Hamp's head, Winnulu's evidence initially failed to mention this. Bartley must have groaned when, on seeking to reinforce this point during cross examination, Winnulu recalled seeing such a mutilation being committed by Moolooltoo, one of the two companions of the accused. Bartley's attempt to portray Winnulu's evidence as being related to another killing was therefore thrown into doubt and the jury found Mingalta and Malgalta guilty — both were sentenced to death.[34]

But some of the more humanitarian-minded Adelaide citizens who had followed the trial were convinced that an injustice had been done. As well as the doubts about the identity of 'Tommy' and the timing and location discrepancies, the link between the knives and pannikins in the possession of the accused and those owned by Hamp was tenuous. This public disquiet led the Governor to request Chief Justice Cooper to review the case. When he did so, Cooper found the evidence against the two to be substantial, despite the doubts raised. In this case, the Chief Justice argued, the difficulty regarding the identity of the victim had been brought to the attention of the jury and they had made their decision upon it and, accordingly, he refused to recommend overturning the verdict.[35] The Chief Justice's report was sent to Charles Mann for comment and he recommended mercy. However, at the Executive Council meeting of 24 October 1849,[36] there was unanimous agreement not to recommend a pardon or reprieve.[37] Nevertheless, the humanitarian forces within Adelaide were not willing to leave the matter there and they rallied to support the Bishop of Adelaide, who collected scores of signatures petitioning for clemency. The result was that the sentence of the two men was commuted to life imprisonment.[38]

By 1849 settlers in the more remote areas of both Eyre and Yorke peninsulas were in fear of losing their livelihoods, if not their lives, as a result of Aboriginal attacks.[39] Those directly involved in facing Aboriginal attacks threatened violent and illegal action against Aboriginal people on the frontier if the police could not bring the attacks on stock and stockkeepers to a halt.[40] However, the fact that two men could appear in the Supreme Court within months of such calls and receive what can only be described as a fair trial, followed by a judicial review and a public campaign for clemency resulting in the commutation of their death sentences, is an indication of the continuing influence of humanitarian-based ideals within the colony. Nonetheless, there was a growing divide between those of a humanitarian bent and colonists of a more pragmatic attitude. Some settlers were already taking matters into their own hands in ways equally as brutal as any of the Aboriginal actions. Most colonists were aware of instances of European brutality, such as the 1844 Mt Bryan killings and the more recent poisoning of Aboriginal people on Mortlock's station near Coffin Bay.[41] In the minds of a significant number of colonists, including some of influence, considerable sympathy still lay with the Aboriginal people who were facing uncontrolled encroachment onto their lands.

When the death of Charles Beevor, the co-owner of Tornto station on western Eyre Peninsula, became known in early May 1849 these moderate views were initially challenged. However, once the details of this murder became known, sympathetic settlers were once again reassured. For Beevor, murdered by Aboriginal people in April 1849, was considered to have been imprudent at best. His relations with the people who killed him were close and probably involved an ongoing sexual relationship with Yabmanna, the wife of one of his alleged killers. The night before the murder, several Aboriginal people (including Nintalta and Yabmanna) slept overnight at his hut and a disagreement culminated in Beevor being speared.[42] After ransacking the hut, the attackers fled but the police had little difficulty in tracking them down and arrests were soon made.[43] Tried at the same sessions as Mingalta and Malgalta, Yabmanna was found not guilty of assisting in the murder of Beevor, but both Kulgulta and Mingulta were found guilty of the crime. These two men, brought up for sentencing on the same day as Hamp's killers, also received the death sentence.[44] In their case though, the evidence had been straightforward and there was no room for protest over the verdict.[45] Kulgulta and Mingulta were hanged on 9 November 1849.[46]

On 9 May 1849 the party following the trail from the site of Beevor's murder heard of the murder of Ann Easton, the wife of one of Vaux's shepherds at Lake Hamilton. Two days earlier, after the young woman had refused rations to a group of Aboriginal people, they had returned and forced their way into her isolated hut.[47] The party of police and civilians was outraged by this rape and murder. They pushed on in hard pursuit of Beevor's killers but most of the Port Lincoln volunteers were forced to withdraw when their horses were exhausted.[48] When word reached the party of a clash at nearby Horne's station, they moved in to surround a nearby Aboriginal camp. Acting Police Commissioner Tolmer ordered the troopers to attack and in the resulting affray three Aboriginal people[49] were killed and five captured, including Bakilti and his female companion Puterpynter, who were charged with the murder of Ann Easton.[50] Bakilti was already known to the authorities (as 'Jem Brown'), having been found guilty of assaulting a shepherd the year before. Although there was initially considerable hostility towards the accused couple among Adelaide residents, this faded somewhat when the weakness of the evidence against them became known. At their Supreme Court trial in late September 1849, the prosecution collapsed when an Aboriginal witness gave evidence that Bakilti 'was outside the hut cutting grass, and that another blackfellow (not in custody) named Malpita, did the deed'.[51] The Judge's summing up suggested that the two accused were little more than opportunistic thieves, who had stolen clothing and rations from the Easton hut after the killers had left. He recommended acquittal on the murder charge and the jury agreed. However, they brought in a guilty verdict on a lesser charge of assault on a shepherd and both Bakilti and Puterpynter were gaoled for two years with hard labour.[52]

Settlers on Yorke Peninsula were also facing sporadic but at times determined resistance to their takeover of Aboriginal land in the late 1840s. Most of the attacks were on flocks rather than on shepherds, but in early August 1849 William Scott was reported missing from his hut near Hardwicke Bay. When Corporal McCulloch investigated he encountered an Aboriginal man, Wilcuramalap, shepherding a large number of Scott's sheep. Once captured, Wilcuramalap led the police to the body of the shepherd. He was charged with Scott's murder but was later acquitted.[53] During his interrogation, however, he gave police information about another murder, that of Thomas Armstrong in July 1849. Armstrong, a shepherd on Stephen's station, had been fatally speared in an attack by several Aboriginal people.[54] Subsequently, Tulta was arrested, but in March 1850 the prosecution conceded that it had no real case against him.[55]

In May of the following year another Yorke Peninsula shepherd, Bagnall, was killed. Aboriginal trackers led an unsuccessful search for the killers, during which the police investigation uncovered a likely motive for this murder: apparently Bagnall had trained his dog to attack Aboriginal people indiscriminately. Several Aboriginal people had made complaints about this to the police in the months preceding his death and Bagnall had been warned about the growing ill feeling against him.[56] In September four Aboriginal men were arrested and charged with his murder: Marrippa, Warrippa, Yellarri and Ngiyeri. A key Aboriginal witness, Mithra, absconded from police custody, delaying proceedings until he was recaptured in February 1852.[57] During the trial, the prosecution decided not to proceed with the charges against Yellarri. Defence counsel made much of the issue of provocation, with the result that the remaining three men were found guilty of manslaughter only.[58]

Marrippa was sentenced to twelve months' imprisonment with hard labour while Warrippa and Ngiyeri received six months each.⁵⁹

In 1851 the east coast of Eyre Peninsula was 'in a very disturbed state, consequent upon the aggressions of the natives'.⁶⁰ A severe drought in this area during the summer of 1850–51 meant that Aboriginal clans were feeling the impact of no longer having unrestricted access to their traditional water resources — clashes over waterholes were inevitable. At Lipson's Cove in April 1851 shepherd George Jenks was found dead, apparently killed with his own axe.⁶¹ Port Lincoln police suspected that Kambalta had been involved. The previous January he had been implicated in the robbery of Constable Kenning's hut at nearby Salt Creek and had been found guilty of receiving stolen goods after Jenks had given evidence against him.⁶² As a result, the suspicion was that he had orchestrated the attack on Jenks in revenge for that earlier incrimination. When confronted, Kambalta resisted arrest and attempted to spear his captors but was taken into custody. Although Kambalta was committed for trial, the local magistrate noted that the evidence against him was 'very unsatisfactory'.⁶³ Investigations suggested that Kambalta may have arranged for others to carry out the deed. The details of this alleged conspiracy came to light because of a sexual relationship between Marialta, Kambalta's wife, and one of Jenks' colleagues, James Fuller. The night before the attack she had warned Fuller to stay clear of Jenks' hut and when this became known, she and a companion, Ngamalta, were arrested as accessories to murder. However, the evidence was 'insufficient to sustain the indictment'⁶⁴ and the case against them was dropped.

Attention then turned to apprehending the men it was alleged had been incited to commit the murder. Thought to be Pangkala men from north of Franklin Harbour, they were pursued by police troopers. In May 1851 two men, Mangultu and Cooliltie, were arrested after being found with objects from Jenks' hut.⁶⁵ They were tried as being accessories to murder: Mangultu was acquitted but Cooliltie was found guilty and sentenced to twelve months in prison.⁶⁶ After serving his sentence he was released but rearrested six years later, this time for the murder of Jenks.⁶⁷ Found guilty on this charge, Cooliltie was sentenced to be hanged but this sentence was commuted.⁶⁸ In a bizarre twist, some months after his release in 1859, Cooliltie was arrested once again and charged for a second time with the murder of Jenks. When the case came up in the Supreme Court, defence counsel Fisher astounded the prosecution by producing evidence of the defendant's previous conviction on the same charge. Not surprisingly the judge 'directed that a man could not be tried twice for the same offence'[69] and found him not guilty.

Soon after the attack on Jenks, another shepherd, William Light, was speared as he emerged from a wurley on Peters' station at Pellara.[70] It was never discovered what the deceased was doing at the time, nor was any clear motive for the killing suggested — but some colonists had their own suspicions. Corporal Geharty[71] and an unnamed Aboriginal constable tracked the attackers from the scene and arrested two men, Kamalta and Tyerrungi.[72] Both were found guilty but not before they impressed several of the officials who had dealings with them.[73] Probably because of the suspicions raised by the circumstances in which Light was killed, the sentence passed upon them was relatively light: twelve months' imprisonment with hard labour.[74] Even so, Kamalta did not have to serve his full term as Port Lincoln residents petitioned for his early release and he was set free in December 1851. Kamalta's subsequent close relationship with the Port Lincoln settlers proved fatal however, as he was accidentally shot dead by Constable Mallelieu in the Port Lincoln Police Station in June 1855.

When Charles Crocker was killed in early March 1851 at Kulura most settlers thought this was simply another murder of a shepherd by Aboriginal people determined to steal sheep and rations. However, the investigation soon raised doubts among local police and officials, particularly that this may have been a murder arranged by another settler with a grievance against Crocker. As the Government Resident in Port Lincoln noted:

> The circumstances connected with this case are, without exception, the most extraordinary that have fallen under my observation during an official experience of upwards of nine years in the habits of the natives of the district. Certain leading features that have stamped every act of violence committed by them on the Europeans were, on this occasion, so completely wanting, that suspicion, based on strong circumstantial evidence, inevitably pointed out a white man as agent; for instance, their murders have always been committed in strong parties, attended by wanton destruction of property, and a barbarous mangling of the head, such as sawing the head, or beating it to a pulp, or burying an axe in it, etc.; besides, they never attempted to cloak their atrocities by any such deliberate measures of concealment

as the sweeping of a floor to efface tracks, or the fastening of a door.[75]

Despite these doubts, the investigation implicated three local Aboriginal people. Kambalta and Kulbilti were arrested and charged with the crime, while Irtabidui, Kulbilti's wife, was indicted as an accessory.[76] Kulbilti confessed to the killing but claimed to have been put up to it by another stockkeeper, John Shepherd.[77] The latter was arrested but when he steadfastly denied any involvement the prosecution decided that it was pointless to proceed against him given that the only evidence was Kulbilti's unsupported statement. Despite a widely held belief among local settlers that Shepherd had instigated the killing, the prosecutions of the three Aboriginal accused still went ahead. Not surprisingly then, Fisher defended the charges vigorously.[78] Although not able to directly accuse Shepherd, Fisher intimated that those in the dock were not solely responsible for the crime. He argued that insufficient evidence had been tendered by the prosecution to justify conviction for either murder or manslaughter but in the end was unable to overcome Kulbilti's confession. The jury acquitted all three on the murder charges but found the two men guilty of manslaughter and they were sentenced to two years' imprisonment with hard labour.[79] Few settlers in the area of the crime were satisfied with this result, most remaining convinced that Shepherd had been the principal instigator. Accordingly, in 1852, several stock owners, perhaps more motivated by pragmatism than any sense of justice, petitioned the Governor for the early release and repatriation of Kambalta and Kulbilti. This would, they argued, forestall further violence in the district by reducing the anger of local Aboriginal people. The Governor agreed and both men were returned to their homelands, where Charles Driver later reported that they were soon regarded as being 'peaceable and obliging'.[80]

Further to the north-west, some groups of the Kokatha could not be so described. By 1850, settlers had consolidated their hold on the coastal lands as far north as Venus Bay but some were imprudent enough to move further north, without adequate support. James Baird was one such risk-taker, convinced that the area around Streaky Bay presented an excellent pastoral opportunity. More prudent settlers had kept clear of the area, aware that earlier clashes between whalers and Aboriginal people had soured race relations along that part of the coast. In late October 1850, Baird and his shepherd, Richard Townsend, were attacked by a large Aboriginal party.[81] Eight hundred sheep were driven off and the next day Baird foolishly set off alone in pursuit of the thieves, leaving Townsend at the station hut. The latter was soon under siege but he managed to slip away at night and walk south to Pinkerton's station to raise the alarm.[82] Constables Smith and Dewson came up from Tungketta police outpost to pursue the offenders. Along with stock owners Pinkerton and Stewart and several of their employees, they set off in search of Baird and the stolen sheep.

On 12 November the party encountered a group of Aboriginal people in charge of several hundred sheep. Without warning, the party galloped into the encampment and opened fire. Two or three Aboriginal people were wounded but all managed to flee into the scrub.[83] Later that day Constable Dewson encountered one of their number, Pulgulta, and took him prisoner.[84] The next day Baird's decomposed body was found in a shallow grave in a salt pan and examination suggested that he had been killed several days earlier.[85] Pulgulta was taken south to Port Lincoln, where he was indicted for murder. On 24 November, Sergeant Geharty, accompanied by several men and an Aboriginal guide, set out to arrest others suspected of involvement in this killing. This party had no difficulty following the tracks of their quarry, as they were driving 300 sheep before them. Although he knew that the men he sought were nearby, Geharty despaired of catching them. By then the Aboriginal people had the advantage as they were able to survive on water pressed from roots while the police party was forced to detour to find water.[86]

While this party was away, Adelaide officials had learned of the affray and that a number of Aboriginal people had been, at the very least, wounded during it. On 30 November the Governor ordered the Protector of Aborigines and Police Commissioner Dashwood to personally investigate the incident to ascertain 'the necessity for the firing' and 'the exact number of the wounded'.[87] In late December these officials, escorted by four police constables and supported by Aboriginal guides and interpreters, headed north from Port Lincoln. Near Lake Hamilton they encountered Constable Smith who was bringing in a prisoner, Poolulta, suspected of involvement in the Baird attacks. Poolulta told them that the attack on Baird had been led by Npungilti and named several others alleged to be involved. Moorhouse and Dashwood arrived in the area of the clash and were told that two men had died as a result of gunshot wounds received in the incident. Only one body could be found and when Moorhouse exhumed it, his examination revealed that the man had been shot in the head from behind. The two officials reported that while the party had been justified in opening fire they had erred by galloping forward unannounced. They also suggested that Baird had contributed to his own demise by pushing north too quickly and foolishly pursuing the sheep thieves alone.[88] When Pulgulta appeared in court[89] language difficulties proved insurmountable, leading the prosecution to abandon the murder charge and proceed with one of stock theft, on which charge Pulgulta was found guilty.[90]

Before the lull in frontier expansion, largely brought on by labour shortages resulting from the 1850s gold rushes, settlers had already pushed into the southern Flinders Ranges, taking over large tracts of land under pastoral leases. In such harsh country, clashes over scarce natural resources were inevitable, with the first being officially recorded in March 1852. James Brown was seventeen years old when he went to work on his family's run and he soon showed the recklessness of youth. Refusing to carry a weapon, he declared his lack of fear of local Aboriginal people. Nevertheless, in mid March 1852 Brown was killed near Lake Torrens. Protector Moorhouse was in the district at the time, investigating the killing of an Aboriginal person. Travelling to the scene with Sergeant Rose, Moorhouse exhumed Brown's body and questioned several local Aboriginal people. This investigation led to the arrest of two Angurignka men on suspicion of murder. They were brought back to Clare where they were remanded by the local magistrate and held in the Kooringa Gaol. However, it was clear that the case would collapse since the only evidence against the two men was 'that the feet of the 2 prisoners responded in length and breadth with the tracks found about the corpse'.[91] But the local Justices of the Peace (JP) were reluctant to admit that there was no real case against the two accused and advised that they needed several weeks to collect more evidence and find witnesses. McDonald JP remanded the prisoners in custody, pending such an investigation.[92] Moorhouse sought their release, arguing that the lack of evidence and communication difficulties made it unlikely that the case could proceed.[93] The Governor agreed and the Colonial Secretary advised the Clare officials of this decision, ordering the Redruth gaoler to set the two men free. However, the local Justices of the Peace were not happy with this decision and cancelled the order on the grounds that new information had been received. McDonald JP then issued a new warrant for the continued remand on the grounds that a vital Aboriginal witness was expected to arrive soon.[94] Eventually the local officials had to admit defeat and both the accused men were 'discharged for want of evidence'.[95] The cautious Protector, probably because of the ill feeling existing in the northern districts towards these two men, personally escorted them back to their clan.

In 1855, the murder of another settler stirred considerable interest within the community. Peter Brown, a shepherd employed on an outpost of Dr McKecknie's[96] station near Franklin Harbour, was killed in June 1855. When police from Mt Remarkable investigated they were told that the perpetrators had gone north. Some months later further information was received from Pinga, a local Aboriginal man who at times worked as a tracker for the police. Apparently Brown's killers had returned to the Franklin Harbour district for a traditional gathering of clans. Police questioning of those in attendance led to the arrest of twelve Pangkala men on charges of sheep theft and murder.[97] Only seven of these men were indicted for murder, including two youths, Errelee and Weelangualla. The latter two were quickly discharged 'in consideration of their tender age'.[98] In December 1855 the case was heard in the Supreme Court, where Bartley defended the five accused and argued especially for the withdrawal of the murder charge against Eelulta. The prosecution refused to give way, insisting that he was at the very least an accomplice in the murder of Brown.[99] Four of the accused were found guilty of murder[100] and Justice Boothby sentenced Eelulta, Palingulta, Weenpulta and Watniltie to be hanged, a sentence which was carried out on 14 January 1856.

In May 1860, a Flinders Ranges' shepherd was killed during a raid on his hut.[101] John Jones' alleged killers, Manyelta and Kainmulta, fled south onto Eyre Peninsula where they were arrested in late June by Constable O'Shanahan and found to be in possession of materials stolen from Jones' hut. Kainmulta managed to escape soon after being taken into custody and Manyelta stood trial alone in August 1860. Stow defended him vigorously but Manyelta was found guilty and sentenced to death.[102] Aboriginal witnesses[103] called by the prosecution gave eyewitness accounts of Jones' death, all agreeing that Manyelta had battered the shepherd with a waddy, after which Kainmulta had speared him. Manyelta's sentence was carried out in early October 1860 at Cooeyanna Police Station near Streaky Bay. Thirty or so Kokatha people were forced to come into the station to witness the hanging and they later took charge of Manyelta's body and buried it nearby. Within

7. Murder and manslaughter

a fortnight, the police became aware of Kainmulta's whereabouts and he was arrested at Mt Wedge. After a committal hearing in Port Lincoln, he was sent to Adelaide and brought to trial in the Supreme Court in December 1860.[104] This time Stow was more successful with his defence, which centred around the sequence of the attack on Jones. Stow argued that Jones was probably already dead when Kainmulta speared him. This was of course impossible to prove, but Stow's line of defence sowed enough doubt in Justice Boothby's mind that he directed the jury to bring in an acquittal on the grounds that the evidence did not justify any other result.[105] This they did and Kainmulta was released without further penalty.[106]

In 1861, there were two murders of women that did much to end whatever sympathy remained for Aboriginal people accused of murdering settlers. The first, of Margaret Impett, a settler at Mt Wedge, occurred in early May 1861. The victim, the wife of a shepherd on Laurence's station, was pregnant at the time of her death and the medical evidence at the inquest and subsequent trial suggested that she had been raped, bashed and left to die. When Mangilti and Karabidne appeared in the Supreme Court in August 1861, charged with this murder, defending counsel Andrews had little to present in their defence. It was accepted that Mrs Impett's murder was sexually motivated and so Andrews resorted to challenging the two men's confessions, on the grounds that they had been obtained under duress. However, Judge Gwynne ruled against him on this point. While admitting that it would be 'dangerous to convict on the confessions alone',[107] Gwynne summed up that the other evidence was strong and advised the jury that the defendants 'could not...be allowed to escape the consequence because they could not understand exactly as we did'.[108] The jury found them guilty and Judge Gwynne sentenced the two to death — both were hanged on 14 September 1861 at Port Lincoln.

The second 1861 rape-murder was committed by a group of Aboriginal people and was generally considered to be even more outrageous as it was committed by Aboriginal men with a long history of contact with Europeans. Mary Rainbird and her two young children, Emma and Robert, were murdered at Hamilton in March 1861. When the bodies were exhumed from their temporary shallow graves, the coroner determined that Mary Rainbird had been raped before being bludgeoned to death. Suspicion quickly fell upon a group of Aboriginal men, well known throughout the district. Indeed, only days before the murder several of their number, mainly in their teens, had been forcibly ejected from Dutton's Anlaby Station after a drunken melee. When the police questioned members of this group, six men were implicated and subsequently arrested. There was considerable confusion when these six were remanded in the Kapunda Court as three of them went under the same name: Warretya.[109]

On their arrival in Adelaide to stand trial, the six men were confronted by angry colonists, many of whom journeyed some distance to see the accused murderers. In the Supreme Court on 16 May 1861, the eldest of the men (Warretya, identified as 'Old Man Jack') was discharged when the prosecution decided not to proceed with charges against him.[110] The prosecution faced the problem of not having any witnesses against the five remaining accused, which they solved by negotiating for one of the men to give evidence for the Crown in return for his freedom. Monnaitya was selected for this task[111] and he testified that Pilta Miltinda had raped and killed Mary Rainbird; Warretya (known as 'Kapunda Robert') had killed the boy; while Warretya (aka 'Goggle-eyed Jemmy') had murdered the girl. In the face of this evidence, the defence resorted to a mitigating plea of drunkenness, suggesting that the men had recently purchased a five-gallon keg of rum. The prosecution relied heavily on circumstantial evidence and the damning statement by Monnaitya. The evidence reforms of 1848–9, which facilitated unsworn evidence, may have had their genesis in a desire to ensure that Aboriginal people could testify against settlers who took the law into their own hands, but here they acted to ensure the conviction of Aboriginal accused. Even so, when the prosecutor summed up, he took no chances and argued strongly for a conviction, not only on the evidence presented to the court but also because of the likelihood that if justice was not seen to be done in this case, then public anger would overflow into illegal retaliation against these and other Aboriginal people in the district. The four men were found guilty and sentenced to death, while the informant Monnaitya was released without penalty.[112] The execution of these four young men in June 1861 raised little protest at the time. In the public mind, there was nothing to mitigate the gang's brutal actions — all but one of the four had been born after European settlement of the area and all were aware of European customs and law. In some eyes, they were living proof of the fallacy of the dictum that the post-settlement generation of Aboriginal people could be successfully assimilated into colonial society.[113]

7. Murder and manslaughter

In January 1861, Theodore Bergooist, a hutkeeper on Swan's property near Fowler's Bay, was fatally speared. Sergeant O'Shanahan went to investigate and arrested two young men, Nelgerie and Titcherie. Nelgerie admitted that he had speared Bergooist twice through the chest before beating him about the head with a waddy, while Titcherie confessed to also being involved in the killing. Defence counsel Andrews challenged the admissibility of these confessions but the judge denied this petition, and the jury returned a guilty verdict.[114] Both men were sentenced to death but a public debate developed over whether this sentence should be carried out. Rumour had it that Bergooist was a violent man, responsible for several assaults on Aboriginal people in the area during the months preceding his death.[115] On hearing these allegations, Protector of Aborigines Murray called for a full inquiry.[116] However, after several colonists came forward in support of the deceased man's propriety in dealing with Aboriginal people, the Advocate General decided against any further investigation.[117] The death sentence stood and Nelgerie and Titcherie were hanged on 7 September 1861.

The following year, further south on the west coast of Eyre Peninsula, William Walker was murdered. A hutkeeper on Marchant's Talia Station, Walker was speared after an argument over rations in March 1862. Surviving long enough to make a statement to fellow workers, Walker gave the names and descriptions of his attackers. He told of Meengulta and two female companions calling at his hut when they ran short of food on their journey from Lake Gairdner to Port Lincoln. When refused flour, the three became abusive. Allegedly, Meengulta threw a spear through the hut window as they departed, striking Walker in the chest.[118] Sergeant Geharty and two Aboriginal constables followed the trio north until, almost a month later, they caught up with them near Lake Gairdner. Meengulta was arrested and brought to Adelaide to face trial for murder. In August 1862, the court heard evidence from Marchant and the man who had discovered Walker, as well as from two Aboriginal witnesses, Chalgulta and Luyelta, who had tracked the three Aboriginal people from the hut until the police arrived to take over the chase.[119] In August 1862 Meengulta was found guilty of murder and sentenced to death,[120] a penalty which was put into effect on 8 September 1862 at Venus Bay.

Between 1836 and 1862, seventy-three Aboriginal people were arrested and charged with murder of settlers, representing thirty-two separate cases. In cases involving twenty-nine individuals, the prosecution was either not proceeded with or abandoned during the trial, leaving 43 Aboriginal people whose fate was decided by juries. Of these, 35 were found guilty of murder[121] with twenty-three being executed. Another five were convicted on the lesser charge of manslaughter. When the cases detailed in this chapter are reviewed, little criticism can be made of the Supreme Court justices, the processes by which they tried the Aboriginal people accused of murder or manslaughter, or the actions of the counsel acting for the defendants. While the indictment of Aboriginal people clearly operated in the interest of protecting European lives and property, this interest did not always overwhelm the rights of the Aboriginal defendants. It can reasonably be argued that, once indicted, Aboriginal defendants received a fair trial in terms of the standards of the day. Indeed, in a number of cases outlined above, the efforts of defending counsel went well beyond that standard. In many of these cases there were difficulties relating to evidence, interpretation and witnesses but in general it seems reasonable to suggest that the benefit of the doubt more often than not went to the Aboriginal defendant. These figures, in themselves, are not necessarily damning of the policy or its implementation, given the level of violence which inevitably occurred on the frontier during the 1840s and 1850s. If the authorities had brought a similar number of settlers before the courts for the killings of Aboriginal people which were known to have been committed during the same period (see chapter 10), then it could be argued that the policy had been implemented in an even-handed way. However, the convictions and executions of Aboriginal people, when placed alongside the lone European found guilty of murdering an Aboriginal person, make it clear that the law primarily operated to protect the interests of the colonists, whatever the rhetoric of equality. This comparison also takes much of the gloss from the fact that Aboriginal people received fair hearings once brought before the Supreme Court, since so many European transgressors were never called to give any account of their actions.

CHAPTER 8
ASSAULT AND ROBBERY

In colonial South Australia it was policy to refer all but minor cases of theft and robbery to either the Adelaide Police Court or the Supreme Court.[1] Accordingly, in relation to assault and robbery cases involving Aboriginal people, we are able to get a reasonably complete picture. What is revealed is a high conviction rate for assault, with twenty-four of the thirty-six Aboriginal people charged being found guilty, twenty of whom received gaol sentences. Eight were found guilty while only four of the defendants were released because the prosecution either declined to proceed or abandoned the prosecution during the case. Possible explanations for this high conviction rate include: the likelihood that settlers did not proceed with prosecutions for assault unless the evidence was clear-cut; that local Justices of the Peace acted as a filter in assault cases, preferring to dismiss charges rather than remand the accused for trial in Adelaide; the reluctance of stock owners to have the case proceed to trial since their employees might well be subpoenaed to give evidence; and an increasing tendency among settlers to act outside the law to punish Aboriginal people who committed what were regarded as minor assaults.

While we might expect that assaults by Aboriginal people upon settlers would be largely confined to the rural districts, where clashes over land and resources were more likely, in fact there were some clashes within Adelaide itself. The town was the initial frontier of contact between the two societies and several factors contributed to early racial tension within its boundaries. First, the high numbers of Aboriginal people who made the journey to Adelaide from surrounding districts in the 1840s strained relations once their novelty waned. For example, Aboriginal attendance at the Queen's Birthday celebrations was 300 in 1840, 400 in 1842, rising to a peak of 800 in 1844,[2] while at least 300 Aboriginal people were permanently living within the town by 1842.[3]

While later some Aboriginal people would actively resist the invasion of their lands, initially many were enthusiastically curious about the newcomers and their town. Second, there was a high turnover of Aboriginal visitors, making European attempts to modify Aboriginal behaviour within the town ineffective. Third, the raising of Aboriginal expectations by the early provision of paid casual work within Adelaide led to resentment when this work proved impermanent. Fourth, the decision by some Aboriginal people to abandon traditional life and live semi-permanently within the town caused concern among town dwellers who had not expected assimilation to be taken so literally.[4] Other factors contributing to tension included Aboriginal forthrightness in demanding reciprocity when obligations were incurred by settlers; language and cultural misunderstandings on both sides; and colonists' expectations that Aboriginal people would behave with deference, gratitude and compliance. Given the number of Aboriginal people visiting or living in and around Adelaide, clashes could be expected but in fact were infrequent. Relatively few cases came before the courts and, where they did so, rated only brief mention in the newspapers of the day.

In respect of Aboriginal people charged with assault, two categories can be identified among these early Adelaide cases: incidents where Aboriginal people were overly zealous in seeking food or money from settlers, and those where Aboriginal people attempted to enforce perceived reciprocal obligations. In the first category, it is clear that some Aboriginal people crossed the line between asking for assistance and intimidation, especially after settlers became less tolerant of begging.[5] By the early 1840s, demands for food and money were common within the town and when refused could provoke threats of violence. In 1841, one newspaper probably overstated the case when it reported that '[n]umerous persons have been threatened and attacked' around town and suggested that it was no longer safe for 'an unprotected female to go from one place to another'.[6] Intimidation was not uncommon, such as the 1843 incident when an Aboriginal man, having been refused money, 'at once pointed his spear, and put himself in a threatening attitude'.[7]

Even so, few cases were regarded as serious enough to warrant arrest and prosecution, although of course the difficulties associated with bringing Aboriginal people before the courts may have discouraged settlers from seeking police intervention. In February 1840 a man known only as 'Jemmy' was found guilty of an assault in these circumstances. Fined one pound, he was unable to pay and in default served a week in the Adelaide Gaol.[8] Three years later 'Williamy' also spent a week in gaol after throwing a spear at Dr. Davey, apparently following his refusal to provide alms.[9] Meanwhile, on the roads leading to Adelaide, some Aboriginal people had reportedly become more insistent in their requests for assistance and, when denied it, 'have not hesitated to procure it by threats and intimidation'.[10] In the town itself residents also encountered similar persistence and implied threats. At times these threats may have been real, although it is difficult to determine Aboriginal motives from European accounts. More often, though, it was a matter of colonists exaggerating the seriousness of interactions. For example, when a colonist recounted an incident near the main Aboriginal camp one night in 1841, claiming a narrow escape after several men ran out in front of him 'shouting, halloing, and dancing before the horse's head', it was more likely simply a case of harassment or intoxicated exuberance.[11]

Another incident which can be placed within this overzealous category occurred at Marion in April 1844, when the insistence of a group of Aboriginal people seeking rations ended with some of their number facing charges for robbery. Having been refused food at a house that autumn morning, these men waited until the male occupants left, perhaps hoping to have more success with the two women of the house. Whether this was intended to be achieved by exploiting their fear or compassion we cannot know, although the fact that these men had been given flour in return for undertaking tasks on numerous occasions in the past points to the latter. One of the occupants, Sarah Stutely, later described the events in court:

> some blacks came to the house and asked me to give them flour; I said I had got none…about two or three minutes later twenty or thirty blacks came, the prisoner was one of them; they pushed me to get into the house, and some got in; I gave them a great quantity of flour.[12]

What seemed to be a simple case of robbery can be seen from another perspective, however. The Aboriginal men made no attempt to harm the women and carried only sticks, not spears or waddies. They initially stood at the door and asked for flour but when they were told that there was none, some of the men pushed past the women. They went to a large sack of flour in the corner of the cottage, pointing to it to show that there indeed was plenty. Even then they did not attempt to take the flour themselves but insisted that Sarah provide them with some, as well as a couple of blankets. Were they robbing Mrs Stutely, forcefully asking for food, or demanding to be given flour in payment for past favours or some perceived obligation? At this point a neighbour intervened and the group left, only to return later when they had to be driven off at gunpoint. Witnesses had little difficulty in identifying one of the men as Caldecotte, well known around Adelaide as a reliable worker and experienced guide. Subsequently, he and two companions were arrested and charged with theft, but the charges against the two unnamed men were dropped when the Stutely sisters failed to identify them.[13] Despite being able to call Moorhouse, Tolmer and the Reverend Meyer as character witnesses, Caldecotte was found guilty and sentenced to transportation,[14] although this sentence was later reduced to three months' imprisonment in the Adelaide Gaol.[15] Within a month a similar incident took place only a few miles away. Another group of men who had travelled up from Encounter Bay demanded bread and tobacco when they visited Mrs Willis' hut. They showed the same reluctance to leave when she 'told them repeatedly to go away as she had nothing to give them',[16] particularly as they could see a large bag of flour through the doorway and could smell fresh-baked bread. Once again the group pushed into the house, perhaps to make it clear that they were not fooled by her denials. They did not press home their demands with threats, finally accepting Mrs Willis' refusal and leaving quietly.

The second category is made up of incidents which, although often depicted by settlers as being indiscriminate and without cause, can be seen more as Aboriginal attempts to enforce obligations or simply to demand fair treatment. Colonists did employ Aboriginal people for a range of tasks within the town — cutting and carrying firewood, clearing trees, gardening, collecting gum and bark — but often reasonable payment was considered to be little more than inadequate rations, a blanket and some discarded clothing.[17] Not unreasonably, Aboriginal people believed that debts were incurred by settlers using their labour, land and resources. For example, when 'Jemmy' was found guilty of an assault on Grace Clark in December 1840, the incident was the result of an argument over payment for work.[18] Two years later, Multyilli was gaoled after a similar altercation with a former employer. After entering Mrs Bennett's house, he demanded fair payment and refused to leave when it was denied. Despite it being clear that his actions arose from his frustration over not being adequately paid, Multyilli was arrested for 'conducting himself in a violent and threatening manner'.[19] Two months later, another unnamed man was involved in a similar incident, although this time he did not stay around to be arrested. He went to the back door of a town house where he had been recently employed cutting firewood and gardening. When the cook refused him some flour an argument developed, resulting in the man allegedly making 'a thrust at the young lady with his spear'.[20] In the following year, in a case where it can be argued that the offenders were provoked, Colcola Waranger and his wife Mareeku were walking through the North Adelaide parklands when one of their dogs chased John Gavan, a dairyman bringing in his cows. Gavan grabbed a branch and killed the dog, inflaming Mareeku to seize hold of the weapon and threaten to strike the dairyman with it. Colcola joined in the ensuing scuffle and subsequently the couple were charged with assault, found guilty and sentenced to two weeks in the Adelaide Gaol.[21] In 1848 'Bob' was charged with assault when he threatened the Follands with his spear when they challenged his taking a melon from their garden.[22] Found guilty in the Police Court, 'Bob' spent one month in gaol.[23]

Few assault cases of a minor nature were considered by the courts, mainly because the official attitude towards the crime of assault was that it was rarely worthy of the trouble of investigation and prosecution. Accordingly, the cases which did come before the courts were those of a more serious nature or those which took place in circumstances where they could not be ignored. When in 1848, for example, hutkeeper Hugh Roy was attacked after he surprised Aboriginal people ransacking his hut, the offenders did not flee when challenged but instead turned on Roy, severely beating him with sticks and waddies. Tilpardnambi, the only one of the group captured, was charged with assault with intent to murder but when the indictment proceedings were heard in the Police Commissioner's Court in December 1848, Fisher persuaded the prosecution to proceed on a lesser charge of assault with intent to steal.[24] When this charge was heard at the March Supreme Court sessions, Tilpardnambi was found guilty and sentenced to eighteen months in gaol.[25] Incidentally, he did not serve his full sentence as his health deteriorated in prison, leading to his release in March 1850. Officials were by then wary of deaths in custody and acted quickly when the sheriff advised that an Aboriginal prisoner's health had declined seriously.[26] As noted in chapter 7, Bakilti and Puterpynter were acquitted on a charge of murder in 1849.[27] However, both had originally been arrested after an alleged assault on a shepherd, Alfred Thompson, and the prosecution proceeded with that charge when the murder charge failed. Found guilty, they were gaoled for two years with hard labour.[28] A month later, at Coutt's station on Yorke Peninsula, a shepherd named John Gall was attacked with waddies during the course of a raid upon his flock. The attackers escaped but, a few days later during an issue of rations specifically arranged with the intent of entrapping some of the raiders, Gall — by then recovered — recognised two of his attackers. Watpa and Koonko were arrested and charged with assault and theft. Brought to Adelaide for trial, the two almost escaped conviction when Gall and Coutts failed to appear as prosecution witnesses.[29] However, court officials were unsympathetic towards country colonists who laid charges but subsequently found the journey to town to attend the resulting court hearing too onerous. In this case the Judge issued warrants requiring the witnesses to attend the March sessions. At this hearing, defence counsel Fisher was able to throw doubt on the identification of Watpa, resulting in the prosecution withdrawing the charges against him.[30] Nevertheless, Koonko was found guilty of assault and received a sentence of four months' imprisonment.[31]

Given rural settlers' self-interest in bringing Aboriginal attackers to justice, one interpretation of the reluctance — or at times outright refusal — of witnesses to attend hearings against Aboriginal people accused of assault was that they feared that the background to the clash would be exposed to public view. For example, in July 1844 Targko Melaitpa was charged with spearing a shepherd, George Halliday. At first this seemed to be a simple case of assault motivated by the hunger of the assailant and his family. Game was scarce and when Targko Milaitpa saw Halliday carrying a dead lamb back to his hut, he asked to be given the lamb just as he had successfully entreated on earlier occasions. When the shepherd refused, apparently by then following less generous instructions from his employer, the Kaurna man resorted to violence. Only when the case came before the court did it come to light that Halliday had frequently slept with Targko's young wife, thereby incurring an obligation that could hardly be swept aside by a tightening of station policy on ration issues to local Aboriginal people. Similarly, in late 1846 in the South-East of the colony, investigation into an affray involving James McKenzie and several Boandik people, soon exposed the European account of the incident as being, at best, incomplete. Stockkeeper McKenzie alleged that he had been attacked without provocation by a man and woman, who made what was described as 'an attempt on his life'.[32] Warrants were issued for the arrest of the couple but when they were brought to Robe it was found that the man had a gunshot wound, apparently inflicted by McKenzie. The local magistrate sought instructions from Adelaide and Moorhouse's subsequent investigation led to the charges against the couple being dropped.[33] Eighteen months later, near Port Lincoln, Kumbulta clashed with a shepherd, Elias Lee, in what also initially looked like an unprovoked assault. However, as the case unfolded after Kumbulta was charged with assault, it became clear that this incident centred on the shepherd's failure to honour a reasonable obligation. It came to light that Lee and Kumbulta were well acquainted and that Lee had been involved in a long-term sexual relationship with a young woman who was related to Kumbulta. Perhaps the clashes between Aboriginal people and settlers in the area during 1849 had cooled Lee's ardour — or he may have been ordered by a cautious employer to sever his intimate link with the local Aboriginal people. Whatever the reason for the change in Lee's attitude, Kumbulta was probably at a loss to understand it. During a heated exchange, Kumbulta hurled a spear at the shepherd, inflicting a slight wound. Kumbulta was arrested and indicted to face a charge of assault in the Supreme Court. Lee proved to be a reluctant witness, failing to appear at the morning session[34] and giving only vague answers when pressed later in the day. Despite a spirited defence by Fisher, who sought to take advantage of Lee's reluctance to testify by dwelling on the 'difficulty of identifying natives',[35] Kumbulta was nevertheless convicted and sentenced to serve twelve months in gaol.[36] In the following year, similar mitigating circumstances came into public view when Karkarra Widlo was charged with an assault against William Bagnall, a shepherd on Rogers' station on Yorke Peninsula. Bagnall claimed that this attack was occasioned by a dispute over water rights but, when the charges were laid, his statement came under closer scrutiny. The local magistrate was suspicious that there was more to the story and noted that Bagnall's statement contained 'discrepancies and contradictory statements'.[37] At the trial, allegations were made that Bagnall owned a dog which he had trained to attack Aboriginal people and that he was involved sexually with local Aboriginal women.[38] However, when these allegations were unable to be substantiated, Karkarra Widlo was found guilty, although his relatively light sentence of three months' imprisonment suggests that the Court gave some credence to the defence arguments.[39]

In a number of assault cases there seems to be somewhat more to the background events and relationships than was revealed at the formal hearing. In mid 1851 several Aboriginal men took part in a robbery of a station hut on Yorke Peninsula. Four of their number (Ngalta, Tantultara, Watpa and Mantamornappa) were subsequently charged with robbery and assault.[40] All four were found guilty and given the standard sentence for this offence — six months with hard labour. There our knowledge of the situation would have ended, were it not for Mantamornappa also being charged (along with two clansmen, Ngurkilli and Partko) with a related assault against Henry Brown. During this hearing it was made clear that Mantamornappa had been employed on the property for some months as a shepherd. In addition, it was revealed that he had only stolen Brown's gun 'for fear it should be used against them by the hutkeeper'.[41] No further details of the relationships involved were revealed in this case, and the result was that the three men were each gaoled for six months.[42] In 1853 one of Gilles' Mt Arden shepherds, Anthony Francis, was severely beaten by Aboriginal people. This crime was portrayed as a brutal unprovoked attack brought about by Francis' refusal to supply his attackers with rations. Indeed, it was serious attack and, had another Aboriginal person not intervened, Francis may well have been killed as his two attackers were inclined to smash in his head with a stone after knocking him to the ground. Yet, despite the severity of this attack the hutkeeper refused to give evidence or even make a full statement, arguing that it was inconvenient to leave the station to do so.[43] The story behind this attack did not come to light and Francis' reasons for not pursuing it through the courts remained unknown, although local settlers may have been aware of the background circumstances and underlying relationships.[44]

Of course, we should not be surprised that closer examination of assault cases reveals that the alleged attackers and the European victim knew each other, often very well. Just as much of today's violence originates within relationships, so too was frontier violence often a result of disagreements between people who had got to know each other well enough to raise expectations, incur obligations or misunderstand motivations. The popular view may be that life on the frontier involved only infrequent meetings with Aboriginal people and that clashes most often occurred when settlers were attacked without warning by marauding Aboriginal people usually unknown to them, but the reality was usually quite different. When Aboriginal people were arrested and charged with assault, it was often because the victims were able to provide police with the names, detailed descriptions and indeed often the current whereabouts of their alleged attackers. This was because, more often than not, those accused had some form of relationship with the hutkeeper or shepherd assaulted. For example, in April 1850, when Yengki was arrested in connection with an assault on a shepherd named Bridges almost two years earlier, the relationships involved were such that the local settlers flatly refused to give evidence against Yengki — he was set free when the police realised that they would be unable to procure an indictment.[45] Similarly, when Berea was charged with assault with intent to commit grievous bodily harm in April 1853, it soon became clear that he was well-known to the victim, John Williams, a settler who had established a run to the east of Mt Arden. Not that this helped in his defence, however, despite the best efforts of Bartley, for Berea was found guilty and sent to gaol for three months.[46]

Although it was not the norm, there were occasionally clashes involving Aboriginal people and settlers who were strangers to each other, usually soon after settlers moved into a new area. For example, also in the Mt Arden area, in August 1853, Richard Mullins was violently attacked when he encountered two Aboriginal men acting suspiciously near his flock. They then drove off sixty of his sheep — none were recovered and the identity of the men remained unknown. In August 1859 a well-sinker, Thomas Shepherd, was attacked by a group of five strangers near Fowler's Bay. Despite being bashed, speared and left for dead, Shepherd managed to make it back to his camp. When Inspector Holroyd investigated this incident, Aboriginal people in the area suggested that three men (known only as 'Billy', 'Georgy' and 'Jacky') were the culprits and subsequently they were arrested.[47] Taken to Port Lincoln and then on to Adelaide to stand trial for assault, the three men appeared in the Supreme Court in September 1859, despite difficulties in communicating with them.[48] This proved not to be a problem as when Shepherd saw the men he confidently declared that none of the accused had been involved in the attack. The three were discharged once it was accepted that this was a case of mistaken identity or false information. However, this was not the last of this particular matter, as in 1862 two other men, Meendeenya and Meenbinya, were charged with the assault. On the way to Adelaide these two men attempted an escape, during which Meendeenya was shot dead by Trooper Morris. This death was made more tragic when once again Shepherd stated that the surviving prisoner was not one of the three men involved in the attack.[49]

There are very few cases involving assault by Aboriginal people upon European women and only one of these where a sexual motive is clearly indicated. In cases such as that against 'Jemmy' in 1852, the rationale for the charge of assault is more related to the fear instilled in the victim than in any physical violence or actual threat thereof. Initially charged with breaking into Edward Syme's house at Allan's Creek, 'Jemmy' was subsequently also indicted for assault when a servant, Mary Savage, claimed that his intrusion had put her 'in bodily fear of her life'.[50] However, once it was clear that no contact or actual threat was involved, 'Jemmy' was acquitted on the latter charge. Not so in the case of 'Billy Goat', however, who was tried in the Clare Court in 1860. Found guilty of an assault on Emma Baker, 'Billy' was sentenced to six months' gaol.[51] Incidentally, he soon escaped but was later recaptured and committed for trial in the Supreme Court.[52] Stow, his defence counsel, put up a strong argument against the charge of escaping from prison, arguing on two grounds: first that the Clare Police lockup was technically not a prison; and second, that 'Billy' had been unlawfully held in custody in the first place, since the Clare Court should never have heard such a serious charge. The Crown Solicitor refuted Stow's latter argument that the Clare Court did not have jurisdiction, expounding on the powers of local magistrates to try such cases. Although this argument was accepted Stow won the day when the Judge dismissed the escaping charge, although 'Billy' was returned to prison to serve out his original sentence. Another 1860 case, against Bungildo, who was originally from the Sydney area, did involve sexual assault. Charged with assault with intent to commit the rape of Caroline Willmer at Tanunda, Bungildo pleaded guilty (on the advice of his counsel, Bartley) to a lesser charge of indecent assault when details of a previous charge for indecent assault eighteen months earlier were given to the Court.[53] Bungildo was gaoled for eighteen months with hard labour.[54]

Only rarely were Aboriginal people brought before the courts charged with assault against other Aboriginal people as police and district officials tended to turn a blind eye to *inter se* assaults. Colonial officials were reluctant to extend the protection of the law to Aboriginal people where violence between themselves did not offend the colonists' own sensibilities. One category of the relatively few *inter se* assaults which was pursued involved attacks by men, usually husbands, against women. In 1846 Pilgalta was tried on a charge of assault occasioning grievous bodily harm, after he was alleged to have speared his wife, Marinna, at a Port Lincoln encampment in June 1846.[55] Although the officials thought the case against him was strong enough to warrant his remand to Adelaide for trial, the jury was reluctant to intervene in a domestic and *inter se* matter and Pilgalta was acquitted.[56] A few years later, when another Aboriginal man from the same district, Munarabidni, was charged with assault upon a young Aboriginal woman, Marnipi, the prosecution collapsed when the European witnesses to the alleged crime could not be found.[57] Despite a determined effort by his counsel, another man charged in similar circumstances in 1860 was not so fortunate.[58] Manancowie (also known as Robert Mannam) allegedly stabbed Heelta after she had spurned his offer of marriage. Although no Europeans were present, the attack took place in the presence of several Aboriginal people who were living in the River Murray port of Mannum.[59] They reported the attack, stressing its seriousness, and agreed to give evidence against Manancowie.[60] Their evidence, along with that of Heelta, still may not have convinced the jury had Manancowie not admitted the attack at his arraignment[61] — an admission that Stow unsuccessfully petitioned to have ruled inadmissible.[62] Found guilty, Manancowie was sentenced to three years' imprisonment.[63]

When officials did press charges in *inter se* cases, often it was because settler interests or public order were threatened in some way. In December 1856, for example, 'Jack' was imprisoned for three months after being found guilty of stabbing a drinking companion, 'Jocko', at Kent Town.[64] A few years later, at Melrose, 'Beautiful Tommy' was charged with assault after a publican intervened as he assaulted a regular Aboriginal patron, 'Jimmy Brandy'.[65] The charge was dismissed when Tommy gave 'an able speech'[66] in his own defence in which he convinced the magistrate that he had been provoked by the drunken 'Jimmy Brandy'. In July 1859, when two Aboriginal patrons of a Robe inn, their names recorded only as 'Gifford' and 'Potbelly', attacked the young Aboriginal ostler employed there, charges of assault were laid. Both men were arraigned for trial at Robe but no record was found of the trial proceeding.[67] In all three cases, not only was alcohol involved but the publicans were also instrumental in having charges laid. It may be more than a coincidence that these three cases occurred at a time where there was increasing public concern about the supply of alcohol to Aboriginal people.

There can be little doubt that many cases of assault by settlers upon Aboriginal people took place during the first twenty-five years of the colony, but few came to the attention of the authorities, let alone eventuated in charges being laid. Most Adelaide settlers turned a blind eye to interracial clashes outside public houses or to instances were settlers committed minor assaults on Aboriginal people within the town. In the rural districts, where settlers of conscience risked public ridicule if they even argued against the killing of Aboriginal people who placed themselves in the way of European interests, it was not likely that they would complain to the authorities if a settler was observed ill-treating or assaulting an Aboriginal person. To warrant action being taken, the assault either had to be generally considered to be excessive or to have been committed upon an Aboriginal person who had special links to other colonists, particularly those in official positions. In 1842, for instance, when Francis Jolly took out his drunken anger on an Aboriginal man, beating and kicking him, the act was not only particularly violent, unprovoked and sustained but also committed in full view of other settlers. A complaint was made in this case and Jolly was arrested and subsequently convicted of assault, to wit 'kicking a native black in the belly, and about the groin and abdomen, in a most savage and inhuman manner'.[68] Two years later, the Protector of Aborigines encouraged a young Aboriginal woman to bring an action of assault against Jemima Sanders, whom it was alleged had assaulted her with a shepherd's crook when the woman sought payment for work done for Sanders. However, when this case came before the court the informant became agitated and, apparently believing that it was she who was on trial, dashed from the court — never to be seen in town again.[69] At times, underlying ill feeling between some settlers and those Aboriginal people who had chosen to live and work within the European community came to the surface. For example, during the 1842 troubles in the Port Lincoln district, a Nauo man named Utulta decided to cooperate with the settlers. Although he was later recruited as a native constable, some settlers never trusted his motives or allegiances as he apparently retained considerable respect and influence within the wider Aboriginal community. On several occasions Utulta was subjected to abuse but in March 1846 George Lawson actually assaulted the Aboriginal constable — he was found guilty and fined twenty pounds, a not insignificant penalty.[70] Three years later the colonial artist ST Gill was threatened with assault charges after his dog attacked Ngungu Ngammin in Adelaide.[71] However, the charge was reduced to that of owning a dangerous dog, which Gill easily managed to evade simply by denying ownership of the errant animal.[72] In November 1853, Frederic Frost was charged with an assault on an Aboriginal stockman employed on Angas' run at Mt Remarkable. Wantulta was a highly regarded stockman and the assault was witnessed by a police officer, who was willing gave evidence against Frost.[73] Even so, Frost was fined only one pound when found guilty.[74] When, in August 1854, 'Jackey' found himself the butt of teasing by a group of young European girls, he was provoked into running after them and swearing. Unfortunately his language offended the sensibilities of a passing colonist, William Taylor. They exchanged harsh words and Taylor took to 'Jackey' with his walking stick. When Moorhouse heard of the incident, he encouraged the victim to lay a complaint of assault and Taylor was brought before the Adelaide Local Court.[75] While the magistrate found Taylor guilty as charged, he determined but a token fine:

> His Worship fined him one shilling, which he handed over to the black, cautioning him at the same time that he must not frighten or run after children.[76]

When another Aboriginal worker, 'Jemmy Rankine', brought a charge of assault against his employer several years later,[77] the latter even admitted that he had horsewhipped the lad. However, the Justice of the Peace was inclined to accept the defence claim that the blows were not serious and so dismissed the charge.[78] Even if an incident involving an assault on an Aboriginal person by a frontier settler was made known to the local Justice of the Peace or Sub-Protector of Aborigines, there was usually little they could do in the face of the elapsed time since the alleged crime, the lack of witnesses and the blatant refusal of settlers to cooperate in any investigation.

There was at times a sexual dimension to assault cases brought by Aboriginal people against settlers but the fact that there was a pre-existing close relationship meant that it was often more difficult for the prosecution to sustain the case, particularly in terms of ensuring that Aboriginal witnesses appeared in the court. When, for example, Thomas Borthwick was charged with assault on an Aboriginal woman in 1851, the witnesses could not be found by the time the matter came before the court and so Borthwick was discharged.[79] A few years later, when Pandalteroo laid a complaint against a Port Lincoln settler named Weaver, the case initially looked clear-cut. The accused man claimed that his stabbing of the young woman had been a result of an affray with several Aboriginal people but the local Sub-Protector was convinced that there was more to the story and carried out his own investigation. There had indeed been an altercation but Weaver had neglected to point out that he had been having sex with the victim for several months prior to the clash. When he found out this, Murray 'advised Pandalteroo to lay an information'.[80] However, rumour had it that Weaver intervened with the witnesses as they did not appear and the case 'accordingly fell to the ground'.[81] Indeed, the only case where a woman sexually involved with a settler successfully sustained a charge of assault was that of Paliana, in 1850, also at Port Lincoln. In this case, William Sawyer was found guilty of assault and fined five pounds.[82] In a different twist on the same theme, when Monarto and Yurnani brought assault charges against Henry Morris in 1849, the two women may have expected support from Yurnani's lover, Christopher Christian. The latter did appear in court but was drunk and disinclined to help the prosecution, which had little choice but to abandon the action.[83]

Even today, assault is a crime which presents some difficulties for police and the courts, given the wide range of actions which can rightly fall within its legal definition and differing public perceptions of what constitutes a minor or serious assault. However, assault can be regarded as something of a litmus test of the implementation of the law, in that it serves to indicate the seriousness with which police and legal authorities regard and implement the law as legislated. In the situation being examined here, official action (or rather inaction) in the category of assault is a telling indicator of the seriousness (or rather lack thereof) with which the law and its agents regarded the implementation of the policy of 'one law for all' — especially when compared with such action when the alleged crime fell within the more serious categories such as of murder or stock theft. Where colonists were themselves the victims it was clearly in their interest to ensure that the law took its course. As we shall see in chapter 10, where Aboriginal people were the victims of murder some prosecutions were brought against European offenders, largely because colonial officials, including senior police, the Protector and the Advocate General, were determined in their prosecution of the policy that Aboriginal people would be equal before the law and, accordingly, be protected by it. However, this cannot be said of the category of assault. Rather, after examining the cases presented in this chapter, one is left with an impression that something of a blind eye was turned to assaults, whether perpetrated by Aboriginal people or settlers. While this might have been the most pragmatic course to take, given the realities of the frontier, it suggests that the policy of equality before the law was one which was more vigorously implemented when it coincided with the interests of the settlers.

CHAPTER 9
PROPERTY OFFENCES

It could be reasonably expected that there would be many cases coming before the courts relating to offences by Aboriginal people against European property, such as theft, larceny, breaking and entering, sheep stealing, stock theft and the killing of stock. This proved not to be the case — for example, only forty-nine Aboriginal people were charged with theft between 1836 and 1862. Of these twenty-four were found guilty, eight not guilty, while in the fifteen remaining cases the prosecution was either abandoned or not proceeded with. Perhaps this small number can be explained by most of the cases being heard by district magistrates, where records are no longer available, but this does not seem to be the case either. Only minor cases within the above categories, namely those involving goods of less than five pounds in value,[1] could be heard in local courts, with all accused in more serious cases being remanded to Adelaide. In fact, the records suggest that where Aboriginal people were involved there was a tendency, if not a firm policy, to remand the accused to Adelaide even where lesser amounts were involved.

Within Adelaide itself there were relatively few thefts by Aboriginal people reported, especially considering the large number of Aboriginal people who came to the capital during the 1840s. This was partly because of the difficulty of identifying Aboriginal offenders but also a general tolerance of Aboriginal people visiting the town and a reluctance by officials to prosecute urban Aboriginal people for minor offences. Not all colonists were sympathetic, however, and at times they insisted on charges being laid. Several points can be made about Aboriginal theft in the towns. First, Aboriginal people themselves had some difficulty understanding the antagonism aroused by their petty thefts, particularly where they felt that the settlers had incurred some personal obligation towards them through their earlier actions. Reciprocity demanded that they be given something in return for their labour or favour, however minor — when they were not so rewarded there seemed little harm in taking something. This was the situation in April 1842, when Pritto Monaitya was arrested while attempting to sell a watch that he had taken while employed to cut firewood — he received one month in gaol and a public whipping.[2] Second, most thefts were minor and often motivated by genuine need, such as when a shirt, a blanket, some flour or a loaf of bread were taken. In the winter of 1841, for example, Yakaria, Puyurin and Wittoari were convicted of the theft of blankets and clothing, each receiving a sentence of twelve months' imprisonment.[3] Indeed, hunger often motivated thefts by otherwise honest town-based Aboriginal people. For example, in 1841 Korda was gaoled for 'stealing a loin of mutton from the shop of Richard Pepperall, value 3s'.[4] Third, some charges involved acts which were more in the nature of disagreements or misunderstandings as to who controlled the resources within the town acres. For example, in 1852 when 'Tommy' and 'Mary' were charged with the theft of firewood from a vacant allotment in Wakefield Street, they were only arrested because some colonists wanted official action taken to deter Aboriginal people from cutting down trees within the town.[5] However, the magistrate was unimpressed by the prosecutor's argument that Aboriginal people were becoming 'quite audacious' in their wood gathering. He declined to allow the charge to proceed, officially on the ground that the owner of the trees was not present to lay an information, having left Adelaide for the Victorian goldfields.[6] Fourth, at times Aboriginal people were exploited by unscrupulous settlers, who used them to steal on their behalf or who profited by 'receiving stolen property from the natives',[7] often deliberately cheating their Aboriginal partner in the process.[8] In 1843, for example, when the police arrested a Kaurna man for theft he led them to the house of his 'employer', Mary Carson. There they found a cache of silverware, most of it stolen by Aboriginal people who had been recruited by Carson.[9]

The overwhelming majority of cases where Aboriginal people were charged with theft involved incidents well outside of Adelaide. Minor thefts of firewood, bread and clothing could be tolerated within the town but when Aboriginal people targeted the property of rural settlers their actions were considered to be more threatening, particularly when this involved the theft of stock. During the period under study here, most cases of property offences coming before the courts related to pastoralism, the economic activity at the heart of the clash between the traditional landowners and colonists. However, a major distinction needs be made here between those cases involving only a small number of sheep and those where large numbers, or indeed the entire flock, were driven off. This distinction is not just one of size or opportunity but rather goes to core of Aboriginal motivations for committing these acts. Almost invariably, where between one and several sheep were taken from the flock, closer examination of the circumstances suggests that the motivating factors behind the theft was the hunger of the offenders and their families, and their sense of entitlement to sheep grazing on their land. Where whole flocks or large portions of them were either taken or killed, the motivation was more likely linked to a desire to strike at the core of the colonial enterprise — the colonists' sheep and cattle.

This basic motivation of hunger perhaps needs to be looked at more closely. One fundamental effect of the alienation of Aboriginal land by settlers was the destruction of traditional food sources, with hunger soon becoming the visible sign of Aboriginal people's loss of control over their land. Within a lifestyle reliant upon regularly finding food nearby, kangaroo and wallaby numbers were crucial. However, these animals were soon — as Reverend Newland noted in 1843 — 'fast disappearing altogether'[10] in the settled districts. Despite general agreement that Aboriginal people should be provided with rations to compensate for this loss, no effective regular distribution system was instituted outside of the major settlements and government stations. While it was an overstatement to claim, as some settlers did, that all Aboriginal depredations were 'committed with the sole purpose of obtaining food or clothing',[11] hunger certainly lay behind many of the attacks on stock. Although this was clear as early as 1840, little was done to avoid repeating the cycle of settlement and consequent Aboriginal hunger as the frontier expanded. Those who observed the situation in the rural districts (such as the Protector and his Sub-Protectors, Government Residents and police officers) argued for increasing ration issues to alleviate the hunger and distress they saw. Successive governments provided some rations (though rarely enough) but often seemed to begrudge doing so. Even as late as 1852, Moorhouse had to argue against further reductions in rations by making a pragmatic link between such a course and Aboriginal attacks, knowing that appeals to humanitarian obligation were no longer heeded:

> I could not recommend any reduction in this item as I think the Government would effect no saving by it: two months hence, outrages would commence, and the cost of capturing, trying, and punishing the offenders would be more than the price of the flour.[12]

At the time, Moorhouse was convinced that the issuing of daily rations had become necessary in the more heavily stocked districts, particularly in the winter months. However, he was told that he assumed too much — Governor Young was not convinced that more funds were needed for Aboriginal rations, arguing that these should only be supplied when 'natives are destitute or are insufficiently supplied from their own sources'.[13] The Protector interpreted the latter statement liberally so that, whenever he had rations available, he distributed them to Aboriginal people.[14] Unfortunately, particularly in more isolated districts, Aboriginal people were reliant largely upon the goodwill of the stock owners themselves, to provide them with either rations or paid work. Both proved to be infrequent and irregular, to the point where, in some districts, Aboriginal people were widely malnourished and, when hard times struck, sometimes 'absolutely on the point of starvation'.[15] Traditional game may have become scarce but an alternative food source, as Moorhouse noted, was now 'scattered over the watered districts'.[16] Not surprisingly, as Charles Driver reported from Port Lincoln, 'the temptation of having food within reach, and with little trouble, [was]... too great for them to bear'.[17] Similarly, a few years later, Tolmer pointed out to his superiors that the people

> inhabiting the interior are driven frequently to commit depredations from hunger, as the flocks and herds of the settlers now advance so far, occupying the country in which they formerly hunted for their subsistence.[18]

Recognising this link between enforced hunger and minor stock theft, some colonists remained reluctant to see Aboriginal people prosecuted for the theft or killing of sheep. As one colonist wrote in 1839, this was something of a moral dilemma:

> we have no right whatever to punish the natives for spearing our sheep; or if we have, they have an equally good right to inflict punishment on us for killing their kangaroos.[19]

Such enlightened views were not just confined to the towns. Stock owners could accept the occasional loss of a lamb and indeed often turned a blind eye to the common practice whereby shepherds offered meat to local Aboriginal people in return for ongoing security, casual labour or sexual favours. The paucity of cases prosecuted where only a few sheep were involved suggests a degree of tolerance among pastoralists — or perhaps simply an unwillingness to commit the resources required to capture such small-scale offenders. This is not to say that no charges were laid in such circumstances but these were very few relative to the widespread 'depredations' on stock reported in the contemporary press. For example, in 1842 Yurki and Narritya were charged with the theft of just one sheep although even in this case the prosecution declined to proceed with the case after the two men had spent several days in the Adelaide Gaol.[20] In the years 1836 to 1852, thirty-three persons were so charged, but in seventeen of these cases the prosecution either declined to proceed or abandoned the case — ten Aboriginal people were found guilty and four not guilty.

By the early 1850s the earlier tendency towards leniency had run its course, with the general view being that the Aboriginal people should by then know better than to steal even one sheep. Of course, this expectation ignored the reality of a moving frontier in which successive and quite separate groups of Aboriginal people were forced to come to terms with the sheep invasion. When, for example, in June 1850, Padlaria was seen taking a single sheep from Rogers' flock on Yorke Peninsula, the stock owner insisted that charges be laid, despite his shepherd being reluctant to proceed. Tried in the Supreme Court in August 1851, Padlaria was strongly defended by Bartley[21] but nevertheless was convicted and sentenced to six months in gaol. Before sentencing, the Judge asked Padlaria why he had stolen the sheep, to which he simply replied: 'I was hungry'.[22] A few days earlier Binarambula had appeared for stealing '1 ewe and 1 lamb, value 6s'[23] but was lucky enough to have the witnesses fail to appear at the hearing, leaving the prosecution with little choice but to abandon their case.[24] At the same sessions Warraki, Kondura and Minora were convicted of stealing 'two wether sheep, value 12s, the property of Allan McFarlan'[25] and each was given a sentence of six months' imprisonment.[26] A few years later, when Nadgiltie, Toocherg, Kokilata and Yarkeltia were found guilty of stealing a sheep each from Maurice's Eyre Peninsula property, they all spent three months in the

Port Lincoln Gaol.[27] Even at the end of the period under study here, Aboriginal people were still being brought before the courts for stealing a sheep or two, such as when Palierie and Nungarinya were brought to Port Lincoln for trial after stealing sheep from Crawford's property near Streaky Bay in June 1862. Convicted, both men were sentenced to twelve months' imprisonment.[28] In the last decade being considered here, the rate of conviction increased considerably, with twenty-two of the thirty-six defendants being found guilty, only six not guilty and prosecution being abandoned in relatively few (eight) cases. The likely reasons for this increase include the improved ability to understand Aboriginal testimony, the judiciary's less stringent requirements on Aboriginal amenability to the law, and pressure by pastoralists for police and the courts to prevent the theft of stock.

Most commonly, however, when Aboriginal people came before the courts charged with stock theft, the motivation was not simply that of hunger. Rather, they were arrested after engaging in what might well be described as a form of economic warfare against the pastoralists. This tactic involved the theft (or simply the driving off and scattering) of a large percentage of the flock at one time. Apart from providing a long-term supply of meat for all members of the clan, this tactic also hit at the stock owner's economic viability since to continue operating he was forced to either expend considerable resources regaining the scattered sheep or purchasing replacement stock. The first attack on stock that can be placed in this category came as early as June 1841, when news reached Adelaide that 'a party of natives had attacked the shepherds at Mr Dutton's station, at Mount Dispersion, and after dangerously wounding one of them, had driven off about eight hundred sheep'.[29] A year later, at Port Lincoln, Moorpar led a party which drove away 500 sheep from Kemp's property and was also involved in the burning of newly built fences at Dutton's station to the north. These larger-scale attacks did not stop — indeed they intensified over the next few years. In 1844, the Scott Brothers lost over 1,000 sheep[30] and Wilkinson also lost a large flock and scores of cattle.[31] At Lake Albert in the spring of 1846 hundreds of sheep were taken from McFarlane's station. Two of his shepherds managed to retrieve all but sixty of this flock and when they returned to the station, they brought with them Ngaloorunger, whom they accused of organising the theft. When his case came up in the Supreme Court it soon became clear that there was no evidence at all against him (other than the shepherds' suspicions) and accordingly he was acquitted and released.[32]

By the mid 1840s, police resources were overstretched and even when they managed to make an arrest, difficulties with interpretation and evidence made it difficult to secure a conviction. For example, when in 1845 'Charley' was charged with stealing almost 200 sheep from a station at Rivoli Bay,[33] no adequate interpreter could be found.[34] The following year, when Ngalkantyirriorn appeared in court charged with stealing fifty lambs from McFarlane's property, an interpreter was found but the prosecution was forced to abandon the case for want of evidence.[35] These and other attacks in the South-East districts threatened the livelihood of several pastoralists and help to explain the severity of the retaliation against Aboriginal people meted out there. Graziers moved to mount 'hunting parties against the natives, and to shoot them indiscriminately',[36] believing that the scale of their losses provided 'just cause for abiding by their own physical force'.[37] Even where the police were called in, such as in 1847 near Cape Northumberland after 300 sheep were stolen, Aboriginal people could not be assured of an arrest and fair trial — the resulting affray between police and Aboriginal people ended when 'four natives were shot'.[38]

On Yorke Peninsula, similar large-scale depredations were made on flocks and herds. Rogers lost more than 200 sheep in August 1855, followed by a similar number only a few weeks later.[39] To his credit, Rogers declined to take the law into his own hands and instead sought legal redress. In total, six men were charged with sheep stealing over these incidents[40] and each received a term of imprisonment of six months when found guilty.[41] In the Mid-North, the theft of a large mob of sheep in late December 1846 provoked a clash between settlers and Aboriginal people, during which three people, including a woman, were fatally wounded. Constable Kenny investigated and subsequently arrested Monaitya and Purri Kudnutya, who were found guilty of stock theft and sentenced to twelve months' imprisonment.[42] However, the former was pardoned on Chief Justice Cooper's recommendation, based on his assistance in 'the recovery of the greater part of the stolen sheep'.[43] A few years later, when a large mob of sheep from Ferguson's and Younghusband's stations were stolen, six men where arrested and charged[44] but it appears that the prosecution abandoned the case soon after the indictment.[45] Stock owners in this district were increasingly becoming frustrated by the law's inability to stem their losses and when, in January 1853, Williams lost some of his flock he took matters into his own hands, shooting the dogs of Aboriginal people suspected of using them to rustle sheep. An argument ensued in which an elderly Aboriginal man was shot by Williams,[46] who later successfully argued that he had been acting in self-defence.[47] Similarly, on Eyre Peninsula, as settlers took flocks northwards along both coasts, there were occasional attacks on their major assets. In 1849, for example, Baird and Sinclair lost more than 1,500 sheep, with the former losing his life in one of the attacks.[48] This was a clear case of a small group of Aboriginal people acting to remove the sheep and their owners from their land, for the sheep were driven north into inhospitable country, where all but a handful soon died from thirst.[49] Following a similar resistance incident in 1855, where a large flock was driven off from Syme's station, Malkeltie was arrested for his involvement. He was found guilty of sheep stealing and sentenced to three months' imprisonment.[50]

Shepherds and station hutkeepers were at the front line of this clash between the two land-dependent cultures. Not surprisingly then, robbery from station huts was a common occurrence throughout the 1840s and, in the later settled districts, well into the 1850s. Shepherds were, by definition, often out with their flocks and their huts were easily broken into. However, the frequency of such offences reported in newspapers and diaries is not reflected in the number of cases brought before the courts. Only thirty-three Aboriginal people were charged with robbery during the twenty-five years under scrutiny here, of whom fifteen were found guilty, five not guilty with the remaining cases abandoned for various reasons. Why was there such a low arrest rate for robbery? The answer lies, first, in the fact that actions commonly described as robbery were often not as serious as that offence implies, particularly when the wider relationship between hutkeepers and Aboriginal people on the frontier is taken into account. Rather than robbery of station huts involving forcible entry by unknown Aboriginal people operating as an organised raiding party, the more usual hut-breaking situation on the South Australian frontier was a more pedestrian affair. Often the offenders were well known to the hutkeeper and with few exceptions the breaking took place while the hutkeeper was well distant. Manipulating or forcing a simple catch on a door, while technically constituting breaking and entering, was not likely to be seen as a serious breach by the Aboriginal perpetrators nor, often, by the hutkeeper himself. In addition, only rarely did the Aboriginal robbers ransack huts, usually only stealing sufficient rations and goods to meet their immediate needs.

Second, just as in the circumstances of some assault cases, incidents where Aboriginal people could have been charged with robbery in fact involved their pressing home what they believed to be genuine claims upon the hutkeeper or station owner. Aboriginal people well understood that the stock owners were making their livelihood at least partly through the use of resources traditionally owned by them. Their occasional insistence on receiving some form of payment or assistance (or, where it was not voluntarily forthcoming, simply taking a reasonable toll) was regarded as offensive by those settlers who failed to appreciate this point of view. For example, in the winter of 1844, when five Aboriginal people approached Mrs Willis' house on the outskirts of Adelaide, they expected to be given rations. Mrs Willis was unsympathetic and they failed to understand her denial, particularly when they could see an abundance of food through the kitchen door. They pushed into the room and helped themselves to bread, flour and tobacco, with the result that two of their number, 'One-eyed Peter' and Mungoringa, were subsequently charged with robbery.[51] When the case came up, Mrs Willis was certain that 'Peter' was not the one-eyed man in the group and he was acquitted.[52] However, Mungoringa was found guilty and sent to gaol for two months.[53]

The general rule seems to be that robberies were often not pursued through the courts. Why then were some cases considered exceptional enough to proceed? First, as in the Willis incident recounted above, it could have been that it involved a forced entry where a woman was home alone. Second, such as in the 1851 case against Kambalta, some robbers simple chose the wrong hut. Police Constable Kennings was not impressed to return from patrol to find the Salt Creek Police Station door ajar and a quantity of food, clothing and tobacco missing. His investigation only managed to recover some of this property, which was found in the possession of Kambalta, but the Judge was not convinced that the defendant had personally entered the hut and so he convicted him only of receiving stolen goods.[54] Third, some stolen goods were more likely to lead to a court appearance than others. For example, when 'Charley' and 'Bonney' Bootha broke into Mrs Young's house at Gawler in 1860 they stole more than food. They ensured their arrest by also taking a bank order which they later presented to the Stockport storekeeper. Both men were found guilty, with 'Charley' being given three years' gaol while 'Bonney' received only eighteen months as he was considered to have played a lesser role in the robbery.[55] Fourth, cases where violence was either threatened or inflicted were more likely to lead to prosecution. When, in 1851, Partko, Ngurkilli and Mantamornappa were arrested after allegedly robbing the hut of one of Coutts' shepherds, it was the fact that they had committed 'robbery with violence' by placing the shepherd 'in bodily fear for his life'[56] which ensured their prosecution. Similarly, when 'Jemmy' was charged with breaking into Edward Symes' house in 1852, the charge apparently was only laid because the housekeeper, Mary Savage, had been 'put in bodily fear of her life'.[57] Fifth, settlers were intolerant of robberies where weapons were stolen, such as in the case of Yarngalta et al.,[58] where six defendants were charged with robbing one of Horne's huts, taking a gun, ammunition and other weapons.[59] Three of the accused were found guilty[60] and imprisoned but in fact they fared better than those of their clan who headed towards the coast when pursued — an unknown number of this group died when driven off the cliffs at Elliston.[61] Finally, settlers could not overlook large-scale thefts of goods such as, in 1850, when Manilti, Panmalta, Mowalta and Winnulu may well have not been charged except that they removed the complete stock of rations (including over 200 pounds of flour) from one of Simms' huts.[62] Similarly, later the same year, robbery charges were probably laid against Mullnullnumelli only because he stripped one of Chambers' huts bare.[63] Cases such as these can be differentiated from the lesser (and usually not prosecuted) instances of robbery not only by the amount of goods stolen but perhaps also by their underlying motivation. Where huts were ransacked, such thefts and robberies may be seen as determined attempts to make life difficult if not untenable for the hutkeeper and, where several attacks were made on the assets of one pastoralist, even to threaten the economic survival of the enterprise.

Pastoralists generally felt that remanding Aboriginal people accused of theft or robbery of huts to Adelaide for trial was inappropriate and impractical. Local magistrates agreed, preferring to deal with any lesser cases themselves. However, Adelaide legal officials were opposed to any relaxation of the policy that serious crimes should be heard in Adelaide, with some justification given that most rural Justices of the Peace were themselves stock owners. This was made clear in 1845, when Charles Driver, the Port Lincoln Government Resident and Magistrate, took local action to try to discourage a spate of thefts and robberies on huts in his district. When Yailgatta and Ngumbi were arrested for the robbery of Clay's station at Murinyana, Driver decided to deal with this crime himself rather than commit the two men for trial in Adelaide. Driver approached local elders to encourage them to be involved in administering justice in this case and in early January 1846 all of the

Aboriginal people living in and around the town were assembled. Pastor Schurmann was enlisted to explain the crime to them and to seek the elders' advice as to how it might best be dealt with. Several Aboriginal speakers admonished Yailgatta, with Driver subsequently sentencing him to be flogged. Yailgatta was held in custody until the next full moon, when this sentence was carried out. The local Aboriginal people may have been content with this experiment in summary and collaborative justice but Adelaide officials were outraged, with the Advocate General arguing that this action 'was entirely unwarranted by Law' and declaring that Aboriginal people were 'not to be subjected to punishment, except by competent judicial authority'.[64] Driver was admonished but he was determined to put his point of view, namely that the interests of justice and other Aboriginal people were best served by prompt action at the local level in what he considered to be relatively minor but not infrequent cases:

> in the absence of all legal evidence, the charge of felony, against the native Yailgalta, would not for a moment have been supported. A magistrate, acting simply in his magisterial capacity, would necessarily have dismissed it…looking upon myself as especially entrusted with the general interests of the natives of this district, I deemed it my duty to ascertain the truth and, having done so, to inflict punishment for the actual offence, however inaccessible by law.[65]

In many of the cases where Aboriginal people were prosecuted for stock theft the alleged thieves were either working for colonists at the time of the offence or had previously done so. Aboriginal people often took on work as shepherds, hutkeepers and casual labourers on farms and stations within a relatively short time of the settlers' arrival in the district and it was not long before instances of theft by these employees came to the notice of the authorities. In 1842, only three years after the settlement of Port Lincoln, a Battara man named Nganti was working as a station hand when he was charged with stealing a sheep. Found guilty, he was imprisoned for a few weeks but it seems that his action was regarded as a lapse rather than a serious crime, since Nganti's employer took him back on the payroll on his release.[66] The 1850s, coinciding with a widespread shortage of station labour, saw more cases of Aboriginal people being charged with stealing sheep from their employers, although it is probable that this simply reflects the greater number of Aboriginal people then being employed. In March 1851, shepherds Kurkrunwilla and Muruss were charged with stealing sheep from Rogers' station on Yorke Peninsula, after being caught tying up a sheep and placing it in the bush, to be retrieved later.[67] A few months later, when four men from the same district were charged with robbery from a hut,[68] the hutkeeper gave evidence that all the men were well known to him and that the ringleader in the robbery, Mantamornappa, was employed as a shepherd on the station.[69] Aboriginal shepherds, in the face of the hunger being experienced in their clans, no doubt came under pressure to supply the occasional sheep to their clanspeople. This was widely recognised by settlers and in times of labour shortages minor infringements were often overlooked by station owners, who now needed Aboriginal labour.[70]

However, when Aboriginal people took too great a liberty, stock owners did take action, perhaps mainly to deter others. For example, in May 1853 on Pinkerton's station on Eyre Peninsula, where several Aboriginal people were employed as shepherds, Pinkerton raided two nearby camps and found eight carcases — a greater stock loss than he was willing to tolerate. Six men,[71] none of them his shepherds, were arrested and charged. However, Pinkerton's Aboriginal shepherds were either unable or unwilling to act as interpreters and the prosecution had no choice but to abandon the proceedings.[72] Further south, in the following year, Tennant decided to take action against one of his Aboriginal shepherds when confronted by similar depredations on his flock by relatives of his workers. Puleringa, who had worked diligently as a shepherd for Tennant for over twelve months, was charged and convicted of stealing sheep.[73] Acting on information received in the questioning of Puleringa, the police also charged another four men[74] with receiving stolen goods. On being found guilty these men were imprisoned for one month, while Puleringa, whose crime was considered more serious since it involved a breach of trust, was gaoled for six months with hard labour.[75] Two years later, two Eyre Peninsula men, Nepulto and Meewulta, also fell foul of the European expectation of honesty among employees. Entrusted by Sergeant Eyre to deliver goods to Three Lakes Police Station, these two men allegedly appropriated the goods for their own use — both were convicted and gaoled for one month with hard labour.[76]

Given the frequency of reports in newspapers of the day, especially during the 1840s, relating to Aboriginal 'depredations' on the pastoralists' stock, it is surprising that only five cases were found where Aboriginal people were charged with the killing of stock — two resulted in convictions and the prosecution was abandoned in the other three.

The first case was that of Kalamco who was indicted in September 1842 for killing a calf but set free when the prosecution was abandoned.[77] Two months later, in November 1842, a similar case was heard in the Supreme Court, leading to the conviction of Mukarta[78] on a charge of killing a calf.[79] Originally sentenced to transportation for ten years, Mukarta was not sent to Van Diemen's Land, instead remaining in the Adelaide Gaol for only a few weeks before being pardoned.[80] In this case, the Governor was convinced by the arguments of the Protector of Aborigines, who pointed out the futility of a longer sentence. Moorhouse reported that Mukarta had told him, 'Natta ai bultimi', the literal translation of which was 'I am emptied' but which the Protector maintained was an indication that Murkata would not offend again.[81] In May 1844 Nyarrokyppur[82] was charged with maliciously wounding a sow owned by George Ottaway but the prosecution declined to proceed, for reasons which remain unclear.[83] Almost four years later, the prosecution withdrew its case against another Aboriginal person, Permalooan, who had been charged with killing stock. Accused of 'spearing and destroying' cattle on Samuel Davenport's property in July 1847, Permalooan looked likely to be convicted since two station employees were expected in court to give evidence against him. However, two problems emerged for the prosecution in this case — the European witnesses failed to appear and the Chief Justice suggested that the man in the dock should have been charged with malicious wounding of cattle rather than killing stock, since the cattle in fact had been slaughtered by stockmen after they had judged them too injured to survive.[84] Accordingly, the Attorney General chose not to proceed further and Permalooan was released. The same result was achieved in the final prosecution, that against Walkaoinni. In September 1851 he was charged with 'unlawful spearing of a bullock' belonging to John McPherson of Salt Creek. After spending a few weeks on remand, Walkaoinni was released when once again witnesses failed to appear and the prosecution was forced to abandon the case.[85]

This failure to appear was not uncommon. Throughout the 1840s, the courts experienced difficulties in prosecuting Aboriginal people for stock killing or theft simply because of reluctance by pastoralists and their employees to appear and give evidence against them. In 1842, for example, Driver reported from Port Lincoln that William Saunders, a witness in the trial of Nweka, refused to obey a subpoena, even though a sea passage to Adelaide was provided.[86] As the magistrate at the committal hearing had not bound Saunders over to attend the Adelaide trial, he could not be made to do so. His employer had no intention of insisting that he travel to Adelaide and all the Advocate General could do was to make sure that it was known who was responsible for the abandonment of the prosecution.[87] Following this case, the Attorney General attempted to alleviate the problem by requiring that summonses for witnesses to appear in such cases be delivered by police officers, and that they be served in time for witnesses to make the necessary travel arrangements. This remained the policy throughout the 1840s and 1850s, although in practice police officers combined this duty with others also taking them into the district in question rather than making special trips. This often meant delays in delivery of summons and not infrequently, failure to deliver. For example, in 1844, when summonses were issued for station hands Frederick Covild and Peter Victory to attend a hearing against 'Charley', the Police Commissioner advised the Attorney General that he had no men to spare for this summons-serving duty. Significantly, he suggested that even if the summonses were served, his opinion was that they would simply be ignored.[88]

By as early as the mid 1840s, the widely held view in the rural districts was that it was not worth the expense involved for pastoralists to encourage their employees to travel to Adelaide to testify against Aboriginal people charged with property offences. Even among pastoralists who preferred police action to the more expedient course of taking the law into their own hands, the pursuit, arrest and arraignment of Aboriginal offenders was considered to be enough of a deterrent lesson to other local Aboriginal people without going to the added expense of giving evidence to support a successful prosecution.[89] After all, once they were arrested Aboriginal people accused of offences were usually removed from the district, often in irons, remanded for some weeks at least in local lockups or the Adelaide Gaol and almost always denied bail — punishment enough in the eyes of other members of the same clan. Even prominent South-East pastoralist and Justice of the Peace, Evelyn Sturt, was reluctant to send any of his men to Adelaide when Aboriginal people were charged with stealing some of his sheep, responding to the official request to do so by asking 'whether it is absolutely necessary that the Witnesses should appear'.[90] Nevertheless, Sturt still expected the Adelaide authorities to take some informal action, at least against one of the prisoners:

> As it appears somewhat improbable that the accused will be convicted, I take the liberty of expressing a hope, that if possible,

9. Property offences

the elder native, be not returned to this District during the winter; I know him to be one of the most troublesome and savage blacks of the Tribes.[91]

One case where European witnesses failed to appear was that against Koonko and Watpa,[92] charged with stealing sheep from Coutt's station on Yorke Peninsula. These charges came about as a result of an investigation into an attack on shepherd John Gall, and both Coutts and Gall were subpoenaed to appear. When they failed to arrive, the Chief Justice expressed his annoyance at their non-appearance:

> And yet these people, who manifest such a culpable remissness in furthering the ends of justice, complained of the police for not apprehending the prisoner sooner. They think nothing of sending men on a harassing pursuit of natives charged with offences, nothing of the trouble and expenses of conveying the prisoners to Adelaide, nothing of the waste of time in that Court, and the mischief that must arise from an abortive prosecution.[93]

Koonko and Watpa were remanded until the March sessions, at which the witnesses did appear, although the result (the theft charges were withdrawn) somewhat vindicated their initial reluctance.[94] In the following year, four men from Eyre Peninsula — Manilti, Panmalta, Mowalta and Winnulu — were charged with robbery of a station hut and sent to Adelaide for trial. Again, however, none of the European witnesses appeared and the prosecution lapsed 'in consequence of the non-appearance in due time of the witnesses'.[95]

When the figures for all of the property offences are totalled, 153 Aboriginal people are shown to have been charged, with about fifty per cent (seventy-three) being found guilty, while twenty-three were acquitted. In fifty-nine cases, the prosecution declined to proceed, either before the case came to trial (eighteen) or during the trial itself (thirty-one). The remainder (ten) did not proceed for a variety of reasons. However, a more accurate picture is achieved when cases not involving the theft of stock are removed — these involved theft mainly in the towns and settlements and had little impact on relations between Aboriginal people and pastoralists. When pastoral-related offences (robbery, stock theft and killing) only are considered, these show a total of 104 Aboriginal people charged, with the result that forty-nine were found guilty and fifteen acquitted, while once again there were a high number of cases where the proceedings were abandoned by the prosecution, whether before (twelve) or during (twenty-two) the trial. Early in the period, these abandonments mainly related to difficulties with jurisdiction and language but, as the years progressed, the prosecution more often found that they were hampered by key European witnesses (often employees of the crime's victim) failing to appear or being uncooperative with prosecuting counsel when they did so. Pressure was applied to pastoralists to allow their employees to give evidence against Aboriginal people accused of theft or robbery, but this simply forced some stock owners to look for other solutions to their problem with local Aboriginal people. First, they simply refused to bring minor crimes to the attention of the police and second, declined to prosecute where the matter did come to the notice of the authorities through other sources. Most pastoralists were genuine in their belief that it was counterproductive to prosecute, although some may have simply preferred to mete out their own punishment. If they did agree to prosecute, as one Eyre Peninsula stock owner noted in 1849:

> we have to go about 150 miles to give information against them, which is a matter of great consideration, for it will occupy a week or so, and in that time all the men about the station may be murdered and the provisions stolen.[96]

For example, in 1853, when Sub-Protector Minchin heard of station huts near Mt Arden being robbed of flour and provisions, he could not persuade the two pastoralists involved to even officially report the crimes. They declined his requests, pointing out 'the time they would lose, the chances of a conviction and the probability of their huts being attacked in their absence'.[97] Even when a few weeks later one of these stock owners had a hutkeeper severely bashed by Aboriginal intruders, both he and the injured man declined to press charges, arguing that neither could spare the time to leave the station.[98] The Protector of Aborigines was not prepared to proceed without their support, noting on the file: 'If the injured party declines prosecuting in this case, one cannot see why he should be compelled to do so'.[99] Unfortunately, the loss of faith among pastoralists that the law could deal effectively with theft or attacks by Aboriginal people had a darker consequence, as some of their number moved to take the law into their own hands, as the following chapter reveals.

CHAPTER 10
PROTECTED BY THE LAW?

As we have seen, Governor Hindmarsh's initial proclamation in 1836 made it clear that Aboriginal people in the colony were not only subject to British law but were also protected by it. If the implementation of the policy of legal equality for colonists and Aboriginal people is to be judged as successful, then this protection test needs to be met — that is, that the law did operate to protect at least the lives, if not the lifestyles, of Aboriginal peoples within South Australia. In chapter 7, the other side of the ledger was examined, involving bringing Aboriginal people to book for the killing of settlers — whereby thirty-five Aboriginal people were found guilty of murder, five were convicted of manslaughter and twenty-three executed. The 'one law for all' policy, if it were adhered to in practice, would suggest some similarity in the proportion of indictments and convictions in cases where Aboriginal people met their death at the hands of settlers. In fact, what this chapter reveals is a gross discrepancy between these comparative conviction rates. This failure of the law and its agencies to protect Aboriginal lives, particularly when officials well knew that illegal killings of Aboriginal people were taking place throughout the 1840s and 1850s, is a powerful argument for the view that South Australia not only failed to implement the policy of equal treatment before the law, but made no real attempt to do so.

The May 1839 trials of the alleged murderers of Duffield and Thompson were detailed in chapter 2 but are revisited briefly here because the issue of settlers taking the law into their own hands was raised during these Supreme Court proceedings. In his opening address in the first of these two trials, Prosecutor Charles Mann urged the jury to convict the Aboriginal defendants, at least partly in consideration of and 'mercy' to other Aboriginal people in the colony:

> for if the guilty escape punishment, the poor fellows will be hunted and shot like wild dogs. Remember gentlemen, that the punishment of the guilty is the protection of the innocent. I need not tell you of the fearful excitement that has existed in the minds of the colonists, such feelings only remain in abeyance, they only await the result of these trials, to see whether through the law they will receive that protection which they have an undoubted right to expect from the law; if they do not receive it, I fear they will take the law into their own hands, and the consequences must be dreadful.[1]

Whether this exhortation had any effect on the jury is not known but public tension was certainly reduced by the conviction and execution of two of the six accused men. The resulting calm did not last long, however, as the events of 1840 (see chapter 7) brought the issue of adequate police protection to the surface once again. Fearing that settlers in that district would be provoked into 'violent retaliatory measures against the Aborigines'[2] by young Frank Hawson's death, Governor Gawler issued a proclamation, reaffirming his government's commitment to protecting the colonists, while giving warning that

> any persons who may use violent retaliatory actions against the natives, except in the most urgently necessary actual defence of life and property, will render themselves liable to be dealt with according to the extreme vigour of the law.[3]

It can be argued that the *Maria* punitive expedition, or more accurately the storm of criticism it raised in London, had some influence on the likelihood of settlers taking the law into their own hands. After 1841, the authorities adopted a more cautious line towards dealing with Aboriginal resisters and offenders with, as detailed in chapter 3, the Chief Justice adopting the view that many Aboriginal people did not in fact fall within the jurisdiction of the courts. However, what seemed to be legitimate legal concerns to lawyers, officials and indeed many colonists within Adelaide could easily be construed as legal quibbles by those colonists settling the frontier districts. The connection between the common perception that the treatment of Aboriginal offenders was overly lenient and stock owners moving to operate against Aboriginal people outside of the law was not only a logical one for such frontier-dwellers but also often related to their financial and even personal survival.[4] If the police were not capable of protecting them, at least from repetitious raids and large-scale stock theft, then these owners and their managers could be expected to take their own protective actions. The courts, as a part of the overall system of law and order, were also involved in this assessment. In the eyes of rural colonists, it was bad enough when the police arrived too late or not at all. However, when they actually made an arrest yet failed to gain a conviction because the court either declared its lack of jurisdiction or inability to understand the alleged offender, the frustration of stock owners was understandably considerable. Many believed that swift official retaliatory action, such as that conducted against the Milmenrura in 1840, should have been repeated when other Aboriginal groups posed a threat to pastoral activities.

As early as 1840 the *Adelaide Chronicle* warned officials that, 'in cases of deliberate murder of white settlers',[5] any recognition of mitigating circumstances or allowance of 'exceptional laws' would provoke widespread 'illegal measures of retaliation on the part of the setters'.[6] By 1842 many frontier dwellers were disillusioned with the ability of the police and the courts to bring enough Aboriginal offenders to trial for legal action to achieve any effective deterrent. At Port Lincoln, for example, settlers petitioned for police or military assistance when persistent Aboriginal attacks drove many of the district's rural settlers into the safety of the town.[7] The *Adelaide Examiner*, under the headline 'Port Lincoln Sacrificed', condemned the 'total indifference of the Government to the sacrifice of their lives and property', and demanded to know '[h]ow many murders must take place before Governor Grey intervenes?'[8] Eventually a contingent of soldiers, led by Lt Hugonin, was sent to the district. However, when they failed dismally to prevent further Aboriginal attacks or to apprehend any Aboriginal people involved in earlier incidents, the frustration of the settlers only intensified. Before the soldiers even left the district, settlers were involved in indiscriminate acts of revenge and retaliation, which contributed to what the local magistrate's clerk recorded in his diary as an 'extensive slaughter'[9] of Aboriginal people around Port Lincoln. In other districts also, when Aboriginal depredations threatened European physical or economic survival, pragmatic settlers at times took what one newspaper described as 'illegal measures of retaliation'.[10]

Even so, one is left with the impression that most property owners would have preferred legal means of preventing Aboriginal attacks on their stock and employees. This was, many believed, the 'true way to protect the blacks',[11] for prompt police action would remove the impetus for settlers to take action themselves. Certainly, rural settlers continued to plead and petition for adequate police protection and government action throughout the 1840s. To continue with the Port Lincoln example, when in 1842 the town was facing a determined campaign of Aboriginal resistance,[12] the residents sought urgent police assistance from Adelaide. In early March 1842, after a public meeting held in the Port Lincoln courthouse, representatives of the meeting drafted a letter to the Colonial Secretary.[13] The following month the proprietors of the Port Lincoln Special Survey met at Bentham's house in Adelaide to discuss the security of their investment on Eyre Peninsula. While most of the discussion focussed on how to overcome the shortage of labour in the district, this group also passed the following resolution, which was later communicated to the Colonial Secretary:

> That this meeting being deeply impressed with the atrocity of the murders lately committed at Port Lincoln, the repeated robberies which have taken place at different sheep stations, and the alarming attitude assumed by the native population… beg respectfully to represent to the Colonial Government, the necessity of immediate and decisive measures for apprehending and punishing the perpetrators of those outrages, and prevent the probability of their recurrence.[14]

Other settlers from Port Lincoln raised the issue in the newspapers,[15] with one publicly threatening to deal with the Aboriginal resistance without the aid of the police:

> if the settlers are not protected, they must and will protect themselves, and from the *weight* of their arguments, and the way they would *discharge* their duty, would teach the Port Lincoln savages the same good lesson that was read to them at Encounter Bay.[16]

Three years later, when pastoralists in the South-East faced a similar outbreak of sheep stealing and violence, several signed a petition stating the Rivoli Bay 'settlers will be under the necessity of taking the law into their own hands, to protect their lives and property'.[17] Officials agreed that an increased police presence in the newly settled districts was desirable[18] but funds were not available to meet the demand. By 1846, when the Police Commissioner expressed regret that he did not have the resources to prevent further clashes in the expanding rural areas, he noted that Aboriginal people 'pay by the loss of life, for their encroachments upon property when the settlers are left to be their own judges and redressors'.[19] Even where the resources were found, such as in the case of Port Lincoln in 1842, they were not often effective.[20] Pleas for assistance most often resulted in action that was too late, too limited or inappropriate. Although officials were aware of their responsibility and the consequences of their failure,[21] they did little more than exhort officials to inform settlers of the illegality of such acts, while explaining to local Aboriginal people the likely 'consequences of their repeated attacks'.[22]

The cases in which alleged Aboriginal offenders were acquitted or discharged because of difficulties in establishing jurisdiction or interpreting their evidence have been detailed in chapters 3 and 4. Understandably, these contributed to the view held by settlers in rural districts, and indeed investors within Adelaide, that the courts did not understand their situation in respect of such Aboriginal people. While some moves were made to overcome these difficulties, it is fair to say that evidential reforms and the provision of interpreters were far too slowly adopted when considered from the point of view of stock owners. In 1847, for example, Captain Butler, the Assistant Protector of Aborigines based at Guichen Bay, informed Adelaide officials that the difficulty remained unresolved:

> On the one hand a native can not be punished if he is unable to defend himself from ignorance of what may be urged against him — On the other hand the shepherds and others when they observe that the natives escape punishment are induced to take the law into their own hands; and acting on the principle of self preservation it is impossible to say what may be the result to the Aborigines, as they often suffer without the slightest chance of the aggressors being detected.[23]

Governor Robe read this report but his only advice was that Butler and his clerk take steps to learn the local dialect themselves.[24]

It is impossible to determine the extent to which settlers did take the law into their own hands, since the very nature of the action meant that such incidents were not likely to reach the attention of authorities. As Nathaniel Hailes noted in 1842, 'while the aboriginal atrocities are made well known in all their details, the civilised provocations and reprisals remain to a considerable extent secret'.[25]

However, a number of such incidents are recorded during the 1840s.[26] At Mt Remarkable in 1844, a civilian party fired on a group of Aboriginal people, killing one and wounding two others.[27] Two days later the same civilians struck at another encampment, where 'three Natives lost their lives, two men and one woman'.[28] In the South-East the following year, one settler claimed that stock thefts and attacks on huts had led to organised retaliation by stock owners, arguing that 'the settlers have just cause for abiding by their own physical force, and, by a coalition, to place themselves in an independent position'.[29] In 1846, on Sterling's station in the South-East, a group of men searching for stolen sheep attacked a campsite and 'in the affray three natives were shot'.[30] In 1849, the *Register* quoted passages purportedly written by an overseer on a Yorke Peninsula property, in which he claimed that: '[u]ntil the settlers are allowed to shoot them wherever they are found they will never be quiet'.[31] Indeed, in practice it was not only active resisters and stock thieves who were subject to such retaliatory action. As Magistrate's Clerk Nathaniel Hailes noted in 1842:

> Legal punishment does not always fall on the really guilty party. Neither do showers of bullets propelled among flying [sic] men, women and children select their victims with discretion — nor do spoonsful of arsenic dropped onto flour discriminate the stomachs into which they enter.[32]

South Australian frontier society, even given that it had far fewer ex-convicts than New South Wales, was not a place for the faint-hearted. As labour became scarce in the more remote districts and Aboriginal attacks on stock and huts increased, some employers looked for tougher men to run their stations. Whereas in 1836 to 1840 many shepherds were to some extent sympathetic to the situation of the local Aboriginal people, attitudes hardened during the 1840s as violent confrontation escalated. Guns, swords and whips were carried more frequently in rural districts as this decade progressed and some settlers showed no hesitation in using these against Aboriginal people, as some of the cases detailed below reveal. The extent of this brutality should not be over-generalised, however, as many experienced shepherds and remote hutkeepers knew that their own long-term interests were best met by maintaining peaceful relations with local Aboriginal groups and individuals.

Where civilians were part of a police–civilian party that fired on Aboriginal people, they were not subject to investigation or reprimand

— whatever the inappropriateness of their action. However, when they fired on Aboriginal people while not accompanied by police, settlers were more likely to face an investigation and, at times, formal charges. For example, when Port Lincoln farmer George Lawson fired on Aboriginal people caught stealing his grain in 1846, the Advocate General condemned his action as being more in the nature of punishment than defence:

> No previous attempt had been made to apprehend the offenders, nor is it reasonable to suppose from what is stated that the firing was necessary, either in self defence or to prevent the commission of the offence. It was not even to prevent escape. It seems rather to have been resorted to as a means of vengeance.[33]

An Aboriginal youth had been wounded in this incident but Charles Driver's investigation led him to conclude that Lawson had not fired with any intent to harm. The Advocate General did not concur with this interpretation and criticised Driver for not investigating further.[34]

When settlers fired upon Aboriginal people in the course of recovering stolen sheep, the official view tended towards leniency when an Aboriginal person was wounded or killed. For example, in January 1847, when a civilian party followed an Aboriginal group who had stolen 400 sheep from Ferguson's station at Mt Arden, charges were not laid against any of their number despite four Aboriginal people being shot dead in the resulting clash.[35] A local land-holder, Hughes, was the nearest magistrate and he could see no reason for any indictments. In contravention of the clear policy of the day, no inquest was held. The Police Commissioner, when forwarding the depositions taken by Hughes at the scene to the Advocate General, argued that the 'owners had a right to recover their property, by force if necessary, and they had a right to arrest the offenders in the act of committing a felony'.[36] The Advocate General concurred in this view,[37] although he did comment on the need for a local coroner to be appointed. When informed of the incident, Governor Robe ordered Moorhouse to investigate. However, the only result of the Protector's subsequent visit to the district was that charges of theft were laid against two of the Aboriginal men involved in the affray. At the trial of these two men[38] the Judge expressed the view that the evidence presented suggested that the killing of the four Aboriginal people had been justifiable.[39] In 1852, this issue was again considered, after an Aboriginal man was killed by shepherds employed by Coutts on his Yorke Peninsula station. Following the tracks of a group of Aboriginal people after they had stolen a mob of sheep, shepherds Gill and Parrington were caught unawares when those they were pursuing turned back and attacked them. Opening fire, the shepherds wounded two of the attackers, one fatally. Once again the official view was that the men were justified in firing on the Aboriginal people, as the Advocate General noted:

> In this case it appears that a felony was committed by the stealing, accompanied with violence, of a flock of sheep...the servants of Mr Coutts went in search of the stolen property with a view to recover it, that finding a consideration [sic] portion of the property in the presence of a party of natives, they were attacked before there was any time for parley — that being attacked they had recourse to fire-arms — that one native was seriously perhaps mortally wounded, and another apparently wounded. Under these circumstances and in the absence of the evidence of the natives I am of opinion that the men Gill and Parrington, were justified in firing upon the natives, — and that they have not committed any offence.[40]

Of course, cases of this kind had one thing in common — usually only the Europeans involved were able to effectively put their account of the events.[41] Local magistrates were unlikely to seek out the Aboriginal side of the story, even if they were able to communicate with the Aboriginal people involved. Even though Moorhouse did attempt to investigate many such incidents, he invariably found that the Aboriginal witnesses were no longer in the district by the time he arrived several days or even weeks later.[42] The inevitable delay between any affray and his investigation gave plenty of time for evidence to be tampered with, witnesses to be suborned or threatened and for any eyewitness accounts to be made congruent.[43] Even the Advocate General accepted that these circumstances could easily be exploited by unscrupulous or self-serving settlers:

> At present, too, there is frequently only the testimony of the parties who have been injured in the first instance, who then take the law into their own hands and inflict a summary and possibly wholly unauthorised chastisement, and who then, in the absence of counter testimony, give such a version of the affair as

may justify themselves, and in this manner contrive to escape the punishment they have merited.⁴⁴

Even so, despite these advantages, legal opinions and court decisions did not always go against the Aboriginal defendants. For example, in 1853, after sheep were stolen from Maurice's station near Lake Hamilton, overseer Adam Fartch and his companions set out on horseback to recover them. In the confrontation which followed, four of the Aboriginal people fled into the scrub, whereupon Fartch quickly ran three of them down and took them captive. The fourth man, Minquilti, avoided capture but secretly followed the Europeans and their prisoners back to their campsite.⁴⁵ From a nearby vantage point he witnessed his three companions being beaten by Fartch and his men.⁴⁶ The stockmen then resumed their search for Minquilti and soon found his hiding place. Not about to give himself up to a certain beating, Minquilti defended himself vigorously, inflicting a minor spear wound on Fartch before being captured. Henry Price JP was called but on hearing the stockman's story was reluctant to proceed against Minquilti, believing that Fartch and his men had terrorised the Aboriginal people involved. However, the overseer insisted on preferring charges, including that of attempted murder, and Minquilti was accordingly arraigned. Price reported to the Advocate General that Minquilti had acted reasonably in resisting arrest, a view with which Hanson concurred:

> Mr Fartch appears, upon a mere guess, to have assumed the right of arresting persons against whom no reasonable ground of suspicion existed, he imprisons one and assaults two others, who by leaving free he admits to have been innocent even of being suspected, and he is about to capture a fourth…I can have no doubt that the native was justified in resisting the attempt, and that Mr Fartch is responsible for the injury he has sustained.⁴⁷

At this point Moorhouse intervened, advising Minquilti to counter-charge Fartch for assault. This he did but the case was almost lost when the court 'had great difficulty in understanding'⁴⁸ Minquilti's evidence. However, one of the European stockmen present at the homestead gave evidence which confirmed Minquilti's account, leading to Fartch's conviction for the assault, 'for which a penalty of one Pound was inflicted'.⁴⁹ This was, the point must be made, a rare result.

Indeed, very few Europeans were brought before the courts for crimes against Aboriginal people and it seems certain that for every act of retaliation which came to the attention of the authorities, many more went unrecorded. However, this is not to say that colonists in the 1840s were unaware of what was taking place on the frontier. In fact, violent actions against Aboriginal people were common knowledge among settlers in all districts.[50] A few cases involving Europeans charged with the murder of Aboriginal people did come before the courts. The first of these was in 1841–1842 when charges were laid as a result of Moorhouse's investigation of the death of an Aboriginal man on Metcalf's station, north of Port Lincoln. The Protector was told that the stockman involved, Roach, had acted in self-defence — the deceased 'took his spear and struck him with it and the European took his gun and fired at the Native'.[51] Sceptical of this account, Moorhouse sought more information, whereupon it came to light that Roach had confronted Worta Kudnaitya as he cooked meat over the fire and accused him of stealing a calf. Raising the musket, Roach ordered Worta and his daughter, Katta Murtana, to leave the area. Worta, a man with considerable experience of Europeans, refused to go and a scuffle developed during which Worta was shot dead. His daughter subsequently walked to Adelaide to tell her story to the Protector of Aborigines, whom she had met earlier that year while visiting town with her father. Although her eyewitness account could not be admitted as evidence in court, it did serve to cast doubt on the story recounted later by the settlers and was probably instrumental in convincing Moorhouse to proceed with charges against Roach and his companions.

At Roach's committal hearing in Port Lincoln, his counsel presented two lines of defence — that Worta had speared him in the side just before the fatal shot was fired and that his musket's discharge had been accidental. However, under cross examination Roach's companions failed to confirm his account. Indeed, Cross explicitly denied that Worta's spear thrust had made contact with Roach's body. Apparently Cross had decided against perjuring himself to protect his companion and during cross-examination he denied seeing any sign of Roach's alleged wound, even agreeing to the feasibility of the prosecution's suggestion that Roach would have had the opportunity to slip out of the tent that night to bury Worta's body, presumably in order to prevent its discovery.[52] Roach was remanded in custody and the case referred to the Advocate General, who took it up with the Governor himself.

Governor Grey was explicit in his instructions as to how the law officers should proceed:

> in my opinion this is a very gross case and the European ought if possible to be severely punished…I think this person should… [be] placed on his trial in order fully to convince the settlers at Port Lincoln that such things cannot be done with impunity.[53]

When Roach appeared before the Grand Jury in the Supreme Court in March 1842,[54] he was determined to face the charges in silence.[55] The Grand Jury refused to indict him on the murder charge, instead finding that Roach should answer a charge of manslaughter.[56] Again though, Roach maintained his silence and this, combined with the inadmissibility of Katta's evidence, left the Crown with little to argue and the case collapsed for want of evidence. When discharging Roach, Cooper warned of the 'cloud resting on his character — a dark cloud arising from the suppression of facts,' but it soon became clear that the sympathy of at least the rural element of colonial society was more with Roach than with his victim.[57]

Public support for Roach's acquittal was an indication of the widening differences in attitude between officials and rural settlers regarding the killing of Aboriginal people. Despite official support for the prosecution of settlers who fired upon Aboriginal people after little or no provocation, few settlers were willing to come forward as witnesses and even fewer juries were willing to convict. For example, when Totaninka was shot dead in 1843 while hunting wombats near Mt Bryan, there was little doubt that the man responsible, Murray, had acted without any provocation. However, despite separate and determined investigations, neither Eyre[58] nor Moorhouse[59] could collect enough evidence to warrant even charging Murray. Government officers stationed in country areas, particularly Resident Magistrates and Assistant Protectors of Aborigines, attempted to uphold the law, at times making themselves unpopular within the local settler community for doing so. For example, at Port Lincoln Charles Driver was roundly condemned when he insisted on sending a settler named Connor for trial in Adelaide on a charge of 'feloniously wounding' an Aboriginal person.[60] Connor was acquitted, reinforcing the Port Lincoln colonists' opposition to such prosecutions. This case led to some settlers expressing the view that government officials were out of touch with frontier reality: that 'you hardly dare defend yourself, without being branded as a felon'.[61]

It is also likely that colonists in outlying districts at times conspired to not report affrays or incidents which led to the death of Aboriginal people. There is, of course, no direct evidence of this since cases which were thus concealed obviously did not come to the attention of the authorities. However, this view is supported when one looks more closely at some incidents which did come to official attention. Often these did so only because of actions and coincidences such as the Protector or Police Commissioner passing through the area soon after the affray, Aboriginal people recounting the circumstances of affrays to sympathetic officials, and local settlers having other reasons for bringing the incident to the fore. For example, when in 1843 a young Aboriginal woman was fatally shot, officials would not have been made aware of this were it not for the wider fears of the local Justice of the Peace. In this case George Hawker JP feared that this killing, which had occurred during an altercation between a hutkeeper and a group of Aboriginal people, would provoke widespread attacks by other Aboriginal people in the area north of the Broughton River.[62] Deciding it prudent to request additional police to be stationed in the district, he had little choice but to inform Adelaide of the reasons for his request. This report reached Governor Grey who ordered Moorhouse to investigate. The difference between the views of rural colonists and town-based officials was revealed once Moorhouse arrived in the district. The Mid-North settlers saw the Protector's role as one of dissuading the local Aboriginal people from exacting revenge for this killing and were surprised when he revealed his intention to investigate the circumstances of the killing itself. Within a day or two, the Protector had a clear account of the incident. He arrested the hutkeeper and assured the young woman's relatives that her killer would be 'tried and punished as a murderer'.[63] However, what seemed to the Protector to be a straightforward case of at least manslaughter soon foundered for lack of evidence, when the settlers conspired to erect a wall of silence.

In the Mid-North, in July 1844, another incident occurred, the official reaction to which revealed just how far apart the views of settlers and Adelaide-based officials had drifted. Despite the circumstances of the incident at Mt Bryan, in which six Aboriginal people died, becoming common knowledge within the area, local Justices of the Peace declined to institute proceedings against the settlers involved. Once again, the Protector only heard of the deaths incidentally while meeting with Aboriginal people camped on a neighbouring station, a fact which the Governor found rendered 'the whole affair an exceedingly suspicious one'.[64] As the story of this incident on Hallett's station later emerged, the overseer, William Carter, accompanied by shepherds, William Smith, Charles Spratt and James Pritchard, made a dawn raid on a group of Aboriginal people found with a flock of sheep in their possession.[65] Four of the Aboriginal people were wounded in the initial volley and Carter later admitted killing a man and a woman during this subsequent affray.[66] Henry Price and George Hawker, the local Justices of the Peace, took depositions from the Europeans involved in the incident. Despite William Carter's admission that he had set his dog upon the wounded woman, watched as it savaged her and then 'took the child out of the womb and gave it to his dog to eat',[67] the Justices of the Peace declined to indict him.[68] Two factors combined to bring the matter to official attention: the Aboriginal report of the incident to Moorhouse and the station-owner's belief that the sheep thieves had not been sufficiently punished, leading to his insistence that they be brought to trial for theft. Accordingly, 'Pintia Ngaltya, alias Kangaroo Jack, was tried before the Supreme Court for stealing sheep'.[69] Carter, called to give evidence against Pintia, took the opportunity to retract his earlier statement, swearing that 'he saw no dead natives'.[70] Pintia was acquitted but not before the events of that day had become widely known within the colony. Moorhouse made it clear that he believed this case to be something of a watershed in race relations within the colony, insisting that justice must be seen to be done if there was to be any hope of stopping the indiscriminate killing of Aboriginal people on the frontier.[71] The two local magistrates stuck with their decision not to indict but the Advocate General found aspects of this decision 'very extraordinary'.[72] Governor Grey intervened, insisting that charges be laid against the shepherds but he was persuaded by the Advocate General to delay their arrest, on the grounds that there was as yet insufficient evidence to make a conviction likely. At this point, Police Commissioner Finniss became involved in the case. Worried that settlers would be encouraged further to take the law into their own hands if such a blatant frontier atrocity went unpunished, Finniss ordered Inspector Gordon to accompany Moorhouse to Mt Bryan to investigate the matter further.

Pari Kudnutya, when interviewed by Moorhouse, gave an account of what had happened that day and agreed to lead them to the graves, but as the Protector reported, they 'found the body had been exhumed; the same had been done to the woman's grave'.[73] Believing that this was the work of Europeans bent on destroying evidence, Moorhouse searched the surrounding area and soon found the ashes of a large fire, where he 'examined the ashes and charcoal, and found human teeth and small bones'.[74] The Protector considered this enough evidence to charge Carter and his companions with murder and he and Gordon went to arrest Hallett's shepherds. However, Carter had fled a few days earlier. Smith, Spratt and Pritchard were arrested and faced committal proceedings but without Carter's retracted confession, it was a matter of the word of the Aboriginal witnesses[75] against that of the shepherds. John Hallett, questioned as to what orders he gave on that night, refused to answer on the grounds that he might incriminate himself, with the examining magistrate noting that 'he appeared to know more of the circumstances than he was willing to disclose'.[76] The shepherds were remanded on bail as the Adelaide-based officials did not wish to proceed without Carter standing with them in the dock.[77] Unfortunately, Carter was helped by local settlers and he escaped to Launceston. Police Commissioner Finniss sent an officer to Launceston and Hobart in pursuit only to receive the news that Carter had taken passage to England.[78] Meanwhile, the Grand Jury had found that the other shepherds had no case to answer, mainly because 'the learned Advocate General has not yet determined what course it will be proper for him to take in this case'.[79] In March 1845, after consulting with the Judge, Advocate General Smillie conceded defeat and dropped all proceedings against the shepherds.

Smillie had little choice but to follow the same course the next year, when South-East settler David Morgan was accused of murdering an Aboriginal man. In October 1846 'a report reached the Police Station, that a Native named Pannenum, had been murdered by a European'.[80] Investigations revealed that the two men knew each other well and suggested that Morgan had murdered Pannenum after a falling out. It was alleged that while the men were hunting kangaroo together, Morgan shot young Pannenum and burned his body.[81] However, the efforts of the Adelaide-based officials to establish a motive, or even to throw light on the relationship and the events leading to Pannenum's disappearance, were frustrated by local settlers' reluctance to give any information on the incident or the events leading up to it. When no body could be found and no further information was forthcoming, the Advocate General was forced to report that 'the evidence, though pregnant with suspicion, is insufficient to fix the charge on the accused'.[82] The obstruction, combined with rumours of further killings of Aboriginal people in the area,[83] left officials with a 'melancholy view of the state of this neighbourhood'.[84]

It was not until 1847 that a settler was found guilty of murdering an Aboriginal person, when Thomas Donelly was convicted and executed for the murder of Kingberrie, an Aboriginal man employed on a South-East sheep run.[85] Even then, the circumstances were such that this conviction can be considered more as an aberration than as a sign of any significant attitudinal change among the European community in general or jurymen in particular. Donelly was a former convict, about twenty-eight years old and well known for his violent temper among his fellow stockmen on Davenport's station near Rivoli Bay. On the first day of spring 1846, Donelly argued with some of his co-workers, especially John Watts, who later explained to the court that Donelly had 'slandered his wife's character'.[86] Donelly stormed off the property but the station hands must have suspected he would return, as they instructed Kingberrie to keep watch.[87] Donelly returned four nights later, armed with a pistol, presumably intending to settle his argument with Davenport's men from a position of advantage and surprise. But Kingberrie saw the approach of Donelly and his companion, a ten-year-old Aboriginal lad known as 'Jemmy'. In raising the alarm, Kingberrie drew attention to himself and was shot by Donelly.[88] Donelly fled but was later arrested on the road to Port Fairy. When cautioned, he reportedly replied: 'Oh, I shall say nothing. I know what I am about, they can't hurt me'.[89] He did not realise the singular situation he was in — Donelly was the first colonist to stand trial without the backing and support of his employer and fellow station hands. Indeed, given that he may well have been returning to commit assault, or worse, against his former workmates, the frontier code of loyalty would hardly extend to Donelly. Unlike other similar cases, none of the defendant's companions took steps to destroy incriminating evidence or to ensure that witnesses were unavailable. While adding to the circumstantial evidence against Donelly, none of the witnesses were able to positively place the smoking gun in Donelly's hand. However, eyewitness 'Jemmy' was called to give evidence and despite defence counsel Fisher's objections to his inability to take the oath, was allowed to give his damning account of the events. Speaking 'in fair English',[90] 'Jemmy' stated that: 'Donelly got a gun with him, picanniny gun, shoot blackfellow with it and he sit down hurt very much'.[91] Fisher tried to have his evidence ruled inadmissible on technical grounds, as without Jemmy's evidence there was only circumstantial evidence against his client.⁹² Chief Justice Cooper directed the jury that he was inclined to 'attach credit'⁹³ to Jemmy's statement and suggested that there was 'a very grave case against the prisoner'.⁹⁴ Within two hours the jury brought back a guilty verdict and Chief Justice Cooper sentenced Donelly to be hanged'.⁹⁵ Governor Robe, on receipt of Cooper's report,⁹⁶ saw 'no reason for interference with the ordinary course of justice in this case'.⁹⁷ Accordingly, the death sentence was carried out on 29 March 1847 in front of the Adelaide Gaol and in the presence of over a thousand witnesses.⁹⁸

There is a temptation to see the Donelly case as something of a turning point. After all, within only a few years of European–Aboriginal contact in the South-East of the colony, a settler had been tried and found guilty of the murder of an Aboriginal person. The *Aboriginal Evidence Act*, passed less than three years earlier, had proved to be workable even in the most difficult situation. However, too much should not be made of the Donelly case, it being more of an exception than an indication of any fundamental change in the way the law was operating within the colony. The key to understanding how Donelly came to be convicted lies not in the law or legal processes but in the motivations and actions of his colleagues at Davenport's station. Had Kingberrie not borne the brunt of Donelly's attack, it seems likely that one or more of their number would have faced his vengeance. The stockmen therefore had little reason to want the acquittal of Donelly and none to conceal evidence, refuse to testify or suborn witnesses. If this factor of 'ill-feeling',⁹⁹ as the Chief Justice described it, between Donelly and his workmates had not existed, then events would probably have proceeded differently. It is not unreasonable to suggest that in different circumstances, first, Donelly's companions would have burned and hidden the body rather than bury it conveniently at the homestead where it could be exhumed by officials later; second, the key witness 'Jemmy' would have been encouraged to leave the district, or worse; and third, the men themselves would been reluctant witnesses or would have moved on to another district.

Even where authorities initially were confident of securing a settler's conviction, this often proved difficult. A case in point is that of James Brown, a settler who had established a station near Guichen Bay. When, in September 1848, a mob of his sheep were driven off by Aboriginal people, Brown and his stockkeeper, 'Yorky' Eastwood, set off in pursuit.¹⁰⁰ Finding the suspect group, they fired on them at close range, whereupon 'a blind old man, five women and three children who could not escape were slaughtered on the spot'.[101] The two men sought to conceal their actions by burning the bodies and burying the remains in an unmarked grave. However, two factors brought the incident to the attention of the authorities: Eastwood could not resist bragging about the exploit; and — unbeknown to Brown and Eastwood — they had been observed by two travellers whose attention had been attracted by the gunshots.[102] A colonist named Parker, in company of an Aboriginal woman, Leandernin, had observed the latter stage of the incident. In February 1849, Moorhouse arrived at Guichen Bay to find the colonists in the area less than enthusiastic about his investigation:

> Parker denied all knowledge of the matter, as did others, who were supposed to have heard the affair spoken of in Brown's presence…they were determined to give no evidence to impeach him.[103]

Nevertheless, the persistent Moorhouse managed to find a cooperative witness — Parker's Aboriginal female companion, Leandernin. He convinced this young woman, who was then no longer living with Parker, to make a statement. While she had not seen the actual shooting, Leandernin stated that she and Parker had arrived on the scene in time to see Brown 'with a gun, and on the same spot several natives lying dead, with wounds fresh and bleeding'.[104] The woman then led Moorhouse to the site of the killings, where, as the Protector later reported:

> we found five holes in which had been deposited human bodies. On searching the neighbourhood of the graves, we found fragments of human bones scattered in every direction, faint tracks of natives, of one European and one horse. We continued our examination of the ground for some time, and discovered, about eighty paces from the graves, the remains of a fire, amongst which were portions of calcined human bones, native bags and mats.[105]

Moorhouse was convinced by this that the graves had been exhumed and the bodies burned by Brown, most probably when he heard of the impending investigation. Although this act had made it 'impossible to speak medically of the cause of death'[106] it strengthened the Protector's conviction that Brown was guilty of murder. Eastwood had already signed on as a crew member of a visiting whaler and was not seen in the colony again. Brown stayed on and in early March 1849 was arrested and committed for trial in the Supreme Court at the June sessions.[107] Parker still refused to give evidence and the prosecution had to rely largely on Leandernin's account. However, when the court convened Leandernin did not appear. Constable Burgon stated that he 'believed she was removed away or deterred from appearing'.[108] Despite the suggestion that Brown may have been involved in the non-appearance of this key witness, he was bailed to appear at the December sessions. The police were unable to find any trace of Leandernin, who was by then widely 'supposed to have been made away with'.[109] Accordingly, when Brown appeared before the Supreme Court in December 1849, the prosecution had little choice but to abandon the proceedings against him, on the grounds of insufficient evidence.

In May 1849, the Government Resident at Port Lincoln reported that several Aboriginal people had been found dead on Mortlock's station, in suspicious circumstances.[110] Inspector Tolmer and the Reverend Schurmann were already in the field to the west of Port Lincoln, investigating the murder of Charles Beevor (see chapter 7) and they diverted to arrange for the burial of the bodies.[111] Near the Port Lincoln Mine they found the remains of five persons whom Dr Lawson estimated had been dead for several weeks. An initial search of the area revealed that there were other recently buried bodies nearby and Tolmer surmised that these had been buried by their companions before they too had succumbed to whatever had killed them. Light was thrown on how these deaths had occurred when the party found a piece of flour sacking, apparently contaminated with arsenic.[112] Investigations suggested that this material had originally come from the hut of Patrick Dwyer, a shepherd on Mortlock's station. When interviewed, Dwyer admitted to storing poisoned flour in his hut but claimed it was only used to poison wild dogs. Tolmer was unconvinced, and he suggested that the flour probably had been deliberately poisoned and left in the hut for Aboriginal hut-breakers to find, 'for the purpose of killing them as a punishment'.[113] He decided to arrest Dwyer, despite foreseeing 'great difficulties in making out a case against him, owing to the total destruction of the intestines'[114] of the victims. A conviction would, Tolmer hoped, curtail 'so barbarous a practice'[115] within the district. Local Justice of the Peace, Henry Price, arraigned Dwyer and he was taken to Port Lincoln. When he appeared before Magistrate Driver, Dwyer admitted that he had prepared the poisoned flour soon after his hut was robbed for the second time that year. However, he maintained his story that he had intended to use it solely to poison dogs, adding that he only had the arsenic in his possession because it was used on the station as a sheep dip. Driver remanded Dwyer to a later date but rejected Tolmer's call to refuse bail, arguing that the evidence against Dwyer did not warrant such a course.[116] Within a few days of his release, Dwyer absconded and, with the assistance of settlers in the district, took passage to California.[117]

Aware of the importance of gaining convictions in such cases if rural settlers were to be discouraged from taking the law into their own hands, various officials then sought to avoid any blame for Dwyer's escape. The Advocate General, William Smillie, was unimpressed with the overall handling of the case:

> I must express my regret at the very unsatisfactory issue in the absconding of the accused, which circumstance itself adds strongly to the grounds of the charge.[118]

He took no responsibility for this bungling, however, claiming that Driver and Moorhouse had been in charge of the case.[119] Smillie claimed, indeed, to have issued instructions to remand Dwyer in custody since in his view the evidence clearly warranted the immediate committal of Dwyer for trial. However, Driver was adamant that he had not received any such instructions and 'in the absence of any evidence or the probability of obtaining any within a reasonable period'[120] believed that he had little choice but to bail the hutkeeper.[121]

In August 1849, Moorhouse was sent to Anstey's station at Yorke Peninsula where an affray between Aboriginal people and station employees had been reported.[122] During the course of his enquiries he coincidentally met an Aboriginal man named Melaityappa, who was suffering from three gunshot wounds inflicted several days earlier.[123] The Protector attended to these wounds on the spot, cutting out one of the bullets before deciding that more expert surgery was needed.[124] He brought Melaityappa back to Adelaide, where the Colonial Surgeon removed another ball from his abdomen but failed to save his live.[125] Having once again only learned of this incident by accidentally encountering the victim, Moorhouse was determined to bring the men named by Melaityappa as his attackers before the courts. Two station workers, Harry Jones and Thomas Morris, were duly arrested and charged with 'feloniously shooting with intent to kill',[126] a charge which was amended to murder after the victim's death. Allegedly, Jones and Morris had been out hunting kangaroos when they encountered Melaityappa and a companion, Piaria. After an initially friendly exchange,[127] Jones opened fire. Although wounded, Melaityappa managed to escape with Piaria into thick scrubland where their mounted attackers could not follow. Jones and Morris denied these charges when they appeared in the Supreme Court,[128] even though their defence counsel had, at the earlier hearing, suggested that the two men may have simply been attempting to arrest Melaityappa for the recent murder of Thomas Armstrong, a fellow station employee.[129] At their trial, Jones and Morris declined to take the stand.[130] Their counsel, Stephen, sought to cast doubt on Piaria's evidence, suggesting that it was self-contradictory. Evidence was given about the two men's treatment of local Aboriginal people, but as a separate charge against Morris for assault had already been dismissed in the Police Court[131] Stephen was able to downplay this. In contrast to the attitude shown towards Donelly two years earlier, the sympathy of the gallery was very much with the two accused, as the *Register* reported:

> A moment after the prisoners were placed at the bar, the court became crowded, and continued so until the termination of the proceedings. An expression of commiseration for the prisoners and an anxiety for the result was visible on every face.[132]

Apart from Piaria's eyewitness account and his positive identification of the two men, the evidence presented against Jones and Morris was essentially circumstantial: first, another of Stephens' shepherds testified that he had seen both men with Aboriginal artefacts soon after the incident;[133] and second, the bullet recovered from Melaityappa had markings similar to those on a homemade ball casting mould owned by Jones.[134] This was not enough to overcome the doubts of the jury who were deliberating, it is significant to note, in the year in which several cases against Aboriginal people accused of murder had ended in acquittal (see chapter 7). Jones and Morris were found not guilty and discharged.

A number of factors operated to modify the initial acceptance by most colonists that the law should be left to deal with resisting or troublesome Aboriginal people. First, the early abandonment of the containment policy meant that interaction between Aboriginal people and settlers soon took place outside of the area within which colonial officials could realistically expect to exert control and influence. Second, there was the related inability of the colonial government to maintain a police force capable of moderating behaviour on both sides by a substantial presence in recently settled districts. As one pastoralist noted as early as 1839, such a presence was needed to not only control Aboriginal people but 'at the same time keep their eye upon the white settler'[135] and so discourage retaliatory actions. In the face of potentially ruinous attacks on their stock and an apparent inability of police officers, often stationed two or three days' ride away, to prevent further depredations, remote settlers grew frustrated with official solutions and took steps to ensure their own survival, even if these took them outside of the law. John Hobbs, for example, after appealing for a police presence on the west coast of the Eyre Peninsula in 1849, went on to argue:

> But if this cannot be accomplished, I then say let us punish them ourselves, and we can do more towards the suppression of such crimes in one month, than a mounted police force of a hundred men could do in eighteen months.[136]

This was a public expression of the third factor, namely the hardening of colonists' attitudes towards the Aboriginal people occupying the frontier districts. Aboriginal resistance activities, the shortage of police officers and the perceived inability of the courts to deal with Aboriginal offenders all operated to make it difficult for those settlers outside of the town to continue to support the official policy that Aboriginal people were to be considered as British subjects with equal rights to protection under the law. After the 1849 hangings, despite some settlers expressing their shame at recent developments in race relations,[137] most had lost confidence in the law being able to successfully balance the protection of the interests of both colonists and Aboriginal people. In that year, despite widespread rumours of 'wholesale murder of natives at Rivoli Bay, Port Lincoln and Yorke's Peninsula'[138] no colonists were charged. Reflecting later on his pastoral experience in the 1840s, Charles Bonney MP admitted that he personally knew of 'instances where the frequent unpunished outrages of the aborigines roused the vengeance of the white men, and resulted in the massacre of a whole tribe of natives'.[139]

By this time, some colonists even argued that Aboriginal people should not have come under the protection of citizenship in the first place:

> I think it was a great error of the Home Government to declare the tribes…British subjects…I think that the proper course would have been that our contact and intercourse with them should have been regulated by the law of nations.[140]

While this may not have been the sentiment of the majority, by the early 1850s it was commonly accepted that the situation in the more remote and newly settled districts was, in practical terms, closer to this view than to the official policy. As one settler noted:

> English law is applied to the natives, as British subjects, that is to say, they are <u>punished</u> and partially protected by our laws: but in the far 'bush', a modification of the principle obtains. <u>There</u>, the settler finds that his <u>rifle</u> is the best exponent of the law, and little reeks he when a 'blackfellow' falls.[141]

Clearly, British law had failed the crucial test of whether it could be successfully applied to both settler and Aboriginal person within the new colony — that of protecting Aboriginal people against illegal actions of the settlers themselves.

CHAPTER 11

CONCLUSIONS AND OBSERVATIONS

In considering the 'one law for all' policy and its implementation, there is no doubt that it was a failure, despite the humanitarian intentions of the Colonial Office and the expectation that the colony of South Australia would be more enlightened in its treatment of Aboriginal people than the other Australian colonies. Regardless of the opportunities afforded by a colony founded without convicts at a time when humanitarian views held sway in the corridors of power, and despite the high-minded declarations of concern for Aboriginal welfare, Aboriginal people in South Australia fared no better than their counterparts in other Australian colonies — the agents of dispossession, disease and cultural destruction were little modified by rhetoric or even well-intentioned action on other fronts. In terms of implementation, there can be no doubt that Aboriginal policy within the new colony generally was a dismal failure. This was the case, whether the evaluation is being applied to the general issues such as assimilation and protection or, as is the focus here, to the more specific legal intentions. Reflecting on the events and cases detailed in this book, it is an unavoidable conclusion that Aboriginal people were not in any practical sense equal before the law at any time during the period 1836 to 1862. Legally, Aboriginal people may have been British subjects, entitled to the full protection of the law, but this dictum was only translated into practice when it did not transcend an even more fundamental colonial principle — that of protecting the paramountcy of settlers' interests. As British law was applied in the situations involving Aboriginal people described here, it was revealed primarily as an instrument for protecting the property and personal rights of the colonists. Contrary to the rhetoric, in practice British law operated one-sidedly, a fact which Aboriginal people quite early on in their contact with it came to realise. As Eyre noted in 1843, the Aboriginal people 'only see that their own people are always punished for offences — that the Europeans almost always escape'.[1]

In considering how and why this policy of 'one law for all' failed, the cases discussed in the previous chapters provide ample evidence for the following explanations. Relatively few settlers were ever charged with offences against Aboriginal people, a fact made worse by the general knowledge within the colony that illegal retaliation against them was a common and widespread practice. Even the very few colonists who were charged with the murder of Aboriginal people were able to plead self-defence, or other mitigating factors, and did so successfully in all but one case.[2] Settlers had little to fear from the local courts — in the unlikely event that colonists were called to account for their actions they could stand in the dock confident in the knowledge that their story would be backed up by credible witnesses fluent in the language of the courts; that the committal proceedings would likely be presided over by a Justice of the Peace whose interests and attitudes were similar to their own; and that, if committed to stand trial in the Supreme Court, the judiciary might not favour them but public opinion certainly would. Aboriginal people were only rarely able to turn to the law for protection or justice when they were attacked by other Aboriginal people or by private settlers. The enduring view that South Australia treated its original inhabitants better than did the other Australian colonies is, on closer examination, more myth than fact for, in reality, the rhetoric was rarely translated into practice.

What were the factors contributing to this failure to implement the declared policy? First, there was the failure to maintain the original policy of concentration of settlement within the colony. While not sufficient in itself to change the course of legal events, the restriction of the settled areas to more manageable limits was a necessary condition for the successful application of the protective function of British law. Perhaps, if the frontier had been contained during the early 1840s to the Adelaide Plains and Mid-North districts, then the resources of the Police Commissioner and Protector of Aborigines may have had some chance of coping with the educational, interpreting and investigative requirements placed upon them by Aboriginal–settler contact. However, with the early abandonment of the concentration of settlement principle, these government officials were placed in an impossible situation, in which they could do little more than respond piecemeal to crises as they arose on the advancing frontier. Local Aboriginal people could not be counselled about the effects of land alienation, dialects could not be learned rapidly enough to ensure more than rudimentary communication, and police stations were either understaffed for the tasks confronting them or soon were found to be sited too far inside the advancing frontier. The dispersal of settlement inevitably led to a number of issues that further impeded the ability of the 'one law for all' policy to function: there was a diminution of official control over race relations, the need to spread limited resources more widely, an increase of frontier contact outside of the view of the law and its agencies, less likelihood of settlers and Aboriginal people learning each other's language, and a greater incidence of settlers deciding to take the law into their own hands.

Second, and at least partly as a consequence of the failure to maintain the concentration policy, South Australian colonists lost confidence in the law as being capable of, or even being the most appropriate means of, mediating between colonists and Aboriginal people. Most settlers were probably willing to allow the law the chance to do so, even within newly settled districts troubled by Aboriginal attacks on stock or huts. While some rural colonists no doubt immediately took illegal action against Aboriginal people who infringed upon their interests, this was a minority response in South Australia. In most cases of stock theft or Aboriginal resistance, settlers initially did call upon the colonial authorities for protective and retaliatory action — there was a widely held expectation that it was the responsibility of the police to search out stock thieves, recover stock and arrest the offenders. However, far too many settlers with interests in stock were disappointed with the results achieved by the police force, even when they did respond in time to pursue the culprits.

Perhaps even more important was that even when police actions resulted in arrests, too few could be translated into convictions to satisfy the expectations of the colonists on the frontier stations. This decline of settler confidence in the institution and practice of the law helps to explain the increased adoption within South Australian rural districts of the violent frontier methods seen in the other colonies, despite their being contrary to the humanitarian principles and beliefs espoused as being central to South Australian race relations. It needs to be emphasised, however, that this slide into illegal retaliation was generally not immediate but rather was fuelled by increasing frustration with the legal processes as they applied to Aboriginal people. Even when they acted without police support, most stock owners initially took upon themselves only the role of the police and not that of judge and jury, restricting their activities to the identification and capture of alleged Aboriginal offenders. However, when the courts failed to convict Aboriginal people of whose guilt the prosecuting colonists were certain — whether this failure was because of difficulties related to jurisdiction, evidence or interpretation — these men and their employees moved further away from the rule of law. Faced with financial ruin and a legal system that seemed unable to adapt itself to the realities of the pastoral frontier, some stock owners adopted the ruthless tactics of private retaliation — via the sword, musket and arsenic.

These actions were able to be perpetrated with impunity, at least partly because of a third factor, namely the erosion of the humanitarian values within the colony. Humanitarianism proved to be a weakly held value among the South Australian colonists, quickly swept aside when they realised the fundamental reality that acceptance of Aboriginal rights inevitably meant the diminution of European interests. Many leading settlers were, of course, never committed to such ideals — their overriding concern was to establish a successful colony based upon controlled land sales and a regulated labour supply, not to mention speculative opportunities for themselves. However, it is too harsh a judgement to tar all the settlers with the same 'land-jobbers' brush.[3] The South Australian Commissioners were forced by Lord Glenelg to incorporate humanitarian-based policies into their colonial plans, and many of their public statements on issues regarding Aboriginal people may be dismissed as insincere rhetoric born of cynical pragmatism. However, humanitarianism was a powerful influence on the minds of English people in the 1830s (if less so on their actions) and it is clear that a considerable number of those who emigrated to South Australia in the initial months were sympathetic, at least in theory, to the plight of the Aboriginal people they were about to dispossess.

This concern was limited, however, and the closer their involvement with pastoral and other rural-based activities, the less likely such concerns were to be translated into actions. Understandably, humanitarian ideals were easier to sustain living in Adelaide than when facing the violence of the clashes on the frontier. As the frontier advanced, those in contact with Aboriginal people moved further away from the humanitarian-inspired expressions of goodwill towards those Aboriginal people. Even in Adelaide, as one-sided accounts of life on the frontier were published in newspapers of the day, settlers with little contact with Aboriginal people also hardened in their attitude towards them. The significance of the attitudinal change regarding the rights and role of Aboriginal people within the colony is considerable. It acted to isolate colonial officials who still hoped to control actions on the frontier through the enforcement of English law and added further to the pressure on the Protector of Aborigines, Police Commissioner and Governor to modify the ways in which the law was applied to Aboriginal people. It also reduced the likelihood of swift reform of the law and legal structures to meet the frontier situation in any just way, and encouraged rural landowners to adopt practices based upon avoidance of the law rather than adherence to it, and to resist moves towards legal reforms which might provide a measure of justice for Aboriginal people.

Another factor contributing to this failure to implement the policy towards Aboriginal people was the early abandonment of the notion of assimilating them into colonial society. Largely predicated upon the Protector of Aborigines being able to educate a core of young Aboriginal people, this amalgamation policy was doomed as soon as the special land surveys opened up new areas in distant locations in 1839. Despite the best efforts of government officials, they could not hope to educate young Aboriginal people from all of the groups brought into contact with Europeans. Anyway, the intention to assimilate them into the wider colonial society was a view shared by few in the colony. Its abandonment was significant to the legal situation of Aboriginal people, since it implied separate treatment of Aboriginal people and colonists, including the making of exceptional laws. Certainly the initial legal exceptions may have been made with the best of intentions, being focussed on issues such as restricting access to alcohol and encouraging the education of Aboriginal children. However, the general climate of accepting that Aboriginal people could be treated differently before the law also led to acceptance of delays in reforming the requirements for the acceptance of Aboriginal witnesses, a lack of urgency in taking action to facilitate the interpretation of Aboriginal evidence, and the view that Aboriginal actions *inter se* could continue to fall outside of the view of the law. These results of the acceptance in practice of two laws within the colony did little to encourage either public officials or private colonists to observe, when they dealt with them, the dictum that Aboriginal people were equal before the law.

Another factor contributing to the failure to implement the policy was the inability to develop a court system that was appropriate to the colonial situation. Unthinking faith in English legal structures led to the establishment of a judicial system more suited to the English counties than to a colony with an expanding frontier. Judicial hierarchy ruled supreme in the minds of colonial legal officials and, more understandably perhaps, the Supreme Court Justices. This court, sitting only in Adelaide and supported by inferior courts with overly limited jurisdiction, was not only a costly system but also directly contributed to the decline of the situation on the frontier.[4] Local magistrates were required to remand offenders charged with thefts of greater value than five pounds to higher courts, a restriction which hardly encouraged pastoralists to seek legal remedies when stock were stolen. Except for minor crimes, offenders were remanded to Adelaide with the result that any witnesses had to make a journey of up to several days each way. This was, given the alternative available to settlers — namely of dealing with the issue outside of the law — a system doomed to failure.

Police Commissioner Warburton suggested that a circuit magisterial system be introduced, after his officers had brought an alleged Aboriginal offender '200 or 300 miles to take him before a Magistrate'.[5] This was hardly a radical proposal even though, if introduced, it may well have alleviated two of the problems associated with cases against Aboriginal people: first, the charges would have been brought before a more independent member of the Bench than would be the case in the alternative of granting greater powers to local Justices of the Peace, and second, perhaps stock owners would have be more willing to let the law take its course since the more localised administration of justice would not have inconvenienced the operation of their runs to the same extent as when they were required to send employees long distances to testify. While it is unlikely that such a reform would have prevented the more ruthless pastoralists from exacting illegal retribution upon Aboriginal people, it may well have convinced the many more reasonable stock owners at least to seek legal remedies before resorting to actions outside of the law. However, what makes Warburton's proposal particularly interesting (and of considerable potential to have effected change) was his view that the visiting magistrate should be empowered, perhaps even required, to coopt a local Aboriginal elder to assist him. This man would act more as a 'juryman' than as an assisting magistrate but would have two major roles: he would assist the circuit magistrate to gain the confidence of, and assert influence over, Aboriginal people within the district; and he would be seen to add legitimacy to the judicial determinations in the eyes of Aboriginal people, such that they would 'carry with them conviction to the minds of the tribe...that justice has been done'.[6]

Yet another factor in the failure to implement the policy was the inability of the colonial government to establish and maintain a police force capable of effectively dealing with the interactions between settlers and Aboriginal people in the frontier districts. The reasons behind this failure were partly financial, for the fledgling force was not funded adequately enough to cope with the daunting task facing it once the policy of containment of the boundaries of settlement was abandoned. When financial difficulties then struck the colony, police staffing levels were frozen, such that in 1843 the police establishment still remained only at twenty-nine mounted troopers and seventeen town-based policemen — clearly inadequate given that settlers were by then moving rapidly into new areas. Even so, perhaps more important in the longer term was police policy and administration rather than funding. Despite widespread calls for a flexible response to the clashes between Aboriginal people and settlers,[7] the South Australian police force remained largely out of touch with the realities of the frontier. With a moving frontier, the police had opportunities to learn by their earlier experiences and to adapt their responses and tactics. These opportunities were squandered, however, as the police leadership ignored suggestions from pastoralists, magistrates and even their own constables in the field. They continued a conservative policing approach based upon 'after-the-event' sorties from a network of permanent police stations that were, within months of their establishment, both well behind the frontier and inappropriately staffed. What was needed in these districts was a substantial police presence, able to react quickly to moderate any predatory actions of Aboriginal people threatened by the 'sheep invasion' while 'at the same time keep[ing] their eye upon the white settler',[8] who might be tempted to overreact.[9] Perhaps this could have been achieved in the 1850s, as the frontier advancement slowed somewhat at that time, but unfortunately the gold rushes intervened. As shepherds headed east to make their fortunes, they were often replaced by Aboriginal men and women,[10] but experienced police constables also resigned to try their luck on the diggings. By 1852, the South Australian police force faced a staffing crisis which could not be completely overcome by additional recruitment of Aboriginal constables. On Eyre Peninsula, for example, where clashes between settlers and Aboriginal people were still occurring, the three constables stationed at Tangatta police outpost resigned, prompting the

Port Lincoln Government Resident to voice his fears of a 'recurrence of bloodshed and rapine in that western coast'.[11]

The appointment of Aboriginal constables had been mooted since 1838, but apart from informal temporary recruitment of Aboriginal men as trackers and interpreters, no action was taken until 1842.[12] When Government Residents suggested that they be empowered to appoint local Aboriginal people as constables, colonial officials were reluctant to give them such power, preferring to make their own often inappropriate appointments.[13] Initially it was proposed that Aboriginal constables would be recompensed only by the provision of free housing, clothing and rations, and it was not until 1842 that the Governor agreed to a pay rate of one shilling per day.[14] Not surprisingly, Aboriginal people soon proved themselves to be effective police officers[15] but despite their numbers growing to thirty-eight before the Aboriginal section of the force was abolished in 1856,[16] they were not used to their full potential in South Australia. For example, at both Venus Bay (where by 1853 there were twelve Aboriginal constables)[17] and Moorundie (where six were recruited that same year) the officers in charge had difficulty even finding mounts for them.[18]

All the above explanatory factors are overshadowed by the argument that alienation of Aboriginal land by colonists was the fundamental reason for the failure to implement, generally, Aboriginal policy and, specifically, the policy that Aboriginal people would be equal before the law.[19] This book has quite deliberately, largely for reasons of scope, avoided the complex issue of land rights within the new colony. However, the conclusion cannot be avoided that, regardless of what statements of policy were made about the law and Aboriginal people, or whether these were genuine intentions or not, the successful implementation of the legal policy could not occur within a context where conflict over land rights remained unresolved. Land was the key to reaching an accommodation between the two racial groups within early South Australia, a fact that was reflected in the original plans that land rights would, at least to some degree, be respected.[20] However, the sticking point was that land remained the key to the making of the fortunes of leading colonists. In practice the rapid alienation of Aboriginal land in South Australia, with (despite the rhetoric) no different result for Aboriginal people than in the other Australian colonies, meant that the stage was set for clashes between the traditional landowners and rural settlers. Farmers and pastoralists exercised control over the land and its resources — damming the watercourses, stopping Aboriginal use of fire, fencing large areas, and driving off the native game. It was these clashes that ensured that Aboriginal people would not be treated as equals before the law, especially within the criminal jurisdiction. The law was, despite all the high-minded expressions of intent, essentially meant to protect the interests of the colonists, particularly those with investments in land and stock. When Aboriginal people, whether innocently or deliberately, acted in ways that threatened those interests, then their rights to equal treatment were either questioned, ignored or denied.[21]

In considering the failure of 'one law for all', not only the reasons above, but also the intentions and motivations of the participants are of interest and importance, even if these are difficult areas for historians to tread. Even if we assume that many early South Australian colonists were genuine in their support of the declaration to include Aboriginal people under the rule of British law, why were they so? Was it because of humanitarian concern for Aboriginal lives and lifestyles, or because they saw this as being the most effective way of ensuring Aboriginal assimilation into the new colonial society and economy? And was their rationale for such assimilation based on egalitarian notions or on the idea that assimilation would lessen resistance to the alienation of land so necessary to their own fortunes? Or would assimilation of Aboriginal people help to ensure their own economic success by providing a pool of casual and cheap labour? Alternatively, if one takes the view that the South Australian colonial planners quite cynically moved to appease the humanitarian-minded officials in London, was this pragmatic approach adopted simply to ensure the establishment of the colony, or was it primarily to avoid the threat to an opportunity to amass private fortunes? And, having accepted the policy prescriptions of the Colonial Office, to what extent did the Colonization Commissioners intend to support, or impede, the implementation of those policies once in the colony? The prevailing view among historians is that the colonial planners and early colonists alike were largely motivated by a desire to improve their own material position.[22] There can be no doubt that profit was a central motivation for most colonists — when the colony was only two years old, a visitor observed that profit and speculation had come to dominate the thinking of Adelaide residents: 'It is difficult to meet a man in Adelaide whose ideas are not built upon gold and ivory, and pearls and diamonds'.[23] Such an emphasis could not be kept separate from everyday dealings, nor from considerations of policy and action when the interests of colonists and Aboriginal people clashed.

Whether one considers the statements concerning Aboriginal people made at the establishment of South Australia to essentially constitute a policy, well-intentioned rhetoric or mere cynical cant, what is not in contention is that these statements failed to be translated effectively into practice within the colony. While the humanitarian influence that had a moderating effect on the original plans for the colony failed to be upheld once the settlers were in South Australia, it can be argued that its tenets did have a more lasting influence on the attitudes of a significant number of government officials and private citizens, including at least several of the Adelaide legal community. Concerning the latter, the cases detailed here reveal the efforts of key members of the Adelaide legal fraternity to ensure that Aboriginal people were adequately represented in the courts. Men such as Bartley, Stow and Fisher cannot be accused of being anything but diligent in the way they represented their Aboriginal clients. In the first five years of the Supreme Court's operation, defence counsel were not provided as a matter of policy to Aboriginal defendants, yet no Aboriginal person stood in the dock during this time without benefit of counsel, such was the interest and concern, perhaps even compassion, among legal practitioners regarding Aboriginal interactions with the law. Of course, there may well have been an element of self-interest in lawyers volunteering to take on the defence of Aboriginal people, despite their not being funded by the Advocate General, although this view is more difficult to sustain when the case in point is one of theft or assault rather than murder. From 1842, after the Protector sought approval to fund the appointment of counsel to defend five Aboriginal people awaiting trial,[24] lawyers expected that they would be paid for their services. Moorhouse sought confirmation from the Governor as to whether this was to be standing policy,[25] and eventually received an affirmative answer.[26] At times these counsel put up spirited, determined and creative defence arguments.

As for the judges, the first two appointments to the Supreme Court Bench were at best mediocre — Jeffcott can be best described as an amiable rogue, holding the dubious distinction of being the only British Chief Justice to be tried for murder,[27] while Jickling, a chronic procrastinator, was clearly out of his depth.[28] Luckily for the colony, and indeed many Aboriginal people who would come before him, Charles Cooper proved to be a sound appointment, gaining the respect of the profession and many colonists, if not always their admiration. Cooper clearly had a central role in the events considered in this book, being the judge who presided over many of the cases discussed here, and certainly he was the most influential individual in the implementation of legal policy regarding Aboriginal people during the 1840s and 1850s. While Cooper can be seen as a man grappling with the problems and difficulties of bringing Aboriginal people within the jurisdiction of British law, another interpretation is that his obstinacy and caution in coming to terms with the realities of settler–Aboriginal contact on the frontier prevented, or at the very least hindered, the working out of any legal compromise and reform. Until 1840, Cooper's doubts on the amenability of Aboriginal people to British law had little effect. However, after he advised the Executive Council in 1840 that it could legally wage war upon the Milmenrura clan since their lack of contact with Europeans placed them outside the rule of law, he became more intransigent in his views. It is suggested here that he became somewhat entrapped by that 1840 advice when the resulting expedition led to the illegal executions which attracted considerable criticism. Rather than admit that he had erred in that advice, Cooper continued to maintain that there were exceptions to the rule of English law where Aboriginal people were concerned. If the Milmenrura were exceptional because of their lack of prior contact, then so too were many of those Aboriginal people from frontier districts who appeared in the Supreme Court in the following years.

However, this is not to say that Cooper did not modify his views as the years progressed. In 1842, he reduced his prior contact criterion from a matter of months to several weeks, and four years later brought this back further to encompass only acts committed when Aboriginal people encountered Europeans for the first time. Even so, the colony was ten years old when Cooper finally acquiesced to Governor Robe's suggestion that this prior contact issue was one for consideration by Executive Council after conviction, rather than a reason not to proceed to trial. More importantly, as his practice for several years following 1846 reveals, this acquiescence was not convincing. Denied the right to determine the amenability of Aboriginal people by the prior contact criterion, Cooper used problems relating to language and evidence to justify the dismissal of charges against Aboriginal defendants with little or no prior contact with settlers. Cooper's single-mindedness on this point probably would not have mattered had the situation on the South

Australian frontier been different. Throughout the 1840s and 1850s settlers did continue to push the frontier forward and expected that the rule of law would follow close behind. When the Chief Justice contributed to the ineffectiveness of dealing with Aboriginal transgressions, it can be argued that his actions to some degree also contributed to the decision of some rural settlers to move their own actions outside of the law, to the considerable cost of Aboriginal interests and lives. It can also be argued that Cooper's focus on the issues of amenability, evidence and language meant that he was deterred from considering other approaches which may have dealt more effectively with the situation on the frontier, such as Police Commissioner Warburton's suggestions for circuit courts. Nevertheless, while it may be that his stance was at times not in the long-term interests of Aboriginal people on the frontier, there is little doubt that he acted with their best interests at heart.

The same cannot always be said for the local Justices of the Peace. At the same time as legal officials in Adelaide were denying Resident Magistrates' requests that they have greater input to and freedom within the adjudication of frontier clashes, a system granting magisterial powers to Justices of the Peace was instituted in rural districts. The inherent difficulty with this arrangement lay in the background of the men who put their names forward for this office — all were pastoral leaseholders or landowners, most with at least the potential for conflict of interest when Aboriginal people were involved in offences against persons or property. When one peruses a list of such Justices of the Peace, prominent pastoral names such as Samuel Davenport, Osmond Gilles, John Hallett, John Barton Hack, George Anstey, Charles Bonney and George Hawker illustrate this potential for conflict.[29] As frontier expansion accelerated, this reliance on local stock owners to apply and interpret the law increased, despite the inappropriateness of having them decide on whether shepherds, overseers or Aboriginal people had a case to answer. Admittedly, some Justices of the Peace were aware of this conflict and were scrupulous in their investigations and committal proceedings, but others clearly colluded with neighbouring landowners to conceal and condone crimes against Aboriginal people.[30] When Aboriginal depredations led to settler retaliation, the fact that these less than impartial officials often were called to adjudicate probably contributed to the inability of Adelaide-based officials to prevent the spread of illegal actions against Aboriginal people.[31] As late as 1860, the Advocate General still found it necessary to remind a Justice of the

11. Conclusions and Observations

Peace that 'no magistrate should adjudicate in any case in which he is in anyway interested'.[32]

The other official who features prominently throughout the events and cases detailed within this study is the fourth Protector of Aborigines, Matthew Moorhouse. Unlike his predecessors, Moorhouse was a full-time appointee and no-one could accuse him of not applying himself diligently to the role. It was probably fortunate that he had an optimistic view of life that allowed him, despite successive failures, to focus on new issues relating to Aboriginal people and their welfare. Initially Moorhouse focussed this optimism on encouraging Aboriginal assimilation into the colonial society and its workforce; when that aim failed to be realised he turned his attention to the education of young Aboriginal people. After that enterprise also failed, Moorhouse looked to the fate of Aboriginal people either brought before the courts or who had suffered at the hands of settlers. Gaining wide respect among Aboriginal people in the settled areas, Moorhouse developed a reputation for listening to Aboriginal grievances and pursuing justice on their behalf, even though he rarely had the power to effect fair solutions. He appears throughout many of the events and court cases described in preceding chapters as a dedicated man, determined to investigate illegal actions against, and track down suspected killers of, Aboriginal people. Despite his detailed formal reports, Moorhouse does not give away much about his own motivations in pursuing such an active role in investigations, on a schedule which, given the incidents and their widespread location that he attended in some years, must have been physically punishing. One suggestion is that his ineffectiveness in preventing the massacre after the Rufus affray in August 1841 preyed upon his conscience, leading him to a near-obsessive determination to bring before the courts colonists who took the law into their own hands. It is difficult to assess his success in this arena, since he was often frustrated by conspiracies among settlers, his lack of resources and the distances and delays involved in any such investigations. However, it could be argued that Moorhouse's willingness to travel any distance, at short notice, to investigate any reported illegal retaliatory incident — and to bring his medical knowledge to bear via exhumation — may well have served to make settlers considering taking extra-legal action against Aboriginal people to think twice before doing so.

Nevertheless, despite the willingness of some colonists to take the law into their own hands, one conclusion that can reasonably be made is that a significant number of them, even including some whose interests seemingly were in direct conflict with the interests of the Aboriginal people they were dispossessing, did recognise (and at times struggle with) the problems raised by the colonial enterprise being so based upon the alienation of Aboriginal land and resources. In the accounts and events presented in the preceding chapters, all is not depressing for there is a positive strand running through many of them. Perhaps historians have moved a little too far away from the earlier overly optimistic view that humanitarianism had a major moderating effect on relationships between the settlers and Aboriginal people within this colony. While this reinterpretation is an understandable reaction against the self-laudatory tone of earlier writers on the subject of race relations within South Australia, it has not proved to be completely in accord with the reality of the frontier and courtroom experience exposed through the cases detailed within this study. For, while brutal examples of settlers taking the law into their own hands have been documented, there are also numerous instances where settlers showed considerable tolerance and a clear desire for the police to take action on their behalf, through arresting Aboriginal offenders and dealing with through the legal system. The cases discussed here involving stock theft and assault or worse against station staff do show that many pastoralists were more frustrated than vindictive, more driven to desperate measures than inherently evil, and more willing to have the law deal with the problems caused them by Aboriginal people than to adopt illegal measures of retaliation. The general impression, notwithstanding the several gruesome cases outlined in chapter 10, is not one of settlers immediately or precipitously abandoning the rule of law in their dealings with Aboriginal people. Few moved quickly to take the law into their own hands and most tried to co-exist with Aboriginal people on the new station runs. Of course, it could be counter-argued that deliberate actions were not necessary since passivity and lack of interest would ensure, through the agencies of malnutrition, disease, cultural destruction and migration, that Aboriginal people would not long remain a threat to the pastoral enterprise.

One final question needs to be addressed: Could it have been different in South Australia in terms of treatment of Aboriginal people within the law, or was it inevitable that the rhetoric of their equality before the law would not be matched by reality? In attempting to answer this question, it can be asked whether equality would ever have been enough, even had it been achieved. Certainly, equality before the law could not have delivered justice to the Aboriginal people within South Australia.[33] The situations and circumstances of the settlers and Aboriginal people were not equal and so a policy of equal treatment before the law of one group was guaranteed to result in the Aboriginal people being dispossessed, forced to abandon key aspects of their culture and daily lives, brought before the courts when they resisted such change, and punished when they took measures to cope with the invasion. However, this does point to one of the alternatives which may have served Aboriginal people better than the policy of 'one law for all' — namely, that of recognising a form of legal separatism, allowing traditional Aboriginal law to coexist with that introduced from England, at least until implementation of the policy of assimilation was well advanced. This 'dual law' approach has an initial appeal but realistically cannot be considered as an option which would have operated, in the longer term, to deliver different outcomes for Aboriginal people in early colonial South Australia. Even today, there are such difficulties involved in courts coming to terms with how customary law can operate alongside mainstream law, that it cannot be seen as a realistic option for the judicial system from 1836 to 1862. In any case, such a separatist option could not have survived in the face of the humanitarian influence in the Colonial Office at the time the colony's plans were being finalised. Once the general policy of amalgamation of Aboriginal people into a new colonial society was accepted then the legal system could hardly be predicated on separation.

However, there are some alternative general approaches which realistically could have been adopted and which, to varying degrees, may have positively influenced the subsequent lives and lifestyles of the Aboriginal people enveloped within the new colony's boundaries. First, had greed and impatience not taken hold so strongly in the colony in the initial years of settlement and forced the abandonment of the policy of concentration of settlement, perhaps the outcome would have been different. Had settlements on Eyre and Yorke Peninsulas and in the South-East been delayed for a decade or so (although this in itself would have merely postponed the alienation of land and resources), perhaps it would have allowed time for issues related to the dispossession to be worked through more effectively than they could be in the 'land-grabbing' atmosphere of the 1840s. Had settlement been slowed, then perhaps the unexpected range of Aboriginal languages would have been more effectively coped with and the language issues better handled by the courts than was the case. Perhaps the Protector could have learned more languages, impeded the move of many Aboriginal people to the town, been more effective in educating Aboriginal youth at the Location School, and earlier addressed the issues relating to Aboriginal evidence. These are, of course, speculative and the conclusion reached here is that, while the abandonment of the concentration policy condemned several official initiatives to failure, it is not convincing to argue that it would have kept the colony's boundaries restricted for long enough to have had any real lasting effect on the outcome for Aboriginal people.

It does, nevertheless, point to another factor which could have made a substantial difference to how the law operated in respect to Aboriginal people — the control of land within the colony. Three features of the land policy within South Australia had the potential to make a significant difference to how Aboriginal people coped with European settlement: the reservation of land for Aboriginal use, the acceptance of the concept of compensation for the loss of land, and the direction of a proportion of funds generated from the sale of land in the colony towards the benefit of the Aboriginal people. The Colonization Commissioners, under pressure from the Colonial Office, included a proposal for the protection of Aboriginal land rights in their initial plan for the colony[34] but had no intention of honouring it once in the colony.[35] However, some of the officials appointed took such instructions more seriously, and attempted to implement that policy when surveyed land was placed on the market. As Charles Sturt wrote in 1840:

> aboriginal inhabitants…have an absolute right of selection prior to all Europeans who have settled in it during the last four years, of reasonable positions of the choicest land, for their especial use and benefit, out of the very extensive districts over which, from time immemorial, these aborigines have exercised distinct, defined and absolute rights of proprietary and hereditary possession.[36]

Simply reserving twenty per cent of the land for Aboriginal use may have led only to the worst sections of each surveyed district being set aside, but the policy was that the Protector would have prior selection rights on behalf of the traditional owners, thus making it a policy provision with real potential to ease the burden of land alienation. A knowledgeable and sensitive Protector of Aborigines would have been able to reserve land that was either of particular significance to Aboriginal people or which was likely to bring the best rent if leased to the colonists. This radical proposal was too much for the colonists, however, and when Moorhouse proceeded to put it into practice, the opposition was fierce and effective.[37] The result was that by 1842 all such reserved land was offered for lease to colonists taking up adjacent land.[38] Worse than that, however, was the abandonment of the policy of creating Aboriginal reserves, on orders from London.[39] Had the reserve system been continued, and the reserves used in ways related to their initial intention, perhaps they would have somewhat eased the tension on the frontier. Even if the original intention of the policy was corrupted by simply leasing these reserves back to settlers, at least substantial funds would have flowed into the government coffers — funds which could have been used in ways that may have prevented some of the clashes on the frontier.

However, this is probably too optimistic a view, given that land was the key to the success of both groups within colonial South Australia. It was the essential factor which placed Aboriginal people and settlers in serious competition with each other. The legal policy of 'one law for all' in South Australia operated within the sphere of this wider framework, so that — when European control of the land and its resources was threatened — the law operated to protect the interests of the colonists above those of the indigenous peoples. Despite the stated intention that Aboriginal people would, as British subjects, have full rights to the protection of the law, the events detailed in this book show a history of delay in granting such a right, a reluctance to grapple with associated legal problems, an inability to develop structures and processes which would ensure some degree of legal equality for Aboriginal people, and the making of exceptional cases to avoid the application of this right where it no longer suited colonists. In early South Australia, despite the early promise and rhetoric, Aboriginal people were never in practice equal before the law. Indeed, the very law which was meant to protect them was often used as just another means of assisting in what was the essential aim of the colony — to make profits based upon the occupation and alienation of the lands of the Aboriginal people.

APPENDIX
CASES INVOLVING ABORIGINAL PEOPLE, 1836 TO 1862

Table 1:   Aboriginal people charged with murder of Europeans 1836–1862
Table 2:   Europeans charged with assault against Aboriginal people 1836–1862
Table 3:   *Inter se* murder cases 1836–1862
Table 4:   *Inter se* manslaughter cases 1836–1862
Table 5:   Aboriginal people charged with assault against Europeans 1836–1862
Table 6:   Aboriginal people charged with assault against other Aboriginal people 1846–1860
Table 7:   Aboriginal people charged with theft 1836–1862
Table 8:   Aboriginal people charged with stock theft 1836–1862
Table 9:   Aboriginal people charged with robbery and hut breaking 1836–1862
Table 10: Aboriginal people charged with stock killing offences 1836–1862

Appendix

Table 1: Aboriginal people charged with murder of Europeans 1836–1862

Name	Year	Victim/s	Verdict	Result
Reppindjeri	1837	Driscoll	No prosecution	Escaped custody
Monichi	1839	Duffield	Not guilty	Released
Parlobooka	1839	Duffield	Not guilty	Released
Yerricha	1839	Duffield	Guilty	Executed May 1839
Picha Cud Nacha	1839	Thompson	Not guilty	Released
Tippa Warricha	1839	Thompson	Not guilty; guilty of assault	Gaoled 12 months
Wang Nucha	1839	Thompson	Guilty	Executed May 1839
Moorcangua	1840	'Maria' survivors	Guilty	Executed by military
Mongarawata	1840	'Maria' survivors	Guilty	Executed by military
Moorpar	1842	Baldock	Guilty — death	Commuted, pardoned
Nultia	1842	Biddle	Guilty — death	Executed April 1843
Moullia	1842	Biddle	Guilty — death	Commuted, pardoned
Nantes	1842	Brown/Lovelock	Prosecution abandoned	Gaoled (theft)
'Williamy'	1842	Littleworth	Guilty — death	Gaoled, pardoned
Boccomola	1842	Littleworth	Guilty — death	Commuted, pardoned
Ngarbi	1843	Stubbs	Guilty (accessory to murder) — death	Executed June 1843
Pantowyn	1845	McGrath	No prosecution	Released
Koorykownimmi	1845	McGrath	No prosecution	Released
Wira Maldira	1845	McGrath	Guilty — death	Executed March 1845
Wekiweki	1845	McGrath	Guilty — death	Commuted, pardoned
Wodla Murkata	1846	Whitney and Scott	Prosecution abandoned	Discharged (language)

Appendix

Table 1 cont.

Name	Year	Victim/s	Verdict	Result
Meiya Murkata	1846	Whitney and Scott	Prosecution abandoned	Discharged (language)
Nakundah Biddeah	1846	Whitney and Scott	Prosecution abandoned	Discharged (language/ evidence)
Tatty Wamboureen	1846	Carney	Prosecution abandoned	Discharged (language/ witnesses)
Tulta	1849	Armstrong	Prosecution abandoned	Released
Nintalta	1849	Beevor	Guilty — death	Commuted, released
Malgalta	1849	Beevor	Guilty — death	Commuted, released
Kulgulta	1849	Beevor	Guilty — death	Executed November 1849
Mingulta	1849	Beevor	Guilty — death	Executed November 1849
Yabmanna	1849	Beevor	Not guilty	Released
Marrippa	1849	Bagnall	Guilty of manslaughter	Gaoled 12 months
Warrippa	1849	Bagnall	Guilty of manslaughter	Gaoled 6 months
Yellarri	1849	Bagnall	Prosecution abandoned	Released
Ngiyeri	1849	Bagnall	Guilty of manslaughter	Gaoled 6 months
Malgalta	1849	Hamp	Guilty — death	Reprieved
Mingalta	1849	Hamp	Guilty — death	Reprieved
Wilcuramalap	1849	Scott	Not guilty	Released
Maingalta	1849	Scott	Guilty, overturned	Discharged
Malyalta	1849	Scott	Guilty, overturned	Discharged
Bakilti	1849	Easton	Not guilty; guilty of assault	Gaoled 2 years
Puterpynter (f)	1849	Easton	Not guilty; guilty of assault	Gaoled 2 years
Kambalta (1)	1851	Crocker	Not guilty; guilty of manslaughter	Gaoled 2 years

Table 1 cont..

Name	Year	Victim/s	Verdict	Result
Kulbilti	1851	Crocker	Not guilty; guilty of manslaughter	Gaoled 2 years
Kambalta (2)	1851	Jenks	Prosecution abandoned	Released
Mangultu	1851	Jenks	Not guilty of being accessory	Released
Cooliltie	1851	Jenks	Guilty of being accessory	Gaoled 1 year
Kamalta	1851	Light	Guilty	Gaoled 1 year
Tyerrungi	1851	Light	Guilty	Gaoled 1 year
Pulgulta	1851	Baird	Prosecution abandoned	Gaoled: theft
'Jemmy'	1852	Richardson	Prosecution abandoned	Released
Unnamed male	1852	James Brown	Prosecution abandoned	Released
Unnamed male	1852	James Brown	Prosecution abandoned	Released
Errelee	1855	Peter Brown	No prosecution	Released
Weelangualla	1855	Peter Brown	No prosecution	Released
Mohaheednie	1855	Peter Brown	No prosecution	Released
Eelanna	1855	Peter Brown	No prosecution	Released
Ghow-ooladna	1855	Peter Brown	No prosecution	Released
Yardna-milkarna	1855	Peter Brown	No prosecution	Released
Nheelulta	1855	Peter Brown	No prosecution	Released
Wodlannah	1855	Peter Brown	No prosecution	Released
Eelulta	1855	Peter Brown	Guilty — death	Executed January 1856
Palingulta	1855	Peter Brown	Guilty — death	Executed January 1856
Weenpulta	1855	Peter Brown	Guilty — death	Executed January 1856
Watniltie	1855	Peter Brown	Guilty — death	Executed January 1856
Puttapa 'Bob'	1856	Mitchell	No prosecution	Died in custody
Warrioota	1856	Mitchell	No prosecution	Escaped custody
Cooliltie	1859	Jenks	Discharged	Released

Table 1 cont.

Name	Year	Victim/s	Verdict	Result
Manyelta	1860	Jones	Guilty — death	Executed October 1860
Kainmulta	1860	Jones	Not guilty	Released
Warretya (1)	1861	Rainbird	Prosecution abandoned	Released
Warretya (2)	1861	Rainbird	Guilty — death	Executed June 1861
Warretya (3)	1861	Rainbird	Guilty — death	Executed June 1861
Monnaitya	1861	Rainbird	No prosecution	Released
Tanka Worta	1861	Rainbird	Guilty — death	Executed June 1861
Pilta Miltinda	1861	Rainbird	Guilty — death	Executed June 1861
Mangiltie	1861	Impett	Guilty — death	Executed October 1861
Karabidne	1861	Impett	Guilty — death	Executed October 1861
Nelgerie	1861	Bergooist	Guilty — death	Executed October 1861
Titcherie	1861	Bergooist	Guilty — death	Executed October 1861
Meengulta	1862	Walker	Guilty — death	Executed October 1861

Table 2: Europeans charged with assault or murder against Aboriginal people 1836–1862

Name	Date	Verdict	Sentence	Result
Francis Jolly	1842	Guilty (assault)	Fined	Fined
William Roach	1842	Acquitted	Nil	Released
Jemima Sanders	1844	No prosecution	Nil	Released
George Lawson	1846	Guilty (assault)	Fined 20 pounds	Fined
Peter McDuff	1847	Acquitted (murder)	Nil	Released
James Brown	1849	Acquitted (murder)	Nil	Released
Thomas Donelly	1849	Guilty (murder)	Death	Hanged

Appendix

Table 2 cont.

Name	Date	Verdict	Sentence	Result
George Field	1849	Acquitted (murder)	Nil	Released
Harry Jones	1849	Not guilty (murder)	Discharged	Released
Henry Morris	1849	Prosecution abandoned	Nil	Released
Thomas Morris	1849	Not guilty (murder)	Discharged	Released
William Sawyer	1850	Guilty (assault)	Fined 5 pounds	Fined
James Young	1850	Dismissed (assault)	Nil	Released
Thomas Borthwick	1851	Not known	Not known	Not known
Frederic Frost	1853	Guilty (assault)	Fined 5 pounds	Fined
Adam Fartch	1853	Guilty (assault)	Fined 1 pound	Fined
Weaver	1854	Prosecution abandoned	Nil	Released
William Taylor	1854	Guilty (assault)	Fined 1 shilling	Fined
William Webb	1860	No prosecution	Nil	Released

Table 3: *Inter se* murder cases 1836–1862

Name	Victims	Trial Date	Verdict	Result
'Larry'	Rallooloolyoo	15 Mar 1847	Prosecution abandoned	Released
Nakundah Biddeah	'Charley'	15 Sep 1847	Discharged – court could not communicate	Released
Melaitpa ('Bobbo')	'Mary'	16 Jun 1848	Guilty – death	Commuted
Kambalta	Muliano	29 Jan 1849	No prosecution	On remand for several months before release
Kutromee	Budlaroo	12 Feb 1851	No prosecution	Released
Tukkurm	Maltalta	19 May 1851	Not guilty	Released
Nyalta Wikkanin	Maltalta	19 May 1851	Guilty – death	Reprieved, pardoned

Appendix

Table 3 cont.

Name	Victims	Trial Date	Verdict	Result
Kanga Worli	Maltalta	19 May 1851	Guilty – death	Reprieved, pardoned
Weepin	Mayponin	20 May 1851	Not guilty on Judge's direction to jury	Released
Ngaiere	Mayponin	20 May 1851	Not guilty on Judge's direction to jury	Released
Tarroti	Mayponin	20 May 1851	Not guilty on Judge's direction to jury	Released
Penchungya	Mayponin	20 May 1851	Not guilty on Judge's direction to jury	Released
'Ballycrack'	Warrinyerrimu & Youngmonamen	13 Aug 1852	Guilty – death	Commuted to life, released 1854 (illness)
'Cracking-younger'	Warrinyerrimu & Youngmonamen	13 Aug 1852	Guilty – death	Commuted to life, released 1854 (illness)
'Potpouch'	Warrinyerrimu & Youngmonamen	13 Aug 1852	Guilty – death	Commuted to life, released 1854 (illness)
Kauadla ('Peter')	Watte Watte	9 & 10 May 1853	Guilty – death	Commuted to 2 years' gaol
Ngallabammu	'Billy'	13 Dec 1853	Guilty (manslaughter)	Gaoled 3 years, pardoned 1854
Tinkanor	'Billy'	13 Dec 1853	Guilty (manslaughter)	Gaoled 3 years, pardoned 1854, died before release
Woringena	'Billy'	13 Dec 1853	Guilty (manslaughter)	Gaoled 3 years, pardoned 1854
Tunkanayman	'Billy'	13 Dec 1853	Guilty (manslaughter)	Gaoled 3 years, pardoned 1854
Monboit	Aiding and abetting murder of 'Alick'	17 Feb 1855	Discharged (lack of evidence)	Released

Appendix

Table 3 cont.

Name	Victims	Trial Date	Verdict	Result
Wrochoven	Aiding and abetting murder of 'Alick'	17 Feb 1855	Discharged (lack of evidence)	Released
Marielare	Loorumumpoo	13 Aug 1855	Not guilty	Released
Poowoolupe	Loorumumpoo	13 Aug 1855	Not guilty	Released
Warenboorimen	'Mary'	29 Nov 1855	Guilty (manslaughter)	Gaoled 3 years
Parichboorinen	'Mary'	29 Nov 1855	Guilty (manslaughter)	Gaoled 3 years
Gootoognuyerie	Courkin	17 Aug 1857	Guilty (manslaughter)	Gaoled 6 months
Toorapennie	Courkin	17 Aug 1857	Guilty (manslaughter)	Gaoled 6 months
Meenaltie	Aboriginal person	18 Feb 1859	No prosecution	Released
Mandeltie	Aboriginal person	18 Feb 1859	No prosecution	Released
Minulta	Nulguiltie	18 Feb 1859	No prosecution	Released
Magulta	Nulguiltie	18 Feb 1859	No prosecution	Released
Kaneguiltie	Nulguiltie	18 Feb 1859	No prosecution	Released
Wooloobully	Baldanant	16 May 1859	Not guilty	Released
Langaryn-garynga	Pantwirri	19 Aug 1859	Guilty (manslaughter)	Gaoled 6 months, escaped
Eroyngaree	Pantwirri	19 Aug 1859	Guilty (manslaughter)	Gaoled 6 months
Eight men (names not known)	'Johnny Come'	24 April 1860	Discharged (lack of evidence)	Released
Popeltie	Pinberri	6 Dec 1860	Not guilty	Released
Padneltie	Pinberri	6 Dece 1860	Not guilty	Released

Appendix

Table 4: *Inter se* manslaughter cases 1836–1862

Accused	Charge	Trial	Verdict	Result
Karrende	Manslaughter of Powang	4 Dec 1856	Guilty (jury made a plea for mercy)	Gaoled 3 months
Beerdeah	Murder of 'Bullocky': reduced to manslaughter	17 Aug 1857	Guilty (manslaughter)	Gaoled 6 months
Warreah	Manslaughter	11 Feb 1858	Not guilty (manslaughter): guilty of being an accessory	Gaoled 3 months
Moniah	Manslaughter	11 Feb 1858	Not guilty (manslaughter): guilty of being an accessory after fact	Gaoled 3 months
Piulta	Manslaughter	11 Feb 1858	Guilty — death	Commuted
Cooteroo	Murder of Coodunge: reduced to manslaughter	12 Feb 1858	Guilty	Gaoled 6 months
Midluck	Murder of Coodunge: reduced to manslaughter	12 Feb 1858	Guilty	Gaoled 6 months
Three men (names not known)	Manslaughter of 'Black Jemmy'	21 Aug 1862	Guilty	Gaoled 6 months

Table 5: Aboriginal people charged with assault against Europeans 1836–1862

Name	Year	Verdict	Sentence	Result
'Jemmy'	1840	Guilty	Fined one pound	Defaulted on fine: One week in gaol
'Jemmy'	1840	Guilty	Fined four pounds	Escaped from custody
Pulcanta	1841	Prosecution abandoned	Nil	Released
Multyilli	1843	Guilty	2 weeks' gaol	Gaoled
'Williamy'	1843	Guilty	7 days' gaol	Gaoled
Pinba Malta	1844	Dismissed	Nil	Released

Table 5 cont.

Name	Year	Verdict	Sentence	Result
Colcola Waranger	1844	Guilty	2 weeks' gaol	Gaoled
'Mary' Waranger	1844	Guilty	2 weeks' gaol	Gaoled
Mareeku	1844	Guilty	2 weeks' gaol	Gaoled
Targko Melaitya	1844	Guilty (assault with intent to murder)	15 years' transportation	Gaoled, pardoned March 1847
Karrinanerume	1844	Guilty	3 months' gaol	Gaoled
Kallgin	1844	Guilty	3 months' gaol	Gaoled
Karrinanerume	1844	Guilty	3 months' gaol	Gaoled
Mantyeuldi	1846	Not guilty	Dismissed	Released
'Bob'	1848	Guilty	1 months' gaol	Gaoled
Watpa	1849	Case dismissed	Nil	Released
Tilpardnambi	1849	Guilty (assault with intent to steal)	18 months' gaol	Gaoled, released March 1850 (ill-health)
Koonkoo	1849	Guilty (assault, theft)	4 months' gaol	Gaoled
Kumbulta	1849	Guilty	12 months' gaol	Gaoled
Bakilti	1849	Guilty	24 months' gaol	Gaoled
Yengki	1850	Not guilty	Nil	Released
Karkarra Widlo	1850	Guilty	3 months' gaol	Gaoled
Ngalta	1851	Guilty (assault, theft)	6 months' gaol	Gaoled
Mantamornappa	1851	Guilty	6 months' gaol	Gaoled
Ngurkilli	1851	Guilty	6 months' gaol	Gaoled
Mingeltie	1852	Not guilty	Nil	Released
Perrie	1852	Not guilty	Dismissed	Released
Warrie	1852	Not guilty	Dismissed	Released
Berea	1853	Guilty (assault with intent to commit GBH)	3 months' gaol	Gaoled

Table 5 cont.

Name	Year	Verdict	Sentence	Result
Minquilti	1853	Attempted murder	Dismissed	Released
Nolunna	1854	Guilty	14 days' gaol	Gaoled
Name unknown	1856	Guilty	Not known	Not known
'Billy'	1859	Not guilty	Dismissed	Released
'Georgy'	1859	Not guilty	Dismissed	Released
'Jacky'	1859	Not guilty	Dismissed	Released
Bungildo	1859	Guilty (indecent assault)	18 months' gaol	Gaoled
'Billy Goat'	1860	Guilty (assault, escaping)	6 months' gaol	Gaoled
'Tommy'	1861	Guilty	2 weeks' gaol	Gaoled
Meenbinya	1862	No indictment	Nil	Shot dead while attempting to escape
Meendeenya	1862	No indictment	Nil	Released

Table 6: Aboriginal people charged with assault against other Aboriginal people 1846–1862

Name	Date	Verdict	Sentence	Result
Pilgalta	1846	Not guilty	Dismissed	Released
Nammoingyu	1849	Not guilty	Dismissed	Released
'Jack'	1856	Not guilty	Dismissed	Released
Gifford	1859	Not known	Not known	Not known
'Potbelly'	1859	Not known	Not known	Not known
'Tommy'	1860	Not guilty	Dismissed	Released
Munarabidni	1850	Not guilty	Dismissed	Released
Mowalta	1850	Not guilty	Dismissed	Released
Manancowie	1860	Guilty (malicious wounding)	3 years' gaol	Gaoled

Table 7: Cases of theft involving Aboriginal people in South Australia 1836–62

Name	Year	Crime	Verdict	Result
Roeda	1840	Larceny	Guilty	Not known
Yakaria	1841	Theft	Guilty	Gaoled 12 months
Puyurin	1841	Theft	Guilty	Gaoled 12 months
Wittoari	1841	Theft	Guilty	Gaoled 12 months
Korda	1841	Theft	Guilty	Gaoled 3 weeks
Yapirin	1841	Larceny	Not guilty	Released
Wittau	1841	Theft	Not guilty	Released
Wariarto (f)	1841	Theft	Guilty	Gaoled 1 month and flogged
Pritto Monaitya	1842	Larceny	Guilty	Gaoled 1 month and flogged
Monichi	1842	Larceny	Guilty	Gaoled 14 days
Nwika	1842	Theft	Prosecution abandoned	Released
Keperin	1843	Larceny	Prosecution abandoned	Released
Puyurin	1843	Theft	Prosecution abandoned	Released
Warrinimo	1843	Theft	Guilty	Gaoled 12 months and flogged
Warritya	1843	Theft	Guilty	Gaoled 12 months
Marrutya	1844	Theft, receiving	Indictment failed	Released
Pelli Kertameeri	1844	Theft	Not guilty	Released
Korda	1844	Theft	Not guilty	Released
Yakkari	1844	Theft	Not guilty	Released
Caldecotte	1844	Theft of flour	Guilty	Gaoled 3 months
Marra Warritya	1845	Theft, breaking	Not guilty	Released
Mungutee	1847	Theft	Not known	Not known
Ngauadko (f)	1847	Theft, receiving	Indictment failed	Released
Mingalta	1847	Theft	Prosecution abandoned	Released
Parapooneen	1848	Theft	Guilty	Not known

Appendix

Table 7 cont.

Name	Year	Crime	Verdict	Result
Warapoonen	1848	Theft	Not guilty	Released
Tyin Bop	1848	Theft	Case dismissed	Released
Ngelmammin	1848	Theft	Not known	Not known
Nanto Kertameru	1848	Theft, receiving	Indictment failed	Released
Jimcrack	1849	Theft	No prosecution	Released
Mingalta	1852	Theft of flour	Guilty	Gaoled 14 days
Mingalta	1852	Theft	Guilty	Gaoled 14 days
'Tommy'	1852	Theft	Prosecution abandoned	Released
'Mary' (f)	1852	Theft	Prosecution abandoned	Released
Pilgulta	1854	Theft	Guilty	Gaoled 7 days
Poondalta	1854	Theft	Guilty	Gaoled 7 days
Mantelta	1854	Receiving	Guilty	Gaoled 1 month
Mingilti	1854	Receiving	Guilty	Gaoled 1 month
Nairoo	1854	Receiving	No prosecution	Released
Kooralgidme	1854	Receiving	No prosecution	Released
Name unknown	1854	Theft	Prosecution abandoned	Released
Coodnaltu	1854	Theft	Guilty	Gaoled 14 days
Yambilti	1854	Theft	Prosecution abandoned	Released
Nepulto	1855	Theft	Guilty	Gaoled 1 month
Meewulta	1855	Theft	Guilty	Gaoled 1 month
Ninchulta	1855	Theft	Guilty	Gaoled 3 months
Gerbally (f)	1859	Theft	Guilty	Gaoled 3 months
'Bonney'	1860	Theft	Guilty	Gaoled 18 months
'Johnny' Bootha	1860	Theft	Not guilty	Released

Table 8: Aboriginal people charged with stock theft 1836–1862

Name	Year	Crime	Verdict	Result
Wang Nucha	1839	Sheep stealing	Prosecution abandoned	Tried for murder: guilty and executed
Nantes	1842	Sheep stealing	Guilty	Gaoled 3 months and flogged
Nganti	1842	Sheep stealing	Guilty	Gaoled 3 weeks
Katamio	1842	Stealing a calf	Guilty	Sentenced to transportation but held in gaol instead
Nweka	1842	Sheep stealing	No prosecution	Released
Pinba Malta	1844	Sheep stealing	Not guilty	Released
Penno Ngalta	1844	Sheep stealing	Not guilty	Released
Karri Kudnutya	1844	Sheep stealing	Not known	Not known
Pintia Ngaltya	1844	Sheep stealing	Not guilty	Released
Marra Warritya	1845	Theft, breaking	Not guilty	Released
'Charley'	1845	Sheep stealing	No prosecution	Released after 5 months on remand
Ngaloorunger	1846	Sheep stealing	Not guilty	Released
Ngalkantyirriorn	1846	Sheep stealing	Prosecution abandoned	Released
Monaitya	1847	Sheep stealing	Guilty	Gaoled 6 months, pardoned
Purri Kudnutya	1847	Sheep stealing	Guilty	Gaoled 6 months
'Toby'	1848	Sheep stealing	Indictment failed	Released
Kudnutya (aka 'Tommy')	1848	Sheep stealing	Indictment failed	Released
'Rosy Wine'	1848	Sheep stealing	Indictment failed	Released
'Frying Pan'	1848	Sheep stealing	Indictment failed	Released
Melaitya	1848	Sheep stealing	No prosecution	Released
Watpa	1849	Sheep stealing	Guilty	Gaoled 4 months
Koonko	1849	Sheep stealing	Guilty	Gaoled 4 months
Padlaria	1850	Sheep stealing	Guilty	Gaoled 6 months
Kondura	1851	Stock theft	Guilty	Gaoled 6 months
Minora	1851	Stock theft	Guilty	Gaoled 6 months
Warraki	1851	Stock theft	Guilty	Gaoled 6 months

Appendix

Table 8 cont.

Name	Year	Crime	Verdict	Result
Binarambula	1851	Sheep stealing	No prosecution	Released
Kurkrunwilla	1851	Sheep stealing	Prosecution abandoned	Released
Muruss	1851	Sheep stealing	Prosecution abandoned	Released
Wummorda	1852	Sheep stealing	Guilty	Gaoled 6 months
Malia (1)	1852	Sheep stealing	No prosecution	Released
Malia (2)	1852	Sheep stealing	No prosecution	Released
Pedia	1852	Sheep stealing	No prosecution	Released
Coonie (1)	1852	Sheep stealing	No prosecution	Released
Coonie (2)	1852	Sheep stealing	No prosecution	Released
Warrie	1852	Sheep stealing	No prosecution	Released
Parkilti	1853	Sheep stealing	Not guilty	Released
Pulyelta	1853	Sheep stealing	Not guilty	Released
Unmiltie	1853	Sheep stealing	Not guilty	Released
Kulbulto	1853	Sheep stealing	Not guilty	Released
Wiebmulta	1853	Sheep stealing	Not guilty	Released
Meekalta	1853	Sheep stealing	Not guilty	Released
Kudnutya	1854	Sheep stealing	Guilty	Gaoled 2 months
Calgulta	1854	Sheep stealing	Guilty	Gaoled but escaped
Poyetta	1854	Sheep stealing	Guilty	Gaoled: unknown
Puleringa	1854	Sheep stealing	Guilty	Gaoled 6 months
Mantelta	1854	Receiving (sheep)	Guilty	Gaoled 3 months
Mingilti	1854	Receiving (sheep)	Guilty	Gaoled 3 months
Nairoo	1854	Receiving (sheep)	Guilty	Gaoled 3 months
Kooralgidme	1854	Receiving (sheep)	Guilty	Gaoled 3 months
Nadgiltie	1855	Sheep stealing	Guilty	Gaoled 3 months
Toocherg	1855	Sheep stealing	Guilty	Gaoled 3 months
Kokilata	1855	Sheep stealing	Guilty	Gaoled 3 months
Yarkeltia	1855	Sheep stealing	Guilty	Gaoled 3 months
Tittawitta	1855	Sheep stealing	Guilty	Gaoled 6 months
'Johnny Gumflat'	1855	Sheep stealing	Guilty	Gaoled 6 months
'Johnny Pointpiercer'	1855	Sheep stealing	Guilty	Gaoled 6 months
Yelluna	1855	Sheep stealing	Guilty	Gaoled 6 months
Wodla	1855	Sheep stealing	Guilty	Gaoled 6 months
Kanyanni	1855	Sheep stealing	Guilty	Gaoled 6 months
Malkeltie	1855	Sheep stealing	Guilty	Gaoled 3 months

Table 8 cont.

Name	Year	Crime	Verdict	Result
Four men	1858	Sheep stealing	Prosecution abandoned	Released
Four women	1858	Sheep stealing	Prosecution abandoned	Released
'Johnny' Bootha	1861	Horse stealing, burglary, escaping custody	Guilty (horse stealing, burglary)	Gaoled 3 years
Palierie	1862	Sheep stealing	Guilty	Gaoled 12 months
Nungarinya	1862	Sheep stealing	Guilty	Gaoled 12 months

Table 9: Aboriginal people charged with robbery and hut breaking 1836–1862

Name	Year	Crime	Verdict	Result
'Peter'	1844	Robbery	Not guilty	Released
Mungoringa	1844	Robbery	Guilty	Gaoled 2 months
Marra Warritya	1845	Theft, break & enter	Not guilty	Released
Coodamin	1845	Housebreaking	Not guilty	Released
Ngumbi	1846	Robbery	Prosecution abandoned	Released
Yailgatta	1846	Robbery	Guilty	Flogged
Yarngalta	1849	Robbery	Guilty	Gaoled 2 years
Yabmanna (f)	1849	Robbery	Guilty	Gaoled 3 months
Wirao (f)	1849	Robbery	Guilty	Gaoled 3 months
Yalluma	1849	Robbery	Guilty	Gaoled 3 months
Manilti	1850	Robbery	Prosecution abandoned	Released
Panmalta	1850	Robbery	Prosecution abandoned	Released
Mowalta	1850	Robbery	Prosecution abandoned	Released
Winnulu	1850	Robbery	Prosecution abandoned	Released
Mullnullnumelli	1850	Break & enter	Prosecution abandoned	Released
Ngurkilli	1851	Robbery	Guilty	Gaoled 6 months
Partko	1851	Robbery	Guilty	Gaoled 6 months
Mantamornappa	1851	Robbery	Guilty	Gaoled 6 months

Appendix

Table 9 cont.

Name	Year	Crime	Verdict	Result
Ngalta	1851	Robbery	Guilty	Gaoled 6 months
Watpa	1851	Robbery	Guilty	Gaoled 6 months
Tantultara	1851	Robbery	Guilty	Gaoled 6 months
Kambalta	1851	Robbery	Guilty of receiving	Gaoled 12 months
'Jemmy'	1852	Breaking, theft	Not guilty	Released
Weelunna	1855	Breaking, theft	Guilty	Gaoled 2 months
Wongary	1855	Breaking, theft	Guilty	Gaoled 2 months
Inabuthina	1858	Robbery	Shot resisting arrest 1864	Death: 'justifiable homicide'
Bailpoori	1860	Breaking, theft	Guilty	Gaoled 12 months
Noriah	1860	Breaking, theft	Not guilty	Released
'Jemmy' Goniah	1860	Breaking, theft	Guilty	Gaoled 12 months
'Charley'	1860	Break and enter	Guilty	Gaoled 3 years
'Bonney' Bootha	1860	Break and enter	Guilty	Gaoled 18 months
Palierie	1862	Theft, robbery	Guilty	Gaoled 12 months
Nungarinya	1862	Theft, robbery	Guilty	Gaoled 12 months

Table 10: Aboriginal people charged with stock killing offences 1836–1862

Name	Year	Crime	Verdict	Result
Kalamco	1842	Killing a calf	No record found — assume no prosecution	Not known
Mukarta	1842	Killing stock	Guilty: transportation 10 years	Gaoled in Adelaide; pardoned December 1843
Rongist Merainmilla	1842	Killing stock	Guilty: transportation 10 years	Gaoled in Adelaide; pardoned May 1845
Nyarrokyppur	1844	Malicious wounding of sow	Prosecution abandoned	Released
Permalooan	1847	Killing stock	Prosecution abandoned	Released
Permalooan	1848	Stock theft and killing cattle	Prosecution abandoned	Released
Walkaoinni	1851	Stock killing	Prosecution abandoned	Released

NOTES

Chapter 1

1. By 1836 cases in New South Wales had affirmed that Aboriginal people were 'amenable to the laws of the Colony for offences committed within it'. Burton J, 'Judgement in appeal of Murrell case', quoted by J Hookey, 'Settlement and sovereignty', in P Hanks and B Keon-Cohen (eds), *Aborigines and the law: essays in memory of Elizabeth Eggleston*, Sydney, 1984, p. 3.
2. First *Proclamation*, read by Governor Hindmarsh at Glenelg, 28 December 1836, reprinted in *Register*, 3 June 1837.
3. See D Pike, *Paradise of dissent*, London, 1957, ch. 3, in E Richards (ed.), *Flinders history of South Australia: social history*, Adelaide, 1986, vol. 1, ch. 1.
4. See D Pike, op. cit., pp. 64–73.
5. See J Main, 'The foundation of South Australia', in E Richards (ed.), op. cit., pp. 7–8.
6. See C Rowley, *The destruction of Aboriginal society*, Ringwood, 1972, ch. 5.
7. See H Reynolds, *The law of the land*, Penguin, Ringwood, first edition, 1987, pp. 106–07 and pp. 111–15; S Berg (ed.) *Coming to terms: Aboriginal title in South Australia*, Adelaide, 2010, pp. 11–17.
8. See H Reynolds, *The law of the land*, op. cit. and R Gibbs, 'Relations between the Aboriginal Inhabitants and the first South Australians', *Journal of Royal Geographic Society of South Australia*, vol. 61, 1959–60, pp. 61–78.
9. Lord Glenelg to SA Commissioners, December 1835, quoted in H Reynolds, *The law of the land*, op. cit., p. 106.
10. See H Reynolds, ibid., p. 107.
11. *Letters Patent establishing South Australia*, 19 February 1836, reprinted in S Berg (ed.) op. cit., pp. 312–13.
12. See C Rowley, op. cit., p. 75.
13. See H Reynolds, *The law* of the land, op. cit., p. 115; J Main, op. cit., p. 7; R Gibbs 1959–60, op. cit.; J Summers, 'Colonial race relations', in *Flinders history of South Australia: social history*, Wakefield Press, Adelaide, 1986, p. 285.

14. In 1841 Lord Russell instructed that part of the proceeds of land sales in the Australian colonies should be directed to Aboriginal welfare: 'fifteen per cent of the yearly produce of sales of land should be so applied'. Lord Russell to Governor Gipps, 28 March 1841; this despatch was reprinted in the *Southern Australian*, 23 July 1841.
15. The Adelaide Location School opened in December 1839. See R Foster, 'The Aborigines Location in Adelaide: South Australia's First "Mission" to the Aborigines', *Journal of Anthropological Society of South Australia*, vol. 28, nos. 1–2, 1990, pp. 11–37.
16. See A Pope, 'Aboriginal adaptation to early colonial labour markets', *Journal of Labour History*, no. 54, May 1988, pp. 8–10.
17. The land issue is not dealt with here as it is not directly related to the criminal law and is a major study in itself. See S Berg (ed.) op. cit.; H Reynolds, *The law of the land*, op. cit.
18. This document recognised 'the rights of any Aboriginal natives of the said Province to the actual enjoyment or employment...of any lands now actually occupied or enjoyed by such Natives'. *Letters Patent Establishing South Australia*, op. cit.
19. H Reynolds, *The law of the land*, op. cit., p. 106.
20. ibid., p. 113.
21. In the 1840s Governor Gawler challenged this interpretation, coming up with a plan to allow local clans to select choice portions of any land opened up for settlement. During his term of office 491 hectares were so reserved and his successor Grey continued to make reserve land until directed by London to cease doing so. See Governor Grey to Lord Stanley, 26 May 1843, in *British Parliamentary Papers*, session 1844, vol. 8, p. 337 and Lord Stanley to Governor Grey, 14 November 1843, in *British Parliamentary Papers*, ibid., p. 339. Not that this practice preserved the land rights of Aboriginal people anyway, since reserved land was soon leased to settlers. See Protector's Report, 10 January 1842, Colonial Secretary's Office, 32 of 1842, State Records, Adelaide.
22. See D Pike, op. cit., p. 52.
23. In 1838 additional land in the south was released to meet the demands of the 'preliminary purchasers' who now wanted possession of their acres. The special surveys of 1839–40 were its death knell as wealthy investors selected large areas outside the defined settlement districts, often in areas with relatively high Aboriginal population.
24. A Castles and M Harris, *Lawmakers and wayward Whigs*, Wakefield Press, Adelaide, 1987, p. 55.
25. J Jeffcott, Address to Grand Jury, 13 May 1837, reported in *South Australian Gazette and Colonial Register*, 3 June 1837.
26. South Australia *Supreme Court Act*, 7 William IV, 5, Adelaide, 1837.
27. A Castles and M Harris, op. cit., p. 63.

Notes

28. See R Cranston, 'Aborigines and the law: an overview', *University of Queensland Law Journal*, vol. 8, 1973, p. 62.
29. A Castles, *An Australian legal history*, Law Book Co, Sydney, 1982, p. 536. See also B Hocking, 'Colonial laws and indigenous peoples: past and present law concerning the recognition of human rights of indigenous native peoples in British colonies with particular reference to Australia', in B Hocking (ed.), *International law and Aboriginal human rights*, Melbourne, 1988, pp. 3–18.
30. Judge Advocate Atkins, 'Opinion on the Treatment of Natives', 8 July 1805, Enclosure no. 2 in Governor King, Despatch to Earl Camden, 20 July 1805, Historical Records of Australia, vol. 5, pp. 502–504.
31. Bridges, in his review of Aboriginal people and the law in NSW, points out that Macquarie had already declared Aboriginal people as being outside of his definition of 'British Subject'. Only those Aboriginal people whose behaviour was officially approved were granted the protection of British law. See B Bridges, 'The extension of English law to the Aborigines for offences committed inter se, 1829–1842', *Journal of the Royal Australian Historical Society*, vol. 59, no. 4, December 1973, p. 265.
32. See Bathurst to Darling, 14 July 1825, Historical Records of Australia, vol. 12, p. 21.
33. Allegedly, 'Dirty Dick' was killed by several men from a different clan.
34. See B Bridges, 1973, op. cit., p. 264.
35. Jack Congo Murrell and George Bummary were accused of murdering Bill Jabenguy and Pat Cleary. This case is generally referred to as the Murrell case.
36. See B Bridges, 1973, op. cit., p. 265.
37. Burton J, Judgement in appeal of Murrell case, quoted by J Hookey, op. cit.
38. Judge Willis, quoted in B Bridges 1973, op. cit., p. 267.
39. Bonjon was discharged but, ironically, was murdered soon after, presumably by Aboriginal people seeking to avenge the death of his alleged victim.
40. Australian Law Reform Commission, Report no. 31, *The recognition of Aboriginal customary laws: summary report*, Canberra, 1986, p. 5.

Chapter 2

1. See B Dickey and P Howell, *South Australia's Foundation: Select Documents*, Adelaide, 1986, p. 8.
2. Colonization Commissioners, 'New Colony in South Australia', 4 December 1835, reprinted in B Dickey and P Howell, op. cit., pp. 66–69.
3. ibid., p. 67.
4. *First Annual Report of the Colonization Commissioners for South Australia*, London, 14 June 1836, House of Commons, Sessional Papers, vol. 39, no. 426.

Notes

5. Governor Grey to Colonization Commissioners, 17 July 1835, Governor's Despatches, State Records, Adelaide.
6. *First Annual Report of the Colonization Commissioners for South Australia*, op. cit., p. 8.
7. loc. cit.
8. loc. cit.
9. B Dickey and P Howell, op. cit., p. 8.
10. 4 & 5 William IV, *An Act to empower His Majesty to erect South Australia into a British Province or Provinces and to provide for the Colonization and Government thereof*, 1834.
11. See A Munyard, 'Making a polity: 1836–1857', *Flinders history of South Australia: political history*, op. cit., p. 55.
12. *Letters Patent establishing South Australia*, 19 February 1836, reprinted in B Dickey and P Howell, op. cit., p. 14.
13. See S Berg (ed.) op. cit.; R Gibbs, op. cit.; G Jenkin, op. cit., pp. 35–36.
14. *Order in Council, authorizing the Governor of South Australia acting with others to make Laws, etc.*, 23 February 1836, reprinted in B Dickey and P Howell, op. cit., p. 75.
15. See G Fischer, 'South Australian Colonization Act and Other Related Constitutional Documents', *Adelaide Law Review*, vol. 2, no. 1, 1963–1966, pp. 360–72; P Howell, 'Clearing the cobwebs: a reconsideration of the beginnings of the province of South Australia', *History Forum*, July 1991, p. 5.
16. Governor Hindmarsh, Proclamation read at Glenelg on 28 December 1836, reprinted in *Register*, 3 June 1837.
17. ibid.
18. GF Angas, quoted in C Mann, *Report of Speeches for Hindmarsh on appointment as Governor of South Australia*, London, 1835.
19. loc. cit.
20. Jeffcott, J, Address to Grand Jury, 13 May 1837, op. cit.
21. This was not, of course, the first killing of a European in South Australia. Captain Collett Barker had been speared while exploring the mouth of the Murray in 1832.
22. See G Jenkin, op. cit., pp. 52–53.
23. See R Clyne 1987, op. cit., p. 8.
24. C Mann, Letter to Gouger, 28 July 1837, quoted by G Jenkin, op. cit., p. 53.
25. Protector of Aborigines, Report, 22 September 1837, Colonial Secretary's Office, 372 of 1837, State Records, Adelaide.
26. W Everard, Letter to C Everard, 1838, Mortlock Library, Adelaide.
27. *Register*, 17 March 1838.
28. Governor Hindmarsh, Proclamation, 10 March 1837, printed in the *Register*, 17 March 1838.

Notes

29. *Register*, 27 April 1839.
30. See *Southern Australian,* 15 May 1839.
31. W Williams, Report of Trip, 21 April 1839, *Register*, 11 May 1839.
32. *Register*, editorial, 4 May 1839.
33. *Southern Australian*, 10 May 1839.
34. Governor Gawler, Reply to Petitioners, 17 May 1839, quoted in *Register*, 18 May 1839.
35. Governor Gawler, Reply to Cooper CJ, 21 March 1839, quoted in *Southern Australian*, 3 April 1839.
36. *Southern Australian*, editorial, 24 April 1839.
37. Cooper CJ, Address to Grand Jury, 25 May 1839, quoted in *Register*, 23 October 1839.
38. *Southern Australian*, 1 May 1839.
39. C Mann, Address to Jury, 2 May 1839, reported in *Register*, 25 May 1839.
40. ibid.
41. ibid.
42. ibid.
43. *Register*, 25 May 1839.
44. Cooper CJ, Remarks on sentencing, reported in *Register*, 25 May 1839.
45. Cooper CJ, Comments in Supreme Court, 23 May 1839, reported in *Register*, 25 May 1839.
46. ibid.
47. *Register*, 1 June 1839.
48. See K Hassell, op. cit.; S Lendrum, 'The Coorong Massacre: Martial Law and the Aborigines at First Settlement', *Adelaide Law Review*, vol. 6, no. 1, 1977–78, pp. 26–43; J Hamann, 'The Coorong Massacre', *Flinders Journal of History and Politics*, vol. 3, 1973.
49. Governor Gawler, Minute to Council of Government, 15 September 1840, printed in *Government Gazette*, 17 September 1840.
50. Governor Gawler, Instructions to O'Halloran, tabled at Council of Government, 15 September 1840, *Government Gazette*, 17 September 1840.
51. See R Foster, R Hoskings and A Nettleback, *Fatal collisions: the SA frontier and the violence of memory*, Wakefield Press, Adelaide, 2001, pp. 13–28.
52. Police Commissioner, Report, *Government Gazette*, 10 September 1840.
53. Governor Gawler, Letter to Chief Justice, 12 August 1840, Colonial Secretary's Office, 511 of 1840, State Records, Adelaide.
54. Cooper CJ provided his advice in writing but was also summoned to attend the Council of Government to put his views personally. See Minutes of Council of Government, 12 August 1840.
55. Cooper CJ, Letter to Governor, 12 August 1840, op. cit.
56. See S Lendrum, 'Special legal problems relating to the Aborigines in the first fifteen years after settlement', LLB thesis, University of Adelaide, 1976.

57. Advocate General, Address to Council of Government, 15 September 1840, *Government Gazette*, 17 September 1840.
58. *Register*, editorial, 12 September 1840.
59. *Government Gazette*, 13 August 1840.
60. *Register*, editorial, 22 September 1840.
61. *Southern Australian*, editorial, 25 September 1840.
62. Governor Gawler, Letter to Petitioners, 15 October 1840, reprinted in *Register*, 24 October 1840.
63. For example, the Aborigines Protection Society publicly condemned the actions of both O'Halloran and Gawler in a report which would have been read widely in London in early 1841. See Aborigines Protection Society (South Australia), *Third Report*, 1841, reprinted in *Register*, 4 December 1841.
64. The Council of Government met on 15 September 1840. Its membership was the Governor, Colonial Secretary, Advocate General, Surveyor General and Assistant Commissioner.
65. The meeting of 15 September 1840 received considerable newspaper coverage.
66. Governor Gawler, Address to Council of Government, 15 September 1840, *Government Gazette*, 17 September 1840.
67. ibid.
68. Advocate General, Address to Council of Government, 15 September 1840, *Government Gazette*, 17 September 1840 (emphasis in original).
69. See S Lendrum, 1976, op. cit., p. 15.
70. Advocate General, Address to Council of Government, 15 September 1840, op. cit.
71. ibid.
72. Governor Gawler, Minute to Council of Government, 15 September 1840, *Government Gazette*, 17 September 1840.
73. See M Moorhouse, Minutes of Evidence, 'Report of Select Committee on the Aborigines', Adelaide, October 1860, *SA Parliamentary Papers*, 1860, vol. 2, no. 165, p. 98.
74. Advocate General, Address to Council of Government, 15 September 1840, op. cit.
75. ibid.
76. ibid.
77. See *Register*, editorial, 3 October 1840.
78. S Lendrum 1977–1978, op. cit., p. 33.
79. Governor Gawler, Address to Council of Government, 15 September 1840, *Government Gazette*, 17 September 1840.
80. Governor Gawler, Address to Council of Government, 30 September 1840, *Government Gazette*, 1 October 1840.
81. See S Lendrum 1977–1978, op. cit., p. 28.

Notes

82. Hope to Law Officers of the Crown, 26 October 1841, quoted in S Lendrum 1976, p. 36. Lendrum notes that the opinion was given on 27 March 1841.
83. Lord Stanley to Governor Grey, 14 December 1841, *Governor's Despatches*, Mortlock Library, Adelaide.
84. See A Tolmer, *Reminiscences of an Adventurous and Chequered Career at Home and in the Antipodes*, London, 1882, p. 193.
85. Certainly these clans had just cause to mount their attacks against drovers and stock. See G Jenkin, op. cit.; R Clyne 1982, op. cit.
86. See R Foster, R Hoskings and A Nettleback, op. cit., pp. 29–43.
87. See Police Commissioner, Letters re Inman Affray, 25 May 1841, Colonial Secretary's Office, 235 of 1841, State Records, Adelaide.
88. T O'Halloran, Diary, 5 May 1841, quoted in J Bull, *Early Experiences of Life in South Australia*, Adelaide, 1884, p. 201.
89. See W Field, Letter to Colonial Secretary, 20 May 1841, Colonial Secretary's Office, 23 of 1841, State Records, Adelaide.
90. Report of public meeting, 25 May 1841, *Southern Australian*, 28 May 1841.
91. Minute read to Council of Government meeting, 10 July 1841, in Governor Grey to Lord Russell, 3 August 1841, *British Parliamentary Papers*, vol. 7, pp. 285–86.
92. Despatches were sent, for example, on 28 and 31 May, 11 June and 3 August 1841.
93. Governor Grey to Lord Russell, 11 June 1841, *Governor's Despatches*, Mortlock Library, Adelaide.
94. Police Commissioner, Report, 27 June 1841, printed in *Southern Australian*, 6 July 1841.
95. ibid.
96. Report of Murray Expedition, *Southern Australian*, 6 August 1841.
97. Memorandum to Magistrates, July 1841, enclosure in Governor Grey to Lord Russell, 31 December 1842, *British Parliamentary Papers*, vol. 7, p. 272.
98. Protector of Aborigines, Report from Lake Bonney, 4 September 1841, reprinted in *Southern Australian*, 14 September 1841.
99. ibid.
100. *Register*, editorial, 18 September 1841.
101. ibid.
102. *Adelaide Examiner*, 19 October 1841.
103. Resolutions of Magistrate's Enquiry into Rufus Affray, September 1841, reported in *Register*, 25 September 1841.

Chapter 3

1. *R v Murrell and Bummary*. See B Bridges, 'The Aborigines and the law: New South Wales 1788–1855', *Teaching History*, December 1970, p. 40.

2. House of Commons, *Report of the Select Committee on Aborigines (British Settlements)*, op. cit.
3. Lord Glenelg to Governor Bourke, 26 July 1837, *Historical Records of Australia*, series 1, vol. 19, p. 47.
4. House of Commons, *Report of the Select Committee on Aborigines (British Settlements)*, op. cit., p. 79.
5. Judge Willis, quoted in B Bridges, 'The extension of English law to the Aborigines for offences committed *inter se*, 1829–1842', *Journal of the Royal Australian Historical Society*, vol. 59, no. 4, December, 1973, p. 267.
6. See P Hasluck, *Black Australians: a survey of native policy in Western Australia, 1829–1897*, Melbourne, 1942.
7. Grey was at this time the Resident Magistrate at King George Sound in Western Australia but he maintained his interest in South Australia and visited Adelaide on his way to London in 1840.
8. G Grey, Speech to Council of Government, 30 September 1840.
9. ibid.
10. Grey succeeded Gawler as Governor on 15 May 1841.
11. Cooper CJ, Address to Grand Jury, 3 November 1840, reported in *Adelaide Chronicle*, 4 November 1840.
12. Cooper CJ, Comments in Supreme Court, 23 May 1839, quoted in *Register*, 25 May 1839.
13. Protector of Aborigines, Report of Journey, 15 May 1843, Colonial Secretary's Office, 290 of 1842, State Records, Adelaide.
14. Governor Grey, Note written on cover sheet of Report of Journey, 15 May 1843, ibid.
15. A Murray, Sub-protector's Report, quoted in Protector of Aborigines, Report, 19 August 1854, *Government Gazette*, 24 August 1854, p. 620.
16. These included Mann, Fisher and Bartley.
17. S Lendrum 1976, op. cit., p. 74.
18. *Register*, 20 November 1842.
19. Katamio was not transported but was imprisoned in the Adelaide Gaol.
20. Other instances of *inter se* offences had come to the attention of the authorities during the previous decade but the practice had been not to intervene by prosecuting. See chapter 6.
21. Rallooloolyoo was also known as Ronkurri and 'Jemmy McLean'. See *R v 'Larry'*, Supreme Court Criminal Sessions Record Book, 24 November 1846. See also chapter 6.
22. Bartley, Comments in Supreme Court, 24 November 1846, reported in *Register*, 25 November 1846.
23. Note in *Judges' Common Notebook* 1846–1848, Supreme Court, 26 November 1846.
24. ibid.
25. Supreme Court Criminal Sessions Record Book, 15 March 1847. See also *Register*, 17 March 1847 and Cooper CJ, Letter to Colonial Secretary,

Notes

22 March 1847, Colonial Secretary's Office, 351 of 1847, State Records, Adelaide.
26. Police Commissioner, Letter to Governor, 6 May 1844, Colonial Secretary's Office, 457 of 1844, State Records, Adelaide. Of course, Finniss was mistaken in his view that the Legislative Council had declared Aboriginal people within the protection of the law.
27. See *South Australian*, 12 and 15 May 1846.
28. Cooper CJ, Address to Grand Jury, 2 June 1846, reported in *South Australian*, 9 June 1846.
29. See chapter 7.
30. Governor Grey to Lord Stanley, 3 August 1843, *British Parliamentary Papers*, vol. 8, p. 347. Stanley agreed with the decision to proceed to execution. ibid., p. 350.
31. See chapter 5.
32. Moorhouse noted, early in October: 'During this time means are to be used, either to instruct the prisoners in the English language, or I must use every effort to acquire their dialect, so as to interpret the evidence against them'. Protector of Aborigines, Letter to Colonial Secretary, 5 October 1846, Colonial Secretary's Office, 1223 of 1846, State Records, Adelaide.
33. Supreme Court Criminal Sessions Record Book, 22 September 1846.
34. ibid.
35. Cooper CJ, Note in *Judges' Common Notebook*, September 1846, Supreme Court, Adelaide.
36. ibid.
37. Advocate General, Letter to Colonial Secretary, 16 October 1846, Colonial Secretary's Office, 1276 of 1846, State Records, Adelaide. Note that a copy of this letter, in Cooper's handwriting, is to be found in the *Judges' Common Notebook*, 20 October 1846.
38. See Robe's note attached to Advocate General, Letter to Colonial Secretary, 16 October 1846, Colonial Secretary's Office, 1276 of 1846, State Records, Adelaide. The letter was forwarded to Chief Justice Cooper on 24 October 1846.
39. Cooper CJ, Draft reply to Colonial Secretary, 30 October 1846, *Judges' Common Notebook*, Supreme Court, Adelaide.
40. ibid.
41. On this point I disagree with Lendrum, who argues that Cooper's 1846 and 1847 statements on the jurisdiction were expressed 'in precisely the same terms as that offered by Cooper to Governor Gawler' in 1840. See S Lendrum, 1976, op. cit., p. 63.
42. Colonial Secretary, Letter to Protector of Aborigines, 10 December 1846, Colonial Secretary's Office, 1620 of 1846, State Records, Adelaide.
43. Colonial Secretary, Letter to Advocate General, 10 December 1846, Colonial Secretary's Office, 1619 of 1846, State Records, Adelaide.
44. Colonial Secretary, Letter to Advocate General, 10 December 1846, ibid.

45. Supreme Court Criminal Sessions Record Book, 17 March 1847.
46. Cooper CJ, Draft of Letter to Governor, 23 March 1847, *Judges' Common Notebook*, op. cit.
47. Cooper CJ, 'Observations relating to the trial of native prisoners', 27 March 1847, Colonial Secretary's Office, 383.5 of 1847, State Records, Adelaide.
48. ibid.
49. Governor Robe, Despatches to Earl Grey, 21 and 23 April 1847, *Governors' Despatches*, State Records, Adelaide.
50. Governor Robe, Despatch to Earl Grey, 21 April 1847, op. cit.
51. Governor Robe, Despatch to Earl Grey, 23 April 1847, op. cit.
52. ibid.
53. ibid.
54. *R v Murrell and Bummary* 1836, quoted by J Hookey, op. cit., p. 3.
55. *R v Melaitpa*, Supreme Court Criminal Sessions Record Book, 16 June 1848.
56. Young took office on 2 August 1848.
57. Earl Grey, Despatch to Governor Young, 27 April 1848, State Records, Adelaide.
58. ibid.
59. ibid.
60. For example, see 'An Appeal on behalf of the Aborigines', *Register*, 14 January 1850; Memorial to Governor, 21 December 1855, Colonial Secretary's Office, 4138.5 of 1855, State Records, Adelaide.
61. In another example, pastoralists on the Eyre Peninsula petitioned in 1852 for the early release of Kambalta and Kamalta, imprisoned for the manslaughter of shepherd Charles Crocker.
62. Comment attributed to Corporal Geharty, included in Police Commissioner, Report, 20 July 1848, Colonial Secretary's Office, 1156 of 1848, State Records, Adelaide.
63. Police Commissioner, Report, 2 December 1850, Colonial Secretary's Office, 2726 of 1850, State Records, Adelaide.
64. Supreme Court Criminal Records, 10 February 1851.
65. *Register*, 21 May 1851. This is Rev Schurmann, the Lutheran missionary based at Port Lincoln and a competent speaker of the Kaurna, Battara and Pangkala languages.
66. The McKechnie brothers based much of their success in 'opening up' frontier district country to grazing on their deliberate assimilation of local Aboriginal clans or families into their operations. Groups of Pangkala people were encouraged to attach themselves to McKechnies' shepherds, with many of their number being informally employed to assist. Although this tactic did not make the graziers immune from Aboriginal depredations, it did guarantee the economic survival of their frontier operations. See F Masters, *Saga of Wangaraleednie,* National Trust, Adelaide, 1950.

Notes

67. The men found guilty were Eelulta, Palingulta, Weenpulta and Watniltie. Supreme Court Criminal Records, 30 November; 4 and 7 December 1855. The remaining men (Parnkalta, Milyalta, Willana, Yertumilkurti, Illamma, Kanadlanna) were charged with theft and assisting a murder (see *Indictment Book 1855–58*, Supreme Court Criminal Records) and were later convicted of the former charge in the Adelaide Police Court, each receiving sentences of three months imprisonment. See *Observer*, 8 December 1855.
68. Memorial to Governor, 21 December 1855, Colonial Secretary's Office, 4138.5 of 1855, State Records, Adelaide. This petition was printed in the *Register*, 12 December 1855, and the *Observer*, 29 December 1855.
69. Advocate General, Note to Executive Council, 23 December 1855, attached to Memorial to Governor, 21 December 1855, ibid.
70. Advocate General, Handwritten note on docket cover, Memorial to Governor, ibid.
71. Memorial to Governor, 21 December 1855, op. cit.
72. George Beresford (Governor's private secretary), Letter to Petitioners, 24 December 1855, Colonial Secretary's Office, 4138.5 of 1855, State Records, Adelaide.
73. See Inspector Holroyd, Diary, Mortlock Library, Adelaide.
74. Supreme Court Criminal Records, 12 December 1853.
75. Tinkanor died in custody in December 1854.
76. Supreme Court Criminal Records, 11 February 1858.
77. *R v Wooloobully*, Supreme Court Criminal Records, 9 and 16 May 1859.
78. Fisher, Statement in Supreme Court, 16 May 1859, reported in *Chronicle*, 17 May 1859.
79. Witnesses Kurning and Yananpooaramann both gave the same account of events. Supreme Court Criminal Records, 16 May 1859.
80. Gwynne J, Statement in Supreme Court, 16 May 1859, reported in *Chronicle*, 21 May 1859; *Advertiser*, 17 May 1859.
81. Piulta was scheduled to be hanged on 6 March 1858.
82. *Register*, 24 February 1858; *Observer*, 20 and 27 February 1858.
83. *Register*, 24 February 1858.
84. Piulta served a sentence in gaol but the actual length of this term is not clear in the records.
85. *Register*, editorial, 17 February 1860.
86. ibid.
87. See chapter 10.
88. See Supreme Court Criminal Records, 16 and 17 May 1861; *Register* 15 and 20 March 1861; *Advertiser*, 20 and 25 March 1861.
89. The major debate in May and June 1861 centred on alcohol controls, since alcohol had been implicated in the Rainbird killings.

Chapter 4

1. See chapter 2 for details of this case.
2. This was because of the danger of self-incrimination. See A Castles 1982, op. cit., p. 532 and B Attwood, 'Aborigines and Academic Historians: Some Recent Encounters', *Australian Historical Studies*, vol. 24, no. 94, April 1990.
3. See Lord Normanby to Governor Gipps, 31 August 1839, *Historical Records of Australia*, series 1, vol. 20, p. 302.
4. See Lord Russell, Despatch to Governor Hutt, 30 April 1841, in *British Parliamentary Papers*, vol. 8, p. 377.
5. Governor Gawler, Address to Council of Government, 15 September 1840, op. cit.
6. ibid.
7. See *Register*, 3 October 1840.
8. See *Register*, 14 August 1844.
9. G Grey, 'Suggestions with reference to the practicability of improving the moral and social condition of the Aboriginal Inhabitants of Australia', *Register*, 18 April 1840.
10. *R v Roach*, Supreme Court Criminal Sessions Record Book, 10 March 1842. See chapter 10.
11. Assistant Crown Solicitor, Letter to Attorney General, 14 September 1841, Advocate General's Office, 32 of 1841, State Records, Adelaide.
12. See *Adelaide Independent*, 9 September 1842.
13. Supreme Court Criminal Sessions Record Book, 10 March 1842.
14. Resident Magistrate (Moorundie), Annual Report for 1842, 1 February 1843, Colonial Secretary's Office, 170 of 1843, State Records, Adelaide.
15. ibid.
16. ibid.
17. Governor Grey, Note on Resident Magistrate (Moorundie), Annual Report for 1842, ibid.
18. See, for example, *Register*, editorial, 7 August 1844.
19. Correspondent to *Adelaide Observer*, 9 December 1843.
20. E Eyre, Letter to Colonial Secretary, 20 May 1844, Colonial Secretary's Office, 523 of 1844, State Records, Adelaide.
21. ibid.
22. Governor Grey, Note on E Eyre, Letter to Colonial Secretary, ibid.
23. Act No. 8 of 1844: *An Ordinance to allow the Aboriginal Inhabitants of South Australia and the parts adjacent, to give Information and Evidence without the sanction of an Oath.*
24. Act No. 8 of 1844 was passed on 12 August 1844.
25. *Register*, 17 July 1844.
26. ibid.

Notes

27. ibid.
28. Protector of Aborigines, Report for second quarter 1846, 14 July 1846, Colonial Secretary's Office, 879 of 1846, State Records, Adelaide.
29. For example, Teichelmann and Schurmann wrote a grammar in 1841. See CG Teichelmann and CW Schurmann, *The Aboriginal Language of South Australia*, Adelaide, 1840.
30. Act No. 8 of 1844, section 5.
31. Act No. 8 of 1844, Preamble.
32. Act No. 8 of 1844.
33. ibid., section 1.
34. Act No. 8 of 1844, section 5. See A Castles and M Harris, op. cit., p. 23.
35. ibid.
36. See A Castles and M Harris, op. cit., p. 23.
37. Act No. 8 of 1844, section 5.
38. ibid.
39. For example, see *Adelaide Examiner*, 7 April 1842.
40. See *Adelaide Examiner*, 7 April and 15 October 1842; *Register*, 15 August 1849.
41. E Eyre, *Journals of Expeditions*, London, 1845, vol. 2, p. 493.
42. Police Commissioner to Advocate General, Advocate General's Office, 138 of 1844, State Records, Adelaide.
43. Protector of Aborigines, Report, 5 October 1846, Colonial Secretary's Office, 1223 of 1846, State Records, Adelaide.
44. Supreme Court Criminal Sessions Record Book, 12–13 March 1847.
45. Cooper CJ, Comments in Supreme Court, 13 March 1847, reported in *Register*, 17 March 1847.
46. *R v Spratt et al*, Supreme Court Criminal Sessions Record Book, 29 November 1844.
47. Protector of Aborigines, Letter to Colonial Secretary, 14 July 1846, Colonial Secretary's Office, 879 of 1846, State Records, Adelaide.
48. Protector of Aborigines, Letter to Colonial Secretary, 14 July 1846, op. cit.
49. ibid.
50. ibid.
51. Government Resident (Guichen Bay), Letter to Advocate General, 8 January 1847, included in Advocate General, Memorandum re Native Evidence, 21 January 1847, Colonial Secretary's Office, 82 of 1847, State Records, Adelaide.
52. Advocate General, Memorandum re Native Evidence, 21 January 1847, ibid.
53. ibid.
54. Government Resident (Guichen Bay), Report, 31 January 1847, Colonial Secretary's Office, 220 of 1847, State Records, Adelaide.
55. Smillie put this view to Robe in January 1847. See Advocate General, Memorandum re Native Evidence, 21 January 1847, op. cit.

56. Governor Robe, Note on Government Resident (Guichen Bay) Report, 31 January 1847, op. cit.
57. Cooper CJ, Observations relating to the trial of native prisoners, 27 March 1847, Colonial Secretary's Office, 383.5 of 1847, State Records, Adelaide.
58. See Governor's Despatches, No. 38 (21 April 1847) and No. 40 (23 April 1847), State Records, Adelaide. Cooper's observations of 27 March 1847 were included in the former despatch.
59. Colonial Secretary, Letter to Advocate General, 17 April 1848, Advocate General's Office, 48 of 1848, State Records, Adelaide.
60. Act No. 3 of 1848: *An ordinance to facilitate the admission of the unsworn testimony of the Aboriginal inhabitants of South Australia and the parts adjacent.*
61. Acting Judge Mann, Comments in Supreme Court, 11 June 1849, reported in *Register*, 16 June 1849.
62. Act No. 4 of 1849, Act to amend 'An ordinance to facilitate the admission of unsworn testimony of the Aboriginal inhabitants of South Australia and the parts adjacent', Adelaide 1849. Passed by Legislative Council on 25 July 1849.
63. ibid.
64. Proceedings of Legislative Council, 24 July 1849, reported in *Observer*, 28 July 1849.
65. See Protector of Aborigines, Report, 4 July 1849, Colonial Secretary's Office, 1271 of 1849, State Records, Adelaide.
66. See chapter 10 for an account of this incident and indictment.
67. Protector of Aborigines, Report from Port Lincoln, 16 July 1849, Colonial Secretary's Office, 1317 of 1849, State Records, Adelaide.
68. Government Resident, Report from Port Lincoln, 1 July 1849, Colonial Secretary's Office, 1329 of 849, State Records, Adelaide.
69. See Supreme Court Criminal Sessions Record Book, 6 September 1849; Supreme Court Criminal Sessions Record Book, 17 September 1849; *Observer*, 8 September 1849.
70. See chapter 10 for further details of this case.
71. Acting Judge Charles Mann later expressed the view that the inconsistencies in interpretation of the Aboriginal evidence tended 'to induce a conviction that neither the native interpreter or witness could be relied on'. C Mann, Letter to Colonial Secretary, 19 October 1849, Colonial Secretary's Office, 1908 of 1849, State Records, Adelaide. See chapter 5 for details of these concerns.
72. *Observer*, 8 September 1849.
73. ibid.
74. *Register*, 15 August 1849.
75. Supreme Court Criminal Sessions Record Book, 25 September 1849. Yabmanna was also charged with robbery and found guilty on this charge. See *R v Yabmanna*, Supreme Court Criminal Sessions Record Book, 24 September 1849.

Notes

76. Protector of Aborigines, Letter to Colonial Secretary, 8 October 1849, Colonial Secretary's Office, 1850 of 1849, State Records, Adelaide.
77. C Mann, Report to Colonial Secretary, 16 October 1849, Colonial Secretary's Office, 1900 of 1849, State Records, Adelaide.
78. *Register*, 17 November 1849.
79. Protector of Aborigines, Letter to Colonial Secretary, 20 October 1849, Colonial Secretary's Office, 1907 of 1849, State Records, Adelaide.
80. Protector of Aborigines, Report, 8 January 1850, *Government Gazette*, 17 January 1850, p. 46; Sheriff, Letter to Colonial Secretary, 30 October 1849, Colonial Secretary's Office, State Records, Adelaide; Sheriff, Report to Colonial Secretary, 14 November 1849, Colonial Secretary's Office, 2070 of 1849, State Records, Adelaide.
81. *R v Maingulta and Malgalta*, Supreme Court Criminal Sessions Record Book, 26 September 1849.
82. See Cooper CJ, Report to Governor, 27 October 1849, Colonial Secretary's Office, 2118 of 1847, State Records, Adelaide. See chapter 7 for details.
83. Protector of Aborigines, Report relative to native prisoners, 8 October 1849, Colonial Secretary's Office, 1850 of 1849, State Records, Adelaide.
84. Cooper CJ, Direction to jury in *R v Marripa et al.*, 10 February 1852, reported in *Register* 11 February 1852.
85. *R v Hinch*, Supreme Court Criminal Sessions Record Book, 19 March 1849.
86. ibid.
87. *Register*, 21 March 1849.
88. ibid.
89. ibid.
90. *Indictment Book*, 1849, Supreme Court Criminal Records.
91. Fisher, Comments in Supreme Court, 6 December 1849, reported in *Adelaide Observer*, 8 December 1849.
92. Crown Solicitor, Opening Address to Jury, Supreme Court, 13 August 1855, reported in *Adelaide Observer*, 18 August 1855.
93. See Supreme Court Criminal Records, 13 August 1855; *Register*, 14 August 1855; *Adelaide Observer*, 18 August 1855.
94. *R v Moongeltie and Cooliltie*, Supreme Court, 17 February 1860, reported in *Adelaide Chronicle*, 25 February 1860.
95. Advocate General, Note on docket, Colonial Secretary's Office, 1230 of 1852, State Records, Adelaide.
96. ibid.
97. See, for example, Sheriff, Letter to Colonial Secretary, 9 June 1852, Colonial Secretary's Office, 1733 of 1852, State Records, Adelaide.
98. Government Resident (Port Lincoln), Report, quoted in Protector of Aborigines, Report, 9 July 1850, *Government Gazette*, 18 July 1850.
99. C Driver, Report to Protector of Aborigines, 28 February 1851, in Protector of Aborigines, Report, 15 April 1851, Colonial Secretary's Office, 941 of 1851, State Records, Adelaide.

100. *R v Wamboureen*, Supreme Court Criminal Sessions Record Book, 18 March 1848.
101. G Butler, Letter to Advocate General, 21 February 1848, Advocate General's Office, 26 of 1848, State Records, Adelaide.
102. Protector of Aborigines, Evidence in *R v McDuff*, 30 January 1847, reported in *Register*, 3 February 1847 and *Adelaide Observer*, 6 February 1847.
103. Advocate General, Report to Colonial Secretary, 26 July 1849, Colonial Secretary's Office, 1388 of 1849, State Records, Adelaide.
104. Minutes of Evidence, *Report of the Select Committee on Aborigines*, op. cit., p. 80.

Chapter 5

1. Governor Gawler, 'Notes on Aborigines of the Murray', *Register*, 18 January 1840.
2. Bromley's book, published in Halifax in 1820, was titled *An Appeal to the Virtue and Good Sense of the Inhabitants of Great Britain, etc, on Behalf of the Indians of North America*. See W Unrau, 'An International Perspective on American Indian Policy: The South Australian Protector and Aborigines Protection Society', *Pacific History Review*, vol. 45, no. 4, 1976, p. 528.
3. W Bromley, Letter to Angas, September 1837, GF Angas Papers, A461, Mortlock Library, Adelaide.
4. Colonial Secretary, Official Instructions to William Wyatt, 11 August 1837, reprinted in *Register*, 12 August 1837.
5. ibid.
6. W Williams, *Vocabulary of the Language of The Aborigines*, extract quoted in *The Guardian*, 21 September 1839.
7. *The Guardian* said of this work: 'We think that every individual in the Colony who holds intercourse with our sable brethren, should possess a copy'. ibid.
8. CG Teichelmann and CW Schurmann, *Outlines of a grammar, vocabulary and phraseology of the Aboriginal Language of South Australia*, Adelaide, 1840.
9. ibid., p. v.
10. Advocate General, Letter to Colonial Secretary, 28 July 1837, Colonial Secretary's Office, 259 of 1837, State Records, Adelaide.
11. Cooper CJ, Comments in Supreme Court, 25 May 1839, reported in *Register*, 23 October 1839.
12. Advocate General, Memorandum re Native Evidence, 21 January 1847, Colonial Secretary's Office, 82 of 1847, State Records, Adelaide.
13. Police Court Proceedings, 29 August 1849, reported in *Register*, 1 September 1849.
14. *R v Morris and Jones*, Criminal Sessions Record Books, 17 September 1849.

15. Jimcrack's interpreting performance at this trial was impressive enough for him to be used as an interpreter in cases over the next decade.
16. *R v Morris and Jones*, op. cit.
17. *R v Pilgalta*, Criminal Sessions Record Books, 19 September 1846.
18. Government Resident (Port Lincoln), Letter to Advocate General, 6 June 1846, Advocate General's Office, State Records, Adelaide.
19. For example, in the Adelaide Local Court in 1853 Native Constable 'Paddy Smith' was found wanting, his evidence being 'not sufficiently intelligible to be further examined'. *Register*, 8 February 1853.
20. Padneltie and Popeltie were charged with the murder of Pinberri (Pinderri) at Franklin Harbour.
21. *Observer*, 12 December 1860.
22. Supreme Court Criminal Records, 6 December 1860.
23. *Register*, 7 December 1860.
24. Cooper CJ, Observations relating to the trial of native prisoners, 27 March 1847, op. cit.
25. Acting Judge Mann, Report to Colonial Secretary, 19 October 1849, Colonial Secretary's Office, 1908 of 1849, State Records, Adelaide.
26. *R v 'Charley'*, Police Commissioner's Court, 26 May, 31 May and 12 September 1845.
27. ibid.
28. Advocate General, Memorandum re Native Evidence, 21 January 1847, op. cit.
29. ibid.
30. Governor Robe, Despatch to Earl Grey, 10 March 1847, Governors' Despatches, State Records, Adelaide.
31. See also chapter 3.
32. Police Commissioner's Court, 12 May 1846, reported in *South Australian*, 15 May 1846.
33. *South Australian*, 12 and 15 May 1846; *South Australian*, 9 June 1846.
34. Criminal Sessions Record Books, 2 June 1846. See also Police Commissioner, Letter to Colonial Secretary, 8 August 1846, Colonial Secretary's Office, 979 of 1846, State Records, Adelaide.
35. Police Commissioner, Letter to Colonial Secretary, 2 June 1846, Police Outgoing Letter Book, 118 of 1846, State Records, Adelaide.
36. Proceedings in Police Commissioner's Court, 27 May 1846, reported in *Register*, 30 May 1846.
37. Criminal Sessions Record Books, 21 September 1846.
38. ibid.
39. See Advocate General, Letter to Colonial Secretary, 16 October 1846, Colonial Secretary's Office, 1276 of 1846, State Records, Adelaide.
40. *South Australian*, 21 September 1846.
41. Colonial Secretary, Letter to Protector of Aborigines, 10 December 1846, Colonial Secretary's Office, 1620 of 1846, State Records, Adelaide.

Notes

42. *Register*, 23 September 1846.
43. See chapter 3.
44. Namely, the Police Commissioner's Report of December 1846 and Moorhouse's report on the difficulty of interpreting the evidence of the three accused. Protector of Aborigines, Report for fourth quarter 1846, 8 February 1847, Colonial Secretary's Office, 32 of 1847, State Records, Adelaide.
45. Governor Robe, Despatch to Colonial Office, 9 March 1847, Governors' Despatches, State Records, Adelaide.
46. Cooper CJ, Letter to Colonial Secretary, 22 March 1847, op. cit.
47. Adelaide Police Court, 22 July 1846.
48. Also known as Ronkurri and 'Jemmy McLean'.
49. Cooper CJ, Report of Prisoners for Trial, November 1846, in Letter to Colonial Secretary, 7 December 1846, Colonial Secretary's Office, 1467 of 1846, State Records, Adelaide.
50. ibid.
51. Government Resident (Guichen Bay), Report to Colonial Secretary, 31 January 1847, Colonial Secretary's Office, 220 of 1847, State Records, Adelaide.
52. Supreme Court Criminal Sessions Record Book, 8 March 1847 and 20 November 1847.
53. Cooper CJ, Comments in Supreme Court, 8 March 1847, reported in *Observer*, 13 March 1847.
54. Advocate General, Report of Criminal Sessions, 16 September 1847, Colonial Secretary's Office, 1161 of 1847, State Records, Adelaide. See also *Observer*, 18 September 1847.
55. Correspondent to *Register*, 18 September 1847.
56. ibid.
57. Governor Robe, Note on Government Resident (Guichen Bay), Report, 31 January 1847, Colonial Secretary's Office, 220 of 1847, State Records, Adelaide.
58. See Master of Supreme Court, Return of prisoners for trial, 22 September 1847, Colonial Secretary's Office, 1190.5 of 1847, State Records, Adelaide. Duncan Smith was only fourteen years old when granted a stipend of twenty pounds per annum to interpret from Boandik to English. See Protector of Aborigines, Letter to Colonial Secretary, 21 March 1848, Colonial Secretary's Office, 375.5 of 1848, State Records, Adelaide.
59. Adelaide Gaol Records, State Records, Adelaide.
60. Government Resident (Guichen Bay), Report, 31 January 1847, op. cit.
61. Government Resident (Port Lincoln), Report, 2 July 1847, Colonial Secretary's Office, 992 of 1847, State Records, Adelaide.
62. Advocate General, Report of Criminal Sessions, 16 September 1847, op. cit.
63. Government Resident (Port Lincoln), Report, 2 July 1847, op. cit.

64. Mingulta was executed, along with Kingulta, on 9 November 1849 at Port Lincoln.
65. Supreme Court Criminal Sessions Record Book, 21 June 1848.
66. *Register*, 18 March 1848.
67. *Register*, 21 May 1851.
68. Supreme Court Criminal Sessions Record Book, 30 June 1849.
69. *Register*, 26 September 1849.
70. J Easton, Letter to *Register*, 3 October 1849.
71. Protector of Aborigines, Report, 10 June 1852, *Government Gazette*, 17 June 1852.
72. See *R v Kambalta*, Supreme Court Criminal Records, 21 August 1851 and 9 May 1852; *R v Parkilti et al*, Supreme Court Criminal Records, 10 May 1853.
73. The men charged were Parkilti, Pulyelta, Unmiltie, Kulbulto, Wiebmulta and Meekalta. Note: There is some confusion over the names of these men within the official records with each being referred to by another name, giving the incorrect impression that twelve men were charged. See Acting Government Resident (Port Lincoln), Report to Colonial Secretary, 27 July 1853, Colonial Secretary's Office, 2059 of 1853, State Records, Adelaide; *Register*, 11 May 1853; Supreme Court Criminal Records, 10 May 1853.
74. *Register*, 11 May 1853.
75. *R v Parkilti et al.*, op. cit.
76. J McDonald, Letter to Colonial Secretary, July 1852, Colonial Secretary's Office, 1793 of 1852, State Records, Adelaide.
77. Police Commissioner, Report for second quarter 1853, *Government Gazette*, 11 August 1853.
78. Cooper CJ, Comments in Supreme Court, 8 March 1847, op. cit.
79. *R v Ninchulta*, Clare District Court, 21 July 1855 reported in *Register*, 25 July 1855.
80. Magistrate William Robinson, Comment in Clare District Court, 21 July 1855, reported in *Register*, 25 July 1855.
81. Supreme Court Criminal Records, 12 August 1859.
82. Holroyd, Report, October 1859, reprinted in *Observer*, 8 October 1859.
83. See also *R v Mannancowie*, Supreme Court Criminal Records, 18 May 1860.

Chapter 6

1. *R v Congo Murrell* 1836, reported in J Hookey, 1984, op. cit.
2. *R v Bonjon*, Melbourne, 1841. See B Bridges 1973, op. cit., p. 267.
3. Australian Law Reform Commission, Report no. 31, *The recognition of Aboriginal customary laws: summary report*, Canberra 1986, p. 5.

4. In April 1838, Eli-a was found guilty of the murder of another Aboriginal person. Governor Stirling could see little point in applying the death sentence and convinced the Executive Council to commute Eli-a's sentence. See B Reece, 'Laws of the white people: the frontier of authority in early Western Australia', in B Hocking (ed), *International law and Aboriginal human rights*, Melbourne, 1988, p. 111.
5. The latter submitted it for publication in the local press.
6. G Grey, 'Notes on the treatment of Aborigines', 1840, op. cit.
7. ibid.
8. ibid.
9. ibid.
10. ibid.
11. Correspondent to *Register*, 4 November 1840.
12. See R Cranston 1973, op. cit., p. 62.
13. See E Eyre, Report, 20 January 1844, Colonial Secretary's Office, 111 of 1844, State Records, Adelaide.
14. Rallooloolyoo was also known as Ronkurri but preferred his adopted name of 'Jemmy McLean' when dealing with Europeans.
15. Cooper CJ, Comments in Supreme Court, 24 November 1846, reported in *Register*, 25 November 1846.
16. Cooper CJ, 'Observations relating to the trial of native prisoners', 27 March 1847, Colonial Secretary's Office, 383.5 of 1847, State Records, Adelaide.
17. Cooper CJ, Comments in Supreme Court, 24 November 1846, op. cit.
18. ibid.
19. ibid.
20. Bartley, Argument in Supreme Court, 26 November 1846, reported in *Register*, 28 November 1846.
21. Cooper CJ, Letter to Colonial Secretary, 22 March 1847, op. cit.
22. See *R v Biddeah et al* 1846, Supreme Court Criminal Sessions Record Book, 22 September 1846. See chapter 7.
23. Supreme Court Criminal Sessions Record Book, 15 September 1847.
24. 'Viator', Letter to *Register*, 8 December 1847.
25. Supreme Court Criminal Sessions Record Book, 16 June 1848.
26. Bartley, Argument in Supreme Court, 16 June 1848, reported in *South Australian*, 20 June 1848.
27. Cooper CJ, Comments in Supreme Court, 16 June 1848, reported in *South Australian*, 20 June 1848.
28. Cooper CJ, Comments in Supreme Court, 4 December 1849, reported in *Gazette and Mining Journal*, 6 December 1849.
29. ibid.

Notes

30. Protector of Aborigines, quoted in Robe to Earl Grey, 10 July 1848, Governors' Despatches, State Records, Adelaide.
31. Governor Robe to Earl Grey, 10 July 1848, op. cit.
32. Editorial, *Gazette and Mining Journal*, 24 June 1848.
33. ibid.
34. ibid.
35. Editorial, *Gazette and Mining Journal*, 1 September 1849.
36. ibid.
37. *R v Kambalta*, Supreme Court Criminal Sessions Record Book, 29 January 1849.
38. See Acting Judge Mann, Report of prisoners for trial, 13 April 1849, Colonial Secretary's Office, State Records, Adelaide, 708 of 849, State Records, Adelaide. Kambalta led something of a charmed life. Arrested in 1851 for the murder of Charles Crocker, he was released without penalty. In 1852 he was charged with stealing from the Salt Creek Police Station but local residents persuaded the authorities not to proceed on the grounds that a trial was likely to stir up further Aboriginal resistance within the Port Lincoln district.
39. The victim was also known as 'Mary'.
40. Supreme Court Criminal Sessions Record Book, 4 December 1849.
41. Advocate General, Comments in Supreme Court, 4 December 1849, reported in *South Australian*, 7 December 1849.
42. ibid.
43. ibid.
44. Cooper CJ, Comments in Supreme Court, 4 December 1849, op. cit.
45. Supreme Court Criminal Sessions Record Book,, 4 December 1849.
46. Also named 'Tommy Ross' in records.
47. Supreme Court Criminal Records, 10–12 February 1851. It is not clear what reasons lay behind this abandonment of the prosecution.
48. Also named as Tukkuru, Ngalta Wikkanni and Kanguworli in some accounts.
49. Supreme Court Criminal Records, 19 May 1851. Some reports suggest that three men were thus sentenced but this can be attributed to confusion over Ngalta Wikkanni's name, giving the impression that he was two separate men.
50. Supreme Court Criminal Records, 20 May 1851.
51. Editorial, *Register*, 7 June 1851.
52. Government Resident, Quarterly Return, 12 June 1851, Colonial Secretary's Office, CSO 1825 of 1851, State Records, Adelaide.
53. ibid.
54. Presentment of Grand Jury, Supreme Court, 15 May 1851. See *Register*, 16 May 1851.
55. See G Taylor, *A Great and Glorious Reformation: Six Early South Australian Legal Innovations*, Wakefield Press, Adelaide, 2005, pp. 53–8 for detailed

Notes

discussion of the Grand Jury's presentment, which Taylor lists as an early 'call for the recognition of Aboriginal customary law' (p. 57).
56. Government Resident, Quarterly Return, 12 June 1851, op. cit.
57. ibid.
58. ibid.
59. ibid.
60. ibid.
61. See S Lendrum 1976, op. cit., pp. 71–2; G Taylor, op. cit., pp. 56–7.
62. Cooper CJ, Reply to Grand Jury, Supreme Court, 15 May 1851. See *Register*, 16 May 1851.
63. ibid.
64. ibid.
65. Cooper CJ, Statement in Summary, Supreme Court, 19 May 1851, reported in *Register*, 20 May 1851.
66. *R v Tukkurm et al.*, Supreme Court Criminal Records, 19 May 1851.
67. *Gazette and Mining Journal*, 15 May 1851.
68. ibid.
69. *Register*, 17 May 1851.
70. ibid.
71. Cooper CJ, Letter to Colonial Secretary, 26 May 1851, Colonial Secretary's Office, 1564 of 1851, State Records, Adelaide.
72. Cooper CJ, Letter to Colonial Secretary, 10 June 1851, Colonial Secretary's Office, 1727 of 1851, State Records, Adelaide.
73. See J Jickling, Report of Supreme Court Proceedings, 26 May 1851, Colonial Secretary's Office, 1560 of 1851, State Records, Adelaide; Advocate General, Letter to Colonial Secretary, 13 June 1851, Colonial Secretary's Office, 1752 of 1851, State Records, Adelaide.
74. *R v Ballycrack et al*, Supreme Court Criminal Records, 11–13 August 1852.
75. This did not prove to be a long sentence as all three were pardoned in late November 1854, on grounds of failing health. Ballycrack died within days of his release. See Protector's Report, 5 March 1855 in *Government Gazette*, 8 March 1855.
76. Watte Watte had attended the Location School and was widely known in Adelaide.
77. Protector of Aborigines, Evidence at Inquest, 7 April 1853, reported in *Register*, 8 April 1853.
78. Evidence of Tainmunda, Supreme Court, 10 May 1853, reported in *Observer*, 14 May 1853.
79. ibid.
80. *Register*, 11 May 1853.
81. Cooper CJ, Sentencing remarks, Supreme Court Criminal Records, 10 May 1853.
82. *Register*, 28 May 1853.

Notes

83. ibid.
84. ibid.
85. Supreme Court Criminal Records, 12 December 1853.
86. Tinkanor died in custody in December 1854 even though he had already been pardoned on grounds of illness.
87. Supreme Court Criminal Records, 17 February 1855.
88. ibid.
89. *Observer*, 10 February 1855.
90. Supreme Court Criminal Records, 24 May 1855.
91. Supreme Court Criminal Records, 13 August 1855.
92. Crown Solicitor, Summation, Supreme Court, 13 August 1855, reported in *Observer*, 18 August 1855.
93. Boothby J, Summation, Supreme Court, 13 August 1855, reported in *Register*, 14 August 1855.
94. ibid.
95. 'Mary' was killed on 21 September 1855. See *Register*, 30 November 1855.
96. Supreme Court Criminal Records, 29 November 1855; *Observer*, 1 December 1855.
97. J Boothby, Summation, Supreme Court, 29 November 1855, reported in *Observer*, 1 December 1855.
98. ibid.
99. ibid.
100. *Register*, 20 August 1859.
101. Supreme Court Criminal Records, 19 August 1859.
102. *Advertiser*, 3 October 1859.
103. Supreme Court Criminal Records, 6 December 1860.
104. *Observer*, 12 December 1860.
105. Supreme Court Criminal Records, 6 December 1860.
106. Supreme Court Criminal Records, List of prisoners for trial, 10 August 1857.
107. Supreme Court Criminal Records, 17 August 1857; *Observer*, 22 August 1857.
108. Interestingly, this was the first case in which the defence of drunkenness was raised. Acting Judge Mann was at pains to express his concern about the supply of alcohol to Aboriginal people. He named the Everly Inn, where these two men had allegedly obtained the liquor, and urged the authorities to prevent such sales. *Observer*, 22 August 1857.
109. See Supreme Court Criminal Records, 17 and 21 August 1857.
110. Supreme Court Criminal Records, 17 August 1857.
111. Supreme Court Criminal Records, 18 February 1859.
112. ibid.
113. Fisher, Supreme Court, 15 March 1859, reported in *Chronicle*, 21 May 1859.

114. J Gwynne, Supreme Court, 15 March 1859, reported in *Chronicle*, 21 May 1859.
115. *Advertiser*, 17 May 1859; *Chronicle*, 21 May 1859.
116. Legislative Council, Enquiry into Aborigines, 1860, *Minutes of Evidence*, p. 75.
117. ibid.
118. ibid., p. 98.
119. Bishop of Adelaide, Letter to *Register*, 23 November 1857.
120. Police Commissioner, Response to Bishop of Adelaide, *Register*, 23 November 1857.

Chapter 7

1. See P Baille, *Port Lincoln and District: A Pictorial History*, Blackwood, 1978.
2. *Southern Australian*, 29 March 1842.
3. See Government Resident (Port Lincoln), Letter to Colonial Secretary Colonial Secretary's Office, 21 October 1840, 552 of 1840, State Records, Adelaide.
4. See *Adelaide Examiner*, 7 April 1842, 7 and 14 September 1842; Protector of Aborigines, Report, 23 June 1842, Colonial Secretary's Office, 483 of 1842, State Records, Adelaide.
5. Government Resident (Port Lincoln), Letter to Colonial Secretary, 5 October 1840, op. cit.
6. Nantes was sentenced to three months' imprisonment and a public whipping of seventy-five lashes. Supreme Court Criminal Sessions Record Book, 7 September 1842.
7. Supreme Court Criminal Sessions Record Book, 9 September 1842.
8. Protector of Aborigines, Report, 2 July 1845, *Government Gazette*, 17 July 1845.
9. Cooper CJ, Notes in *Judges' Notebook*, 1842, Supreme Court, Adelaide.
10. Supreme Court , *Indictments Book*, 1842.
11. ibid.
12. Supreme Court Criminal Sessions Record Book, 23 March 1843. See also Advocate General, Letter to Colonial Secretary, 24 March 1843, Colonial Secretary's Office, 423 of 1843, State Records, Adelaide.
13. See note made by Governor Grey on Government Resident's Report, 7 April 1843, Colonial Secretary's Office, 504 of 1843, State Records, Adelaide; Government Resident, Report, 1 May 1843, Colonial Secretary's Office, 582 of 1843, State Records, Adelaide.
14. Supreme Court Criminal Sessions Record Book, 20 July 1843.
15. See Protector of Aborigines, Report, 30 June 1842, op. cit.
16. Supreme Court Criminal Sessions Record Book, 13 and 14 March 1845.
17. Adelaide Gaol Records, 1845, State Records, Adelaide.

Notes

18. Supreme Court Criminal Sessions Record Book, 10 June 1845. Wekiweki was reprieved by order of the Governor on 23 June 1845.
19. Supreme Court Criminal Sessions Record Book, 8 March 1847, 20 and 27 November 1847.
20. See chapter 5 for a discussion of this point.
21. Protector of Aborigines, Report, 8 November 1847, Colonial Secretary's Office, 1416 of 1847, State Records, Adelaide.
22. See *Research Notes*, no. 252, Mortlock Library, Adelaide.
23. See *Register*, 1 December 1847; *Observer*, 18 September 1847 and 4 December 1847; *South Australian*, 19 March 1847.
24. Supreme Court Criminal Sessions Record Book, 18 March 1848.
25. Criminal Sessions Record Book, 22 September 1846.
26. Cooper CJ, Letter to Colonial Secretary, 22 March 1847, Colonial Secretary's Office, 351 of 1847, State Records, Adelaide.
27. Nakundah was later charged with (and acquitted of) the murder of 'Charley'.
28. Protector of Aborigines, Report, 4 July 1849, Colonial Secretary's Office, 1271 of 1849, State Records, Adelaide.
29. Police Commissioner, Quarterly Report, 27 July 1848, Colonial Secretary's Office, 1156 of 1848, State Records, Adelaide. See also Government Resident (Port Lincoln), Report, 17 July 1848, Colonial Secretary's Office, 1127 of 1848, State Records, Adelaide.
30. Police Commissioner, Quarterly Report, 27 July 1848, op. cit.
31. Protector of Aborigines, Report, 16 July 1849, Colonial Secretary's Office, 1317 of 1849, State Records, Adelaide.
32. *South Australian*, 28 September 1849.
33. Acting Judge Mann, Report to Colonial Secretary, Colonial Secretary's Office, in 2118 of 1849, State Records, Adelaide.
34. Criminal Sessions Record Book, 22 September 1849.
35. Cooper CJ, Report to Governor, 27 October 1849, Colonial Secretary's Office, in 2118 of 1849, State Records, Adelaide.
36. Acting Judge Mann, Letter to Colonial Secretary, Colonial Secretary's Office, 1900 of 1849, State Records, Adelaide.
37. Note on Cooper CJ, Report to Governor, 27 October 1849, op. cit.
38. Criminal Sessions Record Book, 25 September 1849.
39. *Register*, editorial, 15 August 1849.
40. See, for example, Hobbs, Letter to *Register*, 9 June 1849.
41. Government Resident (Port Lincoln), Report, 1 October 1849, Colonial Secretary's Office, 1906 of 1849, State Records, Adelaide.
42. See *Register*, 26 September 1849.
43. See *Gazette and Mining Journal*, 17 May 1849; *Observer*, 19 May 1849.
44. Criminal Sessions Record Book, 25 September 1849.
45. *Register*, 26 September 1849.
46. *Register*, 17 November 1849.

47. Protector of Aborigines, Report, 4 July 1849, Colonial Secretary's Office, 1271 of 1849, State Records, Adelaide.
48. Government Resident (Port Lincoln), Report to Colonial Secretary, 16 May 1849, Colonial Secretary's Office, 947 of 1849, State Records, Adelaide.
49. Two men and one woman; Police Commissioner, Report, 31 July 1849, Colonial Secretary's Office, 1401 of 1849, State Records, Adelaide.
50. See Protector of Aborigines, Report, 16 July 1849, Colonial Secretary's Office, 1317 of 1849, State Records, Adelaide.
51. *Register*, 27 September 1849.
52. Criminal Sessions Record Book, 25 September 1849.
53. Criminal Sessions Record Book, 11 March 1850.
54. *Register*, 28 July 1849.
55. Criminal Sessions Record Book, 11 March 1850; Protector of Aborigines, Report, 10 April 1850, *Government Gazette*, 18 April 1850.
56. See Protector of Aborigines, Report, 2 October 1851, Colonial Secretary's Office, 713 of 1851, State Records, Adelaide; Protector of Aborigines, Report for final quarter 1851, *Government Gazette*, 5 February 1852.
57. Protector of Aborigines, Report for final quarter 1851, op. cit.
58. Supreme Court Criminal Records, 10 February 1852.
59. One source (*Register*, 11 February 1852) puts the sentences as six months and three months but the Supreme Court Criminal Records (10 February 1852) show them as twelve and six months respectively.
60. Police Commissioner, Report, 27 May 1851, Colonial Secretary's Office, 1577 of 1851, State Records, Adelaide.
61. Police Commissioner, Report, 29 April 1851, Colonial Secretary's Office, 1306 of 1851, State Records, Adelaide.
62. *Register*, 25 August 1851.
63. Protector of Aborigines, Report, 21 July 1851, *Government Gazette*, 24 July 1851.
64. *Register*, 25 August 1851.
65. Government Resident (Port Lincoln), Report, 31 May 1851, Colonial Secretary's Office, 1744 of 1851, State Records, Adelaide.
66. Police Commissioner, Report, 29 April 1851, op. cit.
67. See Supreme Court Criminal Records, 10 May 1857 and 22–23 August 1857.
68. Supreme Court Criminal Records, 5 October 1857.
69. *Chronicle*, 25 February 1860.
70. Police Commissioner, Report, 27 May 1851, Colonial Secretary's Office, 1577 of 1851, State Records, Adelaide; Protector of Aborigines, Report, 10 June 1852, Colonial Secretary's Office, 1711 of 1852, State Records, Adelaide.

Notes

71. Geharty's rank changed from Sergeant to Corporal as he was demoted at various times, for disciplinary reasons.
72. See Police Commissioner, Report, 27 May 1851, op. cit.
73. For example, Driver considered Kamalta to be 'a peaceful and obliging black'. Protector of Aborigines, Report, 10 June 1852, op. cit.
74. Supreme Court Criminal Records, 22 August 1851.
75. Government Resident (Port Lincoln), Report, in Protector of Aborigines, Report, 21 July 1851, ibid.
76. Supreme Court, *Indictments Book*, 1851–1854.
77. Protector of Aborigines, Report, 31 May 1851, Colonial Secretary's Office, 1744 of 1851, State Records, Adelaide.
78. Supreme Court Criminal Records, 22 August 1851.
79. See *Register*, 25 August 1851.
80. Government Resident (Port Lincoln), Report, in Protector of Aborigines, Report, 10 June 1852, op. cit.
81. It may be significant that Henry Baird had been living with an Aboriginal woman, who also had lived briefly with one of Baird's early employees. This women left just before the attacks, going off with an Aboriginal companion, after 'some misunderstanding'. Police Commissioner, Report, 2 December 1850, Colonial Secretary's Office, 2726 of 1850, State Records, Adelaide.
82. Townsend, Statement, 7 November 1850, included in Police Commissioner, Report, 2 December 1850, ibid.
83. Police Commissioner, Report, 27 November 1850, Colonial Secretary's Office, 2660 of 1850, State Records, Adelaide.
84. Police Commissioner, Report, 2 December 1850, op. cit.
85. Government Resident (Port Lincoln), Report, 22 November 1850, Colonial Secretary's Office, 2653 of 1850, State Records, Adelaide.
86. Geharty, Report, *Government Gazette*, 30 January 1851.
87. Governor, Note on Police Commissioner's Report, 27 November 1850, op. cit.
88. Geharty, Journal extract (19–25 November 1850), attachment to Police Commissioner and Protector of Aborigines, Report to Colonial Secretary, 16 January 1851, *Government Gazette*, 30 January 1851.
89. Supreme Court Criminal Records, 10 February 1851.
90. *Register*, 21 May 1851.
91. McDonald JP, Letter to Colonial Secretary, 14 April 1852, Colonial Secretary's Office, 1230 of 1852, State Records, Adelaide.
92. McDonald JP, Letter to Colonial Secretary, 17 May 1852, Colonial Secretary's Office, 1513 of 1852, State Records, Adelaide.
93. Protector of Aborigines, Letter to Colonial Secretary, 29 May 1852, Colonial Secretary's Office, 1607 of 1852, State Records, Adelaide.

94. Sheriff, Letter to Colonial Secretary, 9 June 1852, Colonial Secretary's Office, 1733 of 1852, State Records, Adelaide.
95. Protector of Aborigines, Report, 10 June 1852, Colonial Secretary's Office, 1711 of 1852, State Records, Adelaide.
96. See J McKechnie, Letter to Colonial Secretary, 8 December 1855, Colonial Secretary's Office, 4004 of 1855, State Records, Adelaide.
97. Police Commissioner, Report, 4 June 1855, Colonial Secretary's Office, 2041 of 1855, State Records, Adelaide.
98. Protector of Aborigines, Report, 21 August 1855, *Government Gazette*, 20 September 1855.
99. Supreme Court Criminal Records, 7 December 1855.
100. *Observer*, 8 December 1855.
101. *Observer*, 26 May 1860.
102. Supreme Court Criminal Records, 13 and 17 August 1860.
103. Malkiltie, Poongunyah (aka Poonganya) and Kangnalla.
104. Supreme Court Criminal Records, 6 December 1860.
105. Boothby J, Entry in *Judge's Note Book*, December 1860, Supreme Court, Adelaide.
106. *Observer*, 8 December 1860.
107. Supreme Court Criminal Records, 12 August 1861.
108. ibid.
109. The other three were Pilta Miltinda, Monnaitya and Tanka Worta.
110. Supreme Court Criminal Records, 16 May 1861. Warretya was released two days later.
111. *Advertiser*, 20 May 1861.
112. Supreme Court Criminal Records, 17 May 1861.
113. See *Register*, 20 May 1861; *Advertiser*, 20, 25 and 26 March, 1861.
114. Supreme Court Criminal Records, 12 and 15 August 1861.
115. *Advertiser*, 27 and 28 August 1861.
116. A Murray, Letter to *Advertiser*, 27 August 1861.
117. *Advertiser*, 11 September 1861.
118. See *Advertiser*, 25 March 1862 and *Observer*, 29 March 1862.
119. *Register*, 15 August 1862.
120. Supreme Court Criminal Records, 14 August 1862.
121. This total includes the two men (Moorcangua and Mongarawata) executed under military law at Pilgaru in 1840.

Chapter 8

1. For example, all theft cases involving goods over the value of five pounds and all assaults on Europeans were so required to be remanded. See Colonial Secretary, Letter to Advocate General, 23 December 1848, op. cit.

2. See Protector of Aborigines, Report for final quarter 1844, 10 January 1845, Colonial Secretary's Office, 35 of 1845, State Records, Adelaide; Protector of Aborigines, Report for final quarter 1843, 4 January 1844, Colonial Secretary's Office, 20 of 1844, State Records, Adelaide.
3. See Protector of Aborigines, Report, 14 March 1842, Colonial Secretary's Office, 38 of 1842, State Records, Adelaide.
4. Protector of Aborigines, Report for final quarter 1843, op. cit.
5. See Protector of Aborigines, Letter to Colonial Secretary, 14 March 1839, Colonial Secretary's Office, 39 of 1839, State Records, Adelaide; Protector of Aborigines, Report, 10 February 1842, Colonial Secretary's Office, 32 of 1842, State Records, Adelaide.
6. *Adelaide Chronicle*, editorial, 3 February 1841.
7. Correspondent to *Register*, 4 February 1843.
8. Adelaide Gaol Register, 15 February 1840, State Records, Adelaide.
9. Adelaide Police Court Proceedings, 7 February 1843.
10. Protector of Aborigines, Report for second quarter, 8 July 1843, Colonial Secretary's Office, 812 of 1843, State Records, Adelaide.
11. Correspondent to *Register*, 30 January 1841.
12. Stutely, Evidence in Supreme Court, 5 July 1844 reported in *Register*, 6 July 1844.
13. *Register*, 18 May 1844.
14. *Register*, 11 May 1844.
15. *Register*, 3 July 1844.
16. Willis, Evidence in Police Commissioner's Court, 2 May 1844 reported in *Register*, 25 May 1844.
17. See A Pope, 'Aboriginal adaptation to early colonial labour markets', *Journal of Labour History*, no. 54, May 1988, pp. 1–15.
18. 'Jemmy' was fined £4 but, unable to pay, he was sent to prison for one month. He escaped from the Adelaide Gaol after serving one day and was not seen in town again. Adelaide Gaol Records, December 1840, State Records, Adelaide.
19. *Register*, 11 February 1843.
20. *Register*, 5 April 1843.
21. *Register*, 31 July 1844.
22. *Register*, 19 April 1848.
23. *Observer*, 22 April 1848.
24. Proceedings in Adelaide Police Court, 23 December 1848 reported in *Register*, 27 December 1848 and *Observer*, 30 December 1848.
25. Supreme Court Criminal Sessions Record Book, 16 March 1849.
26. Adelaide Gaol Records, 1850, State Records, Adelaide.
27. Supreme Court Criminal Sessions Record Book, 25 September 1849.
28. ibid.
29. Supreme Court Criminal Sessions Record Book, 28 November 1849.
30. Supreme Court Criminal Sessions Record Book, 13 March 1850.

31. ibid.
32. *Gazette and Mining Journal*, 2 February 1847.
33. ibid.
34. Supreme Court Criminal Sessions Record Book, 14 June 1849.
35. *Gazette and Mining Journal*, 16 June 1849.
36. Supreme Court Criminal Sessions Record Book, 14 June 1849.
37. *Register*, 25 June 1850.
38. Supreme Court Criminal Sessions Record Book, 12 August 1850.
39. Supreme Court Criminal Sessions Record Book, 14 August 1850. Bagnall was found murdered the following year.
40. Supreme Court Criminal Records, 4 August 1851.
41. *Register*, August 15 1851
42. Supreme Court Criminal Records, 14 August 1851
43. Sub-Protector of Aborigines, Report, 11 July 1853, Colonial Secretary's Office, 1692 of 1853, State Records, Adelaide.
44. Protector of Aborigines, Note on Sub-Protector of Aborigines, Report, ibid.
45. Protector of Aborigines, Report for second quarter, 17 July 1849, op. cit. Later in the same year, Yengki was arrested on suspicion of being involved in the Beevor murder but again no solid evidence could be produced.
46. Supreme Court Criminal Records, 10 May 1853.
47. *Observer*, 8 October 1859.
48. *Advertiser*, 29 September 1859.
49. *Observer*, 8 October 1859; *Chronicle*, 1 October 1859.
50. Supreme Court Criminal Records, 22 November 1852.
51. See *Advertiser*, 20 August 1860.
52. Supreme Court, *Indictment Book*, 1858–61.
53. It seems that Bungillo was found not guilty on this earlier charge.
54. Supreme Court Criminal Records, 12 August 1859.
55. Supreme Court Criminal Sessions Record Book, 19 September 1846.
56. Protector of Aborigines, Letter to Colonial Secretary, 5 October 1846.
57. Government Resident (Port Lincoln), Report, quoted in Protector of Aborigines, Report, 31 October 1850.
58. Defence counsel Stow unsuccessfully argued that Manancowie had not been cautioned at the time of his arrest and that he could not have understood the caution in any event.
59. *Advertiser*, 15 August 1860.
60. The witnesses were Remilibilleth, Whowilliama and Manyunkle.
61. One suggestion was that Manancowie had only confessed after being advised to do so by a settler.
62. Supreme Court Criminal Records, 13 August 1860.
63. Supreme Court Criminal Records, 14 August 1860.
64. Proceedings in Adelaide Local Court reported in *Register*, 1 January 1857 and *Observer*, 3 January 1857.

Notes

65. The case was heard in the Mt Remarkable Police Court on 29 March 1860.
66. *Observer*, 7 April 1860.
67. This case was heard in the Robe Police Court on 26 July 1859 and reported in *Register*, 5 August 1859.
68. *Southern Australian*, 18 February 1842. The sentence was a fine of five pounds.
69. See Protector of Aborigines, Report for final quarter 1844, 10 January 1845, op. cit.
70. Government Resident (Port Lincoln), Report, 2 April 1846, Colonial Secretary's Office, 411 of 1846, State Records, Adelaide.
71. Adelaide Police Court, 11 May 1849.
72. *Observer*, 12 May 1849.
73. Protector of Aborigines, Report, 16 May 1854, *Government Gazette*, 25 May 1854.
74. *Register*, 31 May 1854.
75. Adelaide Local Court, 16 August 1854.
76. *Register*, 17 August 1854.
77. *Observer*, 7 July 1860.
78. ibid.
79. Government Resident (Port Lincoln), Report, 31 May 1851, Colonial Secretary's Office, 1744 of 1851, State Records, Adelaide.
80. Sub-Protector (Port Lincoln), Report, included in Protector of Aborigines, Report, 21 August 1855, *Government Gazette*, 20 September 1855.
81. ibid.
82. Government Resident (Port Lincoln), Report, 1 June 1850, Colonial Secretary's Office, 1322 of 1850, State Records, Adelaide.
83. Supreme Court Criminal Sessions Record Book, 3 September 1849.

Chapter 9

1. See Colonial Secretary, Letter to Advocate General, 23 December 1848, op. cit.
2. Supreme Court Criminal Sessions Record Book, 2 May 1842.
3. Supreme Court Criminal Sessions Record Book, 6 November 1841.
4. *Register*, 6 February 1841.
5. *Register*, 20 May 1852.
6. Adelaide Police Court, 19 May 1852.
7. *Register*, 24 February 1843.
8. *Southern Australian*, 15 May 1839.
9. Supreme Court Criminal Sessions Record Book, 20 March 1843.
10. Reverend Newland, *Register*, 3 July 1843.
11. *Southern Australian*, editorial, 19 July 1843.
12. Protector of Aborigines, Report, 13 January 1852, Colonial Secretary's Office, 160 of 1852, State Records, Adelaide.

13. Governor Young, Note on Protector of Aborigines, Report, 13 January 1852, ibid.
14. See Protector of Aborigines, Letter to Colonial Secretary, 5 February 1852, Colonial Secretary's Office, 503 of 1852, State Records, Adelaide.
15. Police Commissioner, Report to Colonial Secretary, 27 May 1851, Colonial Secretary's Office, 1577 of 1851, State Records, Adelaide.
16. Protector of Aborigines, Report for second quarter, 12 April 1843, Colonial Secretary's Office, 495 of 1843, State Records, Adelaide.
17. C Driver, quoted in Protector of Aborigines, Report for second quarter, 2 July 1845, Colonial Secretary's Office, 739 of 1845, State Records, Adelaide.
18. Police Commissioner, Letter to Colonial Secretary, 26 October 1849, Colonial Secretary's Office, 1945 of 1849, State Records, Adelaide.
19. Correspondent to *Register*, 11 May 1839.
20. Adelaide Gaol Records, State Records, Adelaide.
21. *South Australian*, 24 August 1850.
22. Supreme Court Criminal Sessions Record Book, 14 August 1850.
23. Supreme Court Criminal Records, 11 August 1851.
24. ibid.
25. Supreme Court Criminal Records, 13 August 1851.
26. *Register*, 14 August 1851.
27. Protector of Aborigines, Report, 17 December 1855, Colonial Secretary's Office, 1579 of 1855, State Records, Adelaide.
28. *Observer*, 19 July 1862.
29. *Register*, 19 June 1841.
30. *Southern Australian*, 20 August 1844.
31. ibid.
32. Supreme Court Criminal Sessions Record Book, 14 September 1846.
33. 'Charley' was arrested as the alleged ringleader of the raiding group.
34. Police Commissioner's Court, 26 and 31 May 1845.
35. Supreme Court *Indictment Book*, 1845–46.
36. *Southern Australian*, 20 August 1844.
37. Correspondent to *Register*, 4 June 1845.
38. *Gazette and Mining Journal*, 18 September 1847.
39. *Observer*, 3 November 1855.
40. 'Ned' Tittawitta, 'Johnny Gumflat', 'Johnny Pointpiercer', Yelluna, Wodla and Kanyanni.
41. Supreme Court Criminal Records, 1 November 1855 and 18 February 1856.
42. Supreme Court Criminal Sessions Record Book, 12 March 1847.
43. Cooper CJ, Letter to Colonial Secretary, 22 March 1847, Colonial Secretary's Office, 351 of 1847, State Records, Adelaide.
44. Malia (1), Malia (2), Pedia, Coonie (1), Coonie (2) and Warrie.
45. *Indictment Book*, 1852, Supreme Court Criminal Records.

Notes

46. *Register*, 19 January 1853.
47. See McDonald JP, Letter to Colonial Secretary, 31 January 1853, Colonial Secretary's Office, 327 of 1853, State Records, Adelaide.
48. Police Commissioner, Report, 27 November 1850, Colonial Secretary's Office, 2660 of 1850, State Records, Adelaide.
49. Supreme Court Criminal Records, 10 February 1851.
50. *Indictment Book*, 1855, Supreme Court Criminal Records.
51. *Register*, 3 July 1844.
52. Police Commissioner's Court, 2 July 1844.
53. See *Register*, 6 July 1844.
54. Supreme Court Criminal Records, 24 August 1851.
55. Supreme Court Criminal Records, 17 May 1860.
56. Supreme Court *Indictment Book*, 1851.
57. Supreme Court Criminal Records, 22 June 1852.
58. Supreme Court Criminal Sessions Record Book, 24 September 1849.
59. ibid.
60. Yarngalta (two years gaol), Yabmanna (three months gaol) and Wirao (three months gaol). Supreme Court Criminal Records, 24 September 1849.
61. See R Foster, R Hoskings and A Nettleback, op. cit, pp. 47–73.
62. *Register*, 12 August 1850. In this case, the prosecution was abandoned when Simms reneged on his earlier decision to allow his men to attend as witnesses.
63. Supreme Court Criminal Sessions Record Book, 25 November 1850. Here also the prosecution had to be abandoned.
64. Advocate General, Letter to Colonial Secretary, 20 April 1846, Colonial Secretary's Office, 411 of 1846, State Records, Adelaide.
65. Government Resident (Port Lincoln), Reply to Colonial Secretary, 27 May 1846, Colonial Secretary's Office, 741 of 1846, State Records, Adelaide.
66. This proved to be unfortunate for Nganti, as in 1846 he was injured when several logs of wood rolled on him. Government Resident, Report, 10 October 1846, Colonial Secretary's Office, 1283 of 1846, State Records, Adelaide.
67. *Register*, 31 March 1851.
68. Ngalta, Tantultara, Watpa and Mantamornappa.
69. Supreme Court Criminal Records, 14 August 1851.
70. Government Resident (Port Lincoln), Report, 27 July 1853, Colonial Secretary's Office, 2059 of 1853, State Records, Adelaide.
71. Parkilti, Puyelta, Unmiltie, Kulbulto, Wiebmulta and Meekalta.
72. See Supreme Court Criminal Records, 10 May 1853; *Register*, 11 May 1853; *Observer*, 14 May 1853.
73. Sub-Protector, Report to Protector, *Government Gazette*, 25 May 1854.
74. Mantelta, Mingilti, Nairoo and Kooralgidme.

75. Supreme Court Criminal Records, 10 April 1854.
76. Government Resident (Port Lincoln), Report, 21 August 1855, Colonial Secretary's Office, 2457 of 1855, State Records, Adelaide. Both men escaped from the Port Lincoln Lockup on 2 June 1855 — Nepulto was recaptured three days later but Meewulta remained free.
77. *Indictment Book*, 1842, Supreme Court Criminal Records.
78. Also known as Kurse, Kertameru and 'Jemmy'.
79. Supreme Court Criminal Records, 9 November 1842.
80. Adelaide Gaol Records, 1842, State Records, Adelaide.
81. Protector of Aborigines, Report for final quarter 1843, 4 January 1844, Colonial Secretary's Office, 20 of 1844, State Records, Adelaide.
82. Also known as Nyarroykypper and 'Jack'.
83. Supreme Court Criminal Sessions Record Book, 9 May 1844.
84. Supreme Court Criminal Sessions Record Book, 16 March 1848.
85. Supreme Court Criminal Records, 24 November 1851.
86. C Driver, Letter to Advocate General, 12 July 1842, Advocate General's Office, State Records, Adelaide.
87. Advocate General, Letter to C Driver, 14 July 1842, Advocate General's Office, State Records, Adelaide.
88. Police Commissioner, Letter to Advocate General, 28 July 1845, Advocate General's Office, State Records, Adelaide.
89. See *Register*, 5 December 1849.
90. E Sturt, Letter to Colonial Secretary, 25 March 1847, Colonial Secretary's Office, 444 of 1847, State Records, Adelaide.
91. ibid.
92. Supreme Court Criminal Sessions Record Book, 28 November 1849.
93. Cooper CJ, Statement in Supreme Court, 28 November 1849, reported in *Register*, 28 November 1849.
94. Supreme Court Criminal Sessions Record Book, 13 March 1850; *South Australian*, 15 March 1850.
95. Government Resident (Port Lincoln), Report, 2 September 1850, Colonial Secretary's Office, 2194 of 1850, State Records, Adelaide.
96. J Hobbs, Letter to *South Australian*, 9 May 1849.
97. Sub-Protector Minchin, Report to Protector of Aborigines, 24 May 1853, Colonial Secretary's Office, 1362 of 1853, State Records, Adelaide.
98. Sub-Protector Minchin, Report to Protector of Aborigines, 11 July 1853, Colonial Secretary's Office, 1692 of 1853, State Records, Adelaide.
99. Protector of Aborigines, Note on Sub-Protector Minchin, Report to Protector of Aborigines, 11 July 1853, ibid.

Chapter 10

1. Advocate General, Prosecution opening address to jury, Supreme Court, 22 May 1839, reported in *Register*, 29 May 1839.

Notes

2. Governor Gawler, Proclamation made on 17 October 1840 and published in the *Government Gazette*, 22 October 1840.
3. ibid.
4. See J Harvey, *Journal of Events at Port Lincoln*, February–March 1842, Colonial Secretary's Office, 81 of 1842, State Records, Adelaide.
5. *Adelaide Chronicle*, editorial, 31 March 1840.
6. ibid.
7. See *Register,* 7 September 1842.
8. *Adelaide Examiner*, editorial, 15 October 1842.
9. N Hailes, Diary of Life in Port Lincoln, 1842, Mortlock Library, Adelaide.
10. *Adelaide Chronicle*, editorial, 31 March 1841.
11. J Crawford, 'Notes on Aborigines', 1839 published in *South Australiana*, vol. 4, no. 1, March 1965.
12. See J Harvey, *Journal of Events at Port Lincoln*, op. cit.
13. J Harvey, Letter to Colonial Secretary, 8 March 1842, Colonial Secretary's Office, 124 of 1842, State Records, Adelaide; Memorial to Governor, March 1842, Colonial Secretary's Office, 125 of 1842, State Records, Adelaide.
14. Resolution of Port Lincoln Proprietors, reported in *Adelaide Examiner*, 7 April 1842.
15. See *Southern Australian*, 29 March 1842; *Adelaide Examiner*, 7 April 1842.
16. ibid. The reference to Encounter Bay presumably relates to the *Maria* hangings.
17. Leake, Lillicrappe, McIntyre, Frew and Underwood, *South Australian*, 27 May 1845.
18. Protector of Aborigines, Report for second half-year 1841, 10 January 1842, Colonial Secretary's Office, 32 of 1842, State Records, Adelaide.
19. Police Commissioner, Letter to Colonial Secretary, 18 May 1846, Police Letter Book, 100 of 1846, State Records, Adelaide.
20. See Lt Hugonin, Report to Government Resident, 24 April 1842, Colonial Secretary's Office, 236 of 1842, State Records, Adelaide.
21. See Colonial Secretary, Reply to C Driver, 19 April 1844, Colonial Secretary's Office, 395 of 1844, State Records, Adelaide.
22. Protector of Aborigines, Report of Journey to Northern Districts, 15 May 1842, Colonial Secretary's Office, 290 of 1842, State Records, Adelaide.
23. Government Resident (Guichen Bay), Report, 31 January 1847, Colonial Secretary's Office, 220 of 1847, State Records, Adelaide.
24. Governor Robe, Note on Government Resident, Report, 31 January 1847, ibid.
25. N Hailes, op. cit.
26. See Police Commissioner, Letter to Colonial Secretary, 26 November 1846, Colonial Secretary's Office, 1428 of 1846, State Records, Adelaide.
27. Protector of Aborigines, Report, Final quarter 1844, 10 January 1845, Colonial Secretary's Office, 35 of 1845, State Records, Adelaide.

28. ibid.
29. W Boys, Letter to *Register*, 4 June 1845.
30. Protector of Aborigines, Report, Third quarter 1846, 14 August 1846, Colonial Secretary's Office, 1008 of 1846, State Records, Adelaide.
31. *Register*, editorial, 5 September 1849.
32. N Hailes, op. cit.
33. Advocate General, Letter to Colonial Secretary, 20 April 1846, Colonial Secretary's Office, 411 of 1846, State Records, Adelaide.
34. ibid.
35. *Register*, 6 January 1847.
36. Police Commissioner, Letter forwarding Depositions, 6 January 1847, Colonial Secretary's Office, 24 of 1847, State Records, Adelaide.
37. Advocate General, Letter to Colonial Secretary, 8 January 1847, in Colonial Secretary's Office, 24 of 1847, ibid.
38. Supreme Court Criminal Sessions Record Book, 12 March 1847.
39. ibid.
40. Advocate General, Opinion, 19 November 1852, Advocate General's Office, State Records, Adelaide.
41. Advocate General, Opinion, 7 July 1853, Advocate General's Office, State Records, Adelaide; Sub Protector Minchin, Report to Protector of Aborigines, 24 May 1853, Colonial Secretary's Office, 1362 of 1853, State Records, Adelaide; C Driver, Letter to Advocate General, 12 July 1842, Advocate General's Office, State Records, Adelaide.
42. See for example, Government Resident (Guichen Bay), Letter to Advocate General, 22 January 1847, Advocate General's Office, State Records, Adelaide.
43. Government Resident (Robetown), 21 February 1848, Advocate General's Office, State Records, Adelaide.
44. Advocate General, Opinion, 19 November 1852, op. cit.
45. Supreme Court Criminal Records, 8 August 1853.
46. Advocate General, 8 February 1853, Advocate General's Office, State Records, Adelaide.
47. Advocate General, Note in docket advising re attempted murder charge, 30 May 1853, Colonial Secretary's Office, 1268 of 1853, State Records, Adelaide. Also see Advocate General, Opinion, 30 May 1853, Advocate General's Office, State Records, Adelaide.
48. Murray, Acting Government Resident's Report, 7 January 1853, Colonial Secretary's Office, 393 of 1853, State Records, Adelaide.
49. ibid.
50. See *Leicester Chronicle*, 1843, article reprinted in *Southern Australian*, 7 January 1844.
51. Protector of Aborigines, Report for second half-year 1841, op. cit.

Notes

52. Evidence in Resident Magistrate's Court, Port Lincoln, 4 September 1841, reported in *Adelaide Independent*, 19 September 1841.
53. Governor Grey, Memo to Advocate General, 24 December 1841, State Records, Adelaide.
54. Supreme Court Criminal Sessions Record Book, 9 March 1842.
55. *Southern Australian*, 11 March 1842.
56. Supreme Court Criminal Sessions Record Book, 9 March 1842.
57. *Southern Australian*, 11 March 1842. See also *Adelaide Independent*, 18 November 1842.
58. E Eyre, Resident Magistrate's Report, 1 April 1843, Colonial Secretary's Office, 448 of 1843, State Records, Adelaide.
59. Protector of Aborigines, Letter to Colonial Secretary, 7 April 1843, Colonial Secretary's Office, 468 of 1843, State Records, Adelaide.
60. Judge's remarks, Supreme Court, 9 March 1842, reported in *Southern Australian*, 11 March 1842.
61. Correspondent to *Southern Australian*, 29 March 1842.
62. Hawker, Letter to Colonial Secretary, 27 January 1843, Colonial Secretary's Office, 131 of 1843, State Records, Adelaide.
63. Protector of Aborigines, Report on death of woman, 8 February 1843, Colonial Secretary's Office, 182 of 1843, State Records, Adelaide.
64. Colonial Secretary, Letter to Advocate General, 9 November 1844, Advocate General's Office, State Records, Adelaide.
65. C Spratt, Evidence to Supreme Court, reported in *Southern Australian*, 3 December 1844.
66. Namely Nyunnira Boura and his pregnant wife, known to Europeans as 'Mary Ann'.
67. W Carter, Statement, in Protector of Aborigines, Report on Return from Mt Bryan, 7 October 1844, Colonial Secretary's Office, 1120 of 1844, State Records, Adelaide.
68. G Hawker, Deposition, in Protector of Aborigines, Report, 7 October 1844, ibid.
69. Protector of Aborigines, Report for final quarter 1844, op. cit.
70. Advocate General, Letter to Colonial Secretary, 7 November 1844, Colonial Secretary's Office, 1293 of 1844, State Records, Adelaide.
71. Protector of Aborigines, Report for final quarter 1844, op. cit.
72. Advocate General, Letter to Colonial Secretary, 7 November 1844, op. cit.
73. Protector of Aborigines, Letter to Colonial Secretary, 6 December 1844, Colonial Secretary's Office, 1446 of 1844, State Records, Adelaide.
74. ibid.
75. Pari Kudnutya, Parnkarri and Narruthpanna.
76. Police Magistrate, Letter to Colonial Secretary, 20 February 1845, Colonial Secretary's Office, 143 of 1845, State Records, Adelaide.
77. Advocate General, Letter to Colonial Secretary, 18 March 1844, op. cit.

78. Police Commissioner, Report, 3 June 1845, Colonial Secretary's Office, 611 of 1845, State Records, Adelaide.
79. Supreme Court Criminal Sessions Record Book, 10 March 1845.
80. H Price JP, Letter to Colonial Secretary, 19 November 1844, Colonial Secretary's Office, 1388 of 1844, State Records, Adelaide.
81. Police Commissioner, Report, 9 July 1844, Colonial Secretary's Office, 721 of 1844, State Records, Adelaide.
82. Leake, Deposition, 11 December 1844, Colonial Secretary's Office, 1527 of 1844, State Records, Adelaide.
83. One person interviewed during this investigation stated that he had heard of two similar killings in the local area: 'Nolan had shot a black boy for not finding his bullocks… a man of the name of Davy at Curran's had shot a black boy'. McKinnon, Deposition, 22 August 1846, Colonial Secretary's Office, 1096 of 1846, State Records, Adelaide.
84. Police Commissioner, Report, 3 June 1845, Colonial Secretary's Office, op. cit.
85. See *Observer*, 20 March 1847; *Register*, 17 March 1847; *Gazette and Mining Journal*, 20 March 1847.
86. Supreme Court Criminal Sessions Record Book, 12 March 1847. See also Cooper CJ, Report on trial, 22 March 1847, Colonial Secretary's Office, 349 of 1847, State Records, Adelaide.
87. *Register*, 17 March 1847.
88. Evidence of John Smith, Supreme Court Criminal Sessions Record Book, 12 March 1847.
89. Statement reportedly made by Donelly on his arrest, reported in *Observer*, 20 March 1847.
90. Supreme Court Criminal Sessions Record Book, 12 March 1847.
91. Evidence of 'Jemmy', Supreme Court 12 March 1847 reported in *Register*, 17 March 1847.
92. Supreme Court Criminal Sessions Record Book, 15 March 1847.
93. ibid.
94. ibid.
95. ibid.
96. Cooper CJ, Report on trial, 22 March 1847, op. cit.
97. Governor Robe, Note written on Cooper CJ, ibid.
98. Very few Aboriginal people attended the execution, reported in *Register*, 31 March 1847.
99. Supreme Court Criminal Sessions Record Book, 15 March 1847.
100. See R Foster, R Hoskings and A Nettleback, A, op. cit., pp. 74–93.
101. Advocate General, Report to Colonial Secretary, 26 July 1849, Colonial Secretary's Office, 1388 of 1849, State Records, Adelaide.
102. Protector of Aborigines, Report on Visit to South-East District, 6 March 1849, Colonial Secretary's Office, 457 of 1849, State Records.

Notes

103. Advocate General, Report to Colonial Secretary, 26 July 1849, Colonial Secretary's Office, 1388 of 1849, State Records, Adelaide.
104. Protector of Aborigines, Report on Visit to South East District, 6 March 1849, op. cit.; Advocate General, Report to Colonial Secretary, 26 July 1849, Colonial Secretary's Office, 457 of 1849, State Records, Adelaide.
105. Protector of Aborigines, Report on Visit to South East District, op. cit.
106. ibid.
107. *Register*, 7 March 1849.
108. Proceedings in Supreme Court, 15 June 1849, reported in *Register*, 16 June 1849.
109. Advocate General, Report to Colonial Secretary, 26 July 1849, Colonial Secretary's Office, 1388 of 1849, State Records, Adelaide.
110. Price, Report, 21 May 1849, Colonial Secretary's Office, 1001 of 1849, State Records, Adelaide.
111. Police Commissioner, Report to Colonial Secretary, 31 May 1849, Colonial Secretary's Office, 1007 of 1849, State Records, Adelaide.
112. Protector of Aborigines, Report from Port Lincoln, 16 July 1849, Colonial Secretary's Office, 1317 of 1849, State Records, Adelaide.
113. Police Commissioner, Report to Colonial Secretary, 31 May 1849, op. cit.
114. ibid.
115. Inspector Tolmer, Report on Port Lincoln Expedition, 28 August 1849, Colonial Secretary's Office, 1619 of 1849, State Records, Adelaide.
116. ibid.
117. Police Commissioner, Report to Colonial Secretary, 13 October 1849, Colonial Secretary's Office, 1883.5 of 1849, State Records, Adelaide.
118. Advocate General, Letter to Lt Governor, 23 July 1849, State Records, Adelaide.
119. Advocate General, Report to Colonial Secretary, 5 June 1849, Colonial Secretary's Office, 1044 of 1849, State Records, Adelaide.
120. Government Resident, Report, 11 July 1849, Colonial Secretary's Office, 1329 of 1849, State Records, Adelaide.
121. Advocate General, Letter to Lt Governor, 23 July 1849, op. cit. See also Advocate General, Report to Colonial Secretary, 25 June 1849, Colonial Secretary's Office, 1178 of 1849, State Records, Adelaide.
122. Protector of Aborigines, Report, 23 October 1849, *Government Gazette*, 1 November 1849.
123. The date of the attack was probably 12 August 1849.
124. Protector of Aborigines, Report, 23 October 1849, op. cit.
125. Melaityappa died on 31 August 1849.
126. Adelaide Police Court, 29 August 1849, reported in *Register*, 1 September 1849.
127. Piaria, Evidence in Adelaide Police Court, 29 August 1849, reported in *Register*, 1 September 1849.

128. Supreme Court Criminal Sessions Record Book, 17 September 1849.
129. See Protector of Aborigines, Report, 23 October 1849, op. cit.
130. Supreme Court Criminal Sessions Record Book, 17 September 1849.
131. Morris was found not guilty on the charge of having assaulted Monarto and Yurnani by whipping them; *Register*, 5 September 1849.
132. *Register*, 19 September 1849.
133. Wilson, Evidence in Supreme Court, 17 September 1849, reported in *Register*, 19 September 1849.
134. Supreme Court Criminal Sessions Record Book, 17 September 1849.
135. J Crawford, 'Notes on Aborigines', 1839, edited by D Pike and published in *South Australiana*, vol. 4, no. 1, March 1965.
136. J Hobbs, *South Australian*, 9 May 1849.
137. 'SJB', Correspondent to *Register*, 14 January 1850.
138. *South Australian*, 4 September 1849.
139. Bonney, in 'Report of Parliamentary Proceedings', 18 November 1857, reprinted in *Register*, 19 November 1857.
140. 'Pater', Correspondent to *Register*, 7 February 1852. See also *Register*, 12 February 1852.
141. 'SJB', Correspondent to *Register*, 14 January 1850.

Chapter 11

1. E Eyre, Resident Magistrate's Report, 1 April 1843, Colonial Secretary's Office, op. cit.
2. See *R v Donelly*, Supreme Court Criminal Sessions Record Book, March 1847.
3. See J Main, op. cit.; J Cashen, op. cit.
4. For example, even when local court reforms in 1849–50 acknowledged the dominance of the Supreme Court, all cases involving the theft of stock were retained within the higher court's jurisdiction.
5. Legislative Council, Enquiry into Aborigines, 1860, *Minutes of Evidence*, 1860, p. 11.
6. ibid., p. 16.
7. See for example, *Register*, 5 September 1849; *Register*, 12 February 1852; J Crawford, 'Notes on Aborigines', 1839, op. cit.
8. J Crawford, 'Notes on Aborigines', 1839, op. cit.
9. *Register*, editorial, 5 September 1849.
10. See A Pope 1988, op. cit.
11. Government Resident, Report, 14 October 1852, Colonial Secretary's Office, 3209 of 1852, State Records, Adelaide. See also W Hughes, Letter to Colonial Secretary, 21 February 1852, Colonial Secretary's Office, 773 of 1852, State Records, Adelaide.
12. See E Schmaal, 'The native constabulary: South Australian style', *Australian Police Journal*, April 1970, pp. 118–24.

13. See for example, Governor Grey, Note on Government Resident (Port Lincoln), Report, 23 March 1842, Colonial Secretary's Office, 100 of 1842, State Records, Adelaide.
14. Colonial Secretary, Letter to Government Resident (Port Lincoln), Colonial Secretary's Office, 1593 of 1842, State Records, Adelaide.
15. See for example, Government Resident (Port Lincoln), Report, 2 November 1843, Colonial Secretary's Office, 1353 of 1843, State Records, Adelaide.
16. Police Commissioner Warburton was not in favour of the Aboriginal constabulary. See E Schmaal, op. cit., p. 119.
17. Sub-Protector (Port Lincoln), Report, in Protector of Aborigines, Report, 24 May 1853, *Government Gazette*, 2 June 1853.
18. Sub-Protector (Moorundie), Report, in Protector of Aborigines, Report, 24 May 1853, ibid.
19. Other writers have raised the centrality of the clash over land within South Australia to explain why the more general humanitarian policies failed within the colony, despite the declared intentions of the planners and government officials. See H Reynolds, *The law of the land*, op. cit.; R Gibbs 1959–60, op. cit.
20. See H Reynolds, *The law of the land*, op. cit., pp. 100–6.
21. See F Gale 1972, op. cit., p. 39.
22. See J Main, op. cit.; J Cashen, op. cit.; J Summers 1986, op. cit.; R Gibbs 1959–60, op. cit.
23. *Port Phillip Gazette*, 27 October 1838.
24. See Protector of Aborigines, Letter to Colonial Secretary, 23 June 1842, Colonial Secretary's Office, 404 of 1842, State Records, Adelaide.
25. Protector of Aborigines, Letter to Colonial Secretary, 29 October 1842, Colonial Secretary's Office, 807 of 1842, State Records, Adelaide.
26. Protector of Aborigines, Letter to Colonial Secretary, 21 January 1843, Colonial Secretary's Office, 92 of 1843, State Records, Adelaide.
27. See R Hague c.1930, op. cit. and R Hague, *Sir John Jeffcott* (1936) Melbourne University Press, Melbourne, 1963, p. 38.
28. See R Hague c.1930, op. cit., p. 245.
29. List of magistrates and their appointments, 1855, State Records, Adelaide.
30. One example was when, in 1844, the confessed murderer, Carter, was remanded in his own recognizance rather than in custody. He took the opportunity to escape to California.
31. Both the Police Commissioner and the Protector at various times lamented that, in alleged cases of murder, massacre and poisonings on the frontier, the local Justices of the Peace failed to act promptly and effectively to investigate and gather evidence.
32. Advocate General, Letter to McKechnie, 7 November 1860, Advocate General's Office, 52 of 1860, State Records, Adelaide.
33. See Summers 1986, op. cit., p. 302.

34. See H Reynolds, *The law of the land*, op. cit., p. 107.
35. ibid., p. 118.
36. C Sturt, Reply to McLaren et al., 17 July 1840, *Register*, 1 August 1840.
37. See, for example, the *Adelaide Chronicle*, editorial, 3 February 1841.
38. Thirty two leases were arranged in 1842 (see Colonial Secretary, Letter to Advocate General, 11 March 1842, Advocate General's Office, State Records, Adelaide). For further developments on the leases and difficulties in collecting rents, see Protector of Aborigines, Report, 1 January 1843, Colonial Secretary's Office, 145 of 1843, State Records, Adelaide; Advocate General to Crown Solicitor, 9 May 1850, Advocate General's Office, State Records, Adelaide; W Field, Letter to Advocate General, 2 April 1849, Advocate General's Office, State Records, Adelaide; Commissioner for Crown lands, Letter to Advocate General, 5 November 1849, Advocate General's Office, State Records, Adelaide.
39. See H Reynolds, *The law of the land*, op. cit., p. 128.

BIBLIOGRAPHY

PART A: PRIMARY SOURCES

Legislation

State Records, Adelaide, South Australia

South Australia Act, 4 & 5 William IV, An Act to empower His Majesty to erect South Australia into a British Province or Provinces and to provide for the colonization and government thereof, London, 1834.

South Australia *Supreme Court Act*, 7 William IV, 5, Adelaide, 1837.

South Australia, No. 8, 1844, An ordinance to allow the Aboriginal inhabitants of South Australia and the parts adjacent, to give information and evidence without the sanction of an oath, Adelaide 1844.

South Australia, No. 5, 1846, Act to amend 'An ordinance to allow the Aboriginal inhabitants of South Australia and the parts adjacent, to give information and evidence without the sanction of an oath', Adelaide, 1846.

South Australia, No. 3, 1848, An ordinance to facilitate the admission of unsworn testimony of the Aboriginal inhabitants of South Australia and the parts adjacent, Adelaide, 1848.

South Australia, No. 4, 1849, Act to amend 'An ordinance to facilitate the admission of unsworn testimony of the Aboriginal inhabitants of South Australia and the parts adjacent', Adelaide, 1849.

Parliamentary Papers and Reports

Mortlock Library of South Australiana, North Terrace, Adelaide

British Parliamentary Papers, 1841–44, vol. 2.

British Parliamentary Papers, 1841–44, vol. 8.

Colonization Commissioners, 'First Annual Report of the Colonization Commissioners for South Australia', London, June 1836, in *British Parliamentary Papers*.

House of Commons, 'Report of the Select Committee on Aborigines (British Settlements)', 26 June 1837, in *British Parliamentary Papers*, 1841–44, vol. 2.

Legislative Council, South Australia, *Minutes of Evidence to Select Committee on the Aborigines*, September 1860, *SA Parliamentary Papers*, 1860, vol. 2, no. 165.

——, 'Report of Select Committee on the Aborigines', Adelaide, October 1860, *SA Parliamentary Papers*, 1860, vol. 2, no. 165.

South Australian Government Records
State Records, Marion Road, Netley, South Australia

Adelaide Gaol Records, GRG 54/23, State Records, Adelaide.

Adelaide Police Court Minutes 1847–1927, GRG65/1.

Advocate General's Office, Correspondence, State Records, Adelaide.

Colonial Secretary's Office, Letters received 1837–1841, GRG 24/1, State Records, Adelaide.

——, Letters received 1842–, GRG 24/6, State Records, Adelaide.

——, Letters sent, GRG 24/4, State Records, Adelaide.

Governors' Despatches, GRG 2/6/1, State Records, Adelaide.

Government Resident (Port Lincoln), Letter Book, 3/379, State Records, Adelaide.

'Papers Relative to South Australia, presented to Parliament in 1843', printed in *British Parliamentary Papers, Colonies: Australia*, Sessions 1842–1844, vol. 7.

Police Outgoing Letter Books, State Records, Adelaide.

South Australian *Government Gazette*, 1837–1862, State Records, Adelaide.

Supreme Court Depositions 1837–1892, GRG36/3.

——, 1839–1853, GRG36/8.

Supreme Court Correspondence, 1838–1852 GRG36/57.

Supreme Court Indictments and some Depositions 1837–1924, GRG36/1.

Supreme Court of South Australia Records
Archives of Supreme Court of South Australia, Victoria Square, Adelaide

Criminal Sessions Record Books, March 1845 to August 1850.

——, November 1850 to March 1855.

——, August 1855 to August 1863.

South Australian Criminal Records (microfilm series), February 1851 to November 1854.

——, February 1855 to May 1858.

——, August 1858 to August 1861.

——, November 1861 to January 1865.

Supreme Court of South Australia, *Indictment Book 1855–58*.
Supreme Court of South Australia Judges' Common Notebook, 1837 to 1846.
——, June 1846 to August 1848.
Supreme Court of South Australia Judges' Notebooks, 1858.
——, 1859, books 1 and 2.
——, 1860, books 1, 2 and 3.

Diaries and Letters

Mortlock Library of South Australiana, North Terrace, Adelaide

George Fife Angas, Papers.
Everard Papers, Mortlock Library, Adelaide.
Nathaniel Hailes, Diary of Life in Port Lincoln, 1842.
Holroyd (Police Inspector), Diary, Mortlock Library, Adelaide.

Newspapers

Mortlock Library of South Australiana, North Terrace, Adelaide

Adelaide Chronicle
Adelaide Independent
Adelaide Observer
Gazette and Mining Journal
The Guardian
Port Phillip Gazette
South Australian Gazette and Colonial Register
South Australian Register
Southern Australian (*South Australian* after 5 November 1844)

PART B: SECONDARY SOURCES

Theses, Reports and Manuscripts

Adelaide University (History Department and Law School), Australian Legal Records Inventory, Working Paper No. 1, *Supreme Court of South Australia Records*, October 1988.

Australian Law Reform Commission, Report no. 31, *The recognition of Aboriginal customary laws: summary report*. Australian Government Publishing Service, Canberra, 1986.

Brown, H, 'The life and work of Sir Richard Davies Hanson', unpublished manuscript, Mortlock Library, 1953.

Foster, R, 'The Bunganditj: European invasion and the economic basis of social collapse', MA thesis, University of Adelaide, 1983.

Gibbs, R, 'Humanitarian theories and the Aboriginal inhabitants of South Australia to 1860', BA Honours thesis, University of Adelaide, 1959.

Grainger, G, Matthew 'Moorhouse and the South Australian Aborigines c.1839–1856', BA Honours thesis, Flinders University of South Australia, 1980.

Hague, R, 'History of law in South Australia', Unpublished manuscript (PhD thesis, University of Adelaide), copy held in Mortlock Library of South Australiana (PRG 215/1), c.1930.

——, 'Court of Appeals', Unpublished manuscript, Adelaide, 1940. Copy held in Rare Books Collection, Supreme Court, Adelaide.

——, 'Mr Justice Crawford', Unpublished manuscript, Adelaide, 1957. Copy held in Rare Books Collection, Supreme Court, Adelaide.

——, 'Mr Justice Boothby', Unpublished manuscript, c.1961. Copy held in Rare Books Collection, Supreme Court, Adelaide.

Hassell, K, 'The relations between the settlers and Aborigines in South Australia 1836–1860', BA Honours thesis, University of Adelaide, 1921. Facsimile edition published by Libraries Board of South Australia, Adelaide, 1966.

Lendrum, S, 'Special legal problems relating to the Aborigines in the first fifteen years after settlement', LLB thesis, University of Adelaide, 1976.

Books

Baille, P, *Port Lincoln and district: a pictorial history*, Lynton Publications, Blackwood, 1978.

Berg, S (ed.), *Coming to terms: Aboriginal title in South Australia*, Wakefield Press, Adelaide, 2010.

Berndt, R and Berndt, C, *From black to white in South Australia*, Cheshire, Melbourne, 1951.

Brock, P, *Yura and Udnyu: A history of the Adnyamathanha of the North Flinders Ranges*, Wakefield Press, Adelaide, 1985.

Bull, J, *Early experiences of life in South Australia*, Adelaide, 1884, Facsimile edition, State Library of South Australia, 1972.

Castles, A, *An Australian legal history*, Law Book Co, Sydney, 1982.

Castles, A and Harris, M, *Lawmakers and wayward Whigs*, Wakefield Press, Adelaide, 1987.

Clark, CM, *A History of Australia*, Melbourne University Press, Melbourne, 6 volumes, 1962–1987.

Clyne, R, *Colonial blue*, Wakefield Press, Adelaide, 1987.

Dickey, B and Howell, P, *South Australia's Foundation: select documents*, Wakefield Press, Adelaide, 1986.

Eyre, E, *Journals of expeditions of discovery*, 2 vols, London, 1845.

Fels, M, *Good men and true: the Aboriginal Police of the Port Phillip District 1837–1853*, Melbourne University Press, Melbourne, 1988.

Bibliography

Foster, R, Hoskings, R and Nettleback, A, *Fatal collisions: the SA frontier and the violence of memory*, Wakefield Press, Adelaide, 2001.

Gale, F, *Urban Aborigines*, Australian National University, Canberra, 1972.

Hague, R, *Sir John Jeffcott: Judge of the Supreme Court*, Hassell Press, Adelaide, 1936, reprinted by Melbourne University Press, Melbourne, 1963.

——, *The gentle Jickling*, Hassel Press, Adelaide, 1939.

Hallam, S, *Fire and hearth*, Australian Institute of Aboriginal Studies, Canberra, 1979.

Hart, H, *The concept of law*, Clarendon Press, London, 1961.

——, *Essays in jurisprudence and the philosophy of law*, Oxford University Press, Oxford, 1983.

Hasluck, P, *Black Australians: a survey of native policy in Western Australia 1829–1897*, Melbourne University Press, Melbourne, 1942.

Hirst, J, *Adelaide and the country, 1870–1917: their social and political relationship*, Melbourne University Press, Melbourne, 1973.

Historical Records of Australia, Commonwealth Parliament, NSW Government Printer, Sydney.

Hodder, E, *The History of South Australia*, Sampson Low, Marston, London, 1893.

Hodge, C, *Encounter Bay: the miniature Naples of Australia*, Adelaide, 1932.

Jenkin, G, *Conquest of the Ngarrindjeri*, Rigby, Adelaide, 1979.

Liddy, P, *The Rainbird murders*, Peacock, Adelaide, 1993.

Loren, M, *An early history of the Supreme Court of South Australia*, Adelaide, mimeo, October 1987.

——, *History of the Local Court of South Australia 1850–1987*, Adelaide, mimeo, 1987.

——, *A History of the Police and Magistrates Court 1844–1968*, Adelaide, mimeo, 1987.

Mann, C, *Report of Speeches for Hindmarsh on appointment as Governor of South Australia*, London, 1835.

Masters, F, *Saga of Wangaraleednie*, National Trust, Adelaide, 1950.

Mattingley, C, *Survival in our own land*, SA Government Printer, Adelaide, 1988.

McGrath, A, *Born in the cattle: Aborigines in cattle country*, Allen & Unwin, Sydney 1987.

Molony, J, *An architect of freedom: John Hubert Plunkett in New South Wales*, ANU Press, Canberra, 1973.

Mortlock Library of South Australiana, *Research Notes*, Adelaide, various dates.

Napier, C, *Colonization particularly in Southern Australia with some remarks on small farms and overpopulation*, London, 1835. Facsimile printed by Kelly, New York, 1969.
Pike, D, *Paradise of dissent*, Melbourne University Press, Melbourne, 1957.
Pope, A, *Resistance and retaliation*, Heritage Action, Adelaide, 1989.
Reece, R, *Aborigines and colonists: Aborigines and colonial society in New South Wales in the 1830s and 1840s*, Sydney University Press, Sydney, 1974.
Reynolds, H, *The other side of the frontier*, Penguin, Ringwood, 1982.
——, *Frontier: Aborigines, settlers and land*, Allen & Unwin, Sydney, 1987.
——, *The law of the land*, Penguin, Ringwood, first edition, 1987.
——, *With the whites*, Penguin, Ringwood, 1990.
——, *Aboriginal sovereignty: reflections on race, state and nation*, Melbourne, 1995.
Robinson, F and York, B, *The black resistance*, Widescope International, Melbourne, 1981.
Rosser, B, *Up rode the troopers: the Black Police in Queensland*, University of Queensland Press, Brisbane, 1990.
Rowley, C, *The destruction of Aboriginal society*, Penguin, Ringwood, 1972.
Taylor, G, *A great and glorious reformation: six early South Australian legal innovations*, Wakefield Press, Adelaide, 2005.
Teichelmann, CG and Schurmann, CW, *The Aboriginal language of South Australia*, Published by the authors, Adelaide, 1840.
Tolmer, A, *Reminiscences of an adventurous and chequered career at home and in the antipodes*, Sampson Low, Marston, London, 1882.
Torrens, R, *Colonization of South Australia*, Longmans, London, 1835.
Towler, D and Porter, T, *The Hempen Collar: Executions in South Australia 1838–1964: a collection of eyewitness accounts*, Wednesday Press, Adelaide, 1990.
Woodruff, P, *Two million South Australians*, Peacock Publications, Adelaide, 1984.
Yarwood, A and Knowling, M, *Race relations in Australia*, Methuen, Sydney, 1982.

ARTICLES

Attwood, B, 'Aborigines and academic historians: some recent encounters', *Australian Historical Studies*, vol. 24, no. 94, April 1990.
Australian Law Reform Commission, 'Traditional Aboriginal society and its law', in W Edwards (ed.), *Traditional Aboriginal society*, MacMillan, Melbourne, 1998, p. 217ff.

Bibliography

Berndt, R, 'Law and order in Aboriginal Australia', in R Berndt and C Berndt (eds), *Aboriginal Man in Australia*, Angus & Robertson, Sydney, 1965.

Bridges, B, 'The Aborigines and the law: New South Wales 1788–1855', *Teaching History*, December 1970, pp. 40–70.

——, 'The extension of English law to the Aborigines for offences committed *inter se*, 1829–1842', *Journal of the Royal Australian Historical Society*, vol. 59, no. 4, December 1973.

Brock, P, 'Protecting colonial interests: Aborigines and criminal justice', *Journal of Australian Studies*, vol. 12, no. 2, 1997, pp. 120–29.

Cashen, J, 'Owners of labour', *Flinders History of South Australia: Social History*, Wakefield Press, Adelaide, 1986, pp. 105–14.

Clyne, R, 'At war with the natives: from the Coorong to the Rufus, 1841', *Journal of the Historical Society of South Australia*, no. 9, 1982.

Cocks, A, 'Remaking Aboriginal history: a conversation with Bain Attwood', *Another Voice*, vol. 1, no. 1, 1991, pp. 11–15.

Cranston, R, 'Aborigines and the law: an overview', *University of Queensland Law Journal*, vol. 8, 1973, pp. 62–78.

Crawford, J, 'Notes on Aborigines', 1839, edited by D Pike and reprinted in *South Australiana*, vol. 4, no. 1, March 1965.

Davies, S, 'Aborigines, murder and the criminal law in early Port Phillip, 1841–1851', *Historical Studies*, vol. 22, no. 88, April 1987.

Debelle, B, 'Aboriginal customary law and the common law', in E Johnston, M Hinton and D Rigney (eds), *Indigenous Australians and the law*, Cavendish, Sydney, 1997, p. 82ff.

Elkin, P, 'Aboriginal evidence and justice in Northern Australia', *Oceania*, vol. 17, no. 3, 1947.

Fenner, C, 'Growth and development in South Australia', *Proceedings of Royal Geographical Society (South Australia)*, vol. 36, pp. 65–89.

Fischer, G, 'South Australian Colonization Act and other related constitutional documents', *Adelaide Law Review*, vol. 2, 1963–66, pp. 360–72.

Foster, R, 'Aboriginal history and South Australian legal records', *Journal of Anthropological Society of South Australia*, vol. 27, no. 5, 1989, pp. 11–14.

——, 'The Aborigines Location in Adelaide: South Australia's first "mission" to the Aborigines', *Journal of Anthropological Society of South Australia*, vol. 28, nos. 1–2, 1990, pp. 11–37.

Frost, A, 'New South Wales as terra nullius: the British denial of Aboriginal land rights', *Historical Studies*, vol. 19, no. 77, October 1981, pp. 65–76.

Gibbs, R, 'Relations between the Aboriginal inhabitants and the first South Australians', *Journal of Royal Geographic Society (South Australia)*, vol. 61, 1959–60, pp. 61–78.

Griffiths, A, 'Capital punishment in South Australia 1836–1964', *Australian and New Zealand Journal of Criminology*, vol. 3, no. 4, December 1970, pp. 214–22.

Hamann, J, 'The Coorong Massacre', *Flinders Journal of History and Politics*, vol. 3, 1973.

Havermann, P, 'The rule of law, betrayal and reparation' in S Berg (ed.) *Coming to terms: Aboriginal title in South Australia*, Wakefield Press, Adelaide, 2010, pp. 122–47.

Highland, G, 'Aborigines, Europeans and the criminal law', *Aboriginal History*, vol. 14, nos. 1–2, 1990, pp. 182–96.

Hocking, B, 'Colonial laws and indigenous peoples: past and present law concerning the recognition of human rights of indigenous native peoples in British colonies with particular reference to Australia', in B Hocking (ed.), *International law and Aboriginal human rights*, Law Book Co, Melbourne, 1988, pp. 3–18.

Hookey, J, 'Settlement and sovereignty', in P Hanks and B Keon-Cohen (eds), *Aborigines and the law: essays in memory of Elizabeth Eggleston*, Allen & Unwin, Sydney, 1984, pp. 1–18.

Howell, P, 'The South Australia Act', *Flinders history of South Australia: political history*, Wakefield Press, Adelaide, 1986, pp. 26–51.

——, 'Clearing the cobwebs: a reconsideration of the beginnings of the province of South Australia', *History Forum*, July 1991, pp. 4–21.

Jacobs, W, 'The fatal confrontation: early native–white relations on the frontiers of Australia, New Guinea, and America — a comparative study', *Pacific Historical Review*, 1971, pp. 283–309.

Kurreish, V, 'Thompson and the rule of law: jurisprudence and ideology in terra nullius', *Law in Context*, vol. 7, 1989, pp 120–33.

Lendrum, S, 'The Coorong Massacre: martial law and the Aborigines at first settlement', *Adelaide Law Review*, vol. 6, no. 1, 1977–78, pp. 26–43.

Maddock, K, 'Aboriginal customary law', in P Hanks and B Keon-Cohen (eds), *Aborigines and the law: essays in memory of Elizabeth Eggleston*, Allen & Unwin, Sydney, 1984, p. 226ff.

Main, J, 'The Foundation of South Australia', *Flinders history of South Australia: political history*, Wakefield Press, Adelaide, 1986, pp. 1–25.

Markus, A, 'Through a glass darkly: aspects of contact history', *Aboriginal History*, vol. 1, no. 1, 1977.

McCulloch, S, 'Sir George Gipps and eastern Australia's policy towards the Aborigine, 1838–1846', *Journal of Modern History*, vol. 33, no. 3, September 1961, pp. 261–69.

Munyard, A, 'Making a polity: 1836–1857', *Flinders history of South Australia: political history*, Wakefield Press, Adelaide, 1986, pp. 52–75.

Parker, F and Somerville, J, 'What occurred at Holdfast Bay on 28 December 1836?', *Proceedings of the Royal Geographical Society (South Australia)*, no. 38, pp. 53–78.

Pope, A, 'Aboriginal adaptation to early colonial labour markets', *Journal of Labour History*, no. 54, May 1988, pp. 1–15.

Radcliffe-Brown, A, 'Former numbers and distribution of Australian Aboriginals', *Official Yearbook of the Commonwealth of Australia*, Canberra, 1930.

Read, P, 'Good historians and true: revising Aboriginal history', *Victorian Historical Journal*, vol. 61, no. 4, 1990, pp. 291–98.

Reece, R, 'The Aborigines in Australian historiography', in J Moses (ed.), *Historical disciplines and culture in Australasia: an assessment*, University of Queensland Press, Brisbane, 1979, pp. 253–81.

——, 'Laws of the white people: the frontier of authority in early Western Australia', in B Hocking (ed.), *International law and Aboriginal human rights*, Law Book Co, 1988, pp. 110–36.

Reynolds, H, 'Aboriginal–European contact history: problems and issues', *Journal of Australian Studies*, no. 3, June 1978, pp. 52–64.

——, 'Aborigines and European social hierarchy', *Aboriginal History*, vol. 7, no. 2, 1983, pp. 124–33.

Richards, E, 'South Australia observed', in *Flinders history of South Australia: social history*, Wakefield Press, Adelaide, 1986, pp. 1–32.

Schmaal, E, 'The native constabulary, South Australian style', *The Australian Police Journal*, April 1970, pp. 118–24.

Sharp, P, 'Three frontiers: some comparative studies of Canadian, American and Australian settlement', *Pacific Historical Review*, vol. 24, 1955, p. 372ff.

Summers, J, 'The Destruction of the Kaurna', *Australian History Collected Articles*, History Teachers Association of South Australia, mimeograph, 1978.

——, 'Colonial race relations', in *Flinders history of South Australia: social history*, Wakefield Press, Adelaide 1986, pp. 283–311.

Unrau, W, 'An international perspective on American Indian policy: the South Australian Protector and Aborigines Protection Society', *Pacific History Review*, vol. 45, no. 4, 1976, pp. 579–638.

INDEX

Names stating with 'Mc' are interfiled as if spelled 'Mac'; locators in the form '206n94' indicate, for example, page 206, note 94'.

Aboriginal customary law, 8, 11, 12, 83–4, 171
   and *inter se* cases, 70–2, 74, 75, 77–8, 87
   jurors' views, 77–8
   Stevenson's views, 75, 78–9
Aboriginal Evidence Acts, 44–9, 60, 150
   tested in court, 49–53
   see also admissibility of Aboriginal evidence
Aboriginal land rights, 3–5, 10–11, 164–5, 172–3
Aboriginal languages
   Boandik language, 64
   diversity of, 56, 65, 66–7, 171–2
   interpreters *see* interpretation and interpreters
   Kaurna language and speakers, 56–7, 58
   learning by officials, 44, 48, 56, 58–9, 67, 139
   see also language barriers
Aboriginal offenders
   cases (charges and outcomes), 175–8, 179–91
   numbers discharged, 68–9
   see also jurisdiction and amenability of Aboriginal people to British law
Aboriginal people
   in Adelaide, 105–6, 119–20
   and alternative approaches to colonisation, 171–3
   demands for food and money, 14, 106–8
   disputes among *see inter se* cases

education of *see* education of Aboriginal people
employment, 106, 108–9, 129–30
failure of British law to protect Aboriginal people, 135–56
hunger as motivation for theft, 120, 121–4, 127, 130
ignorance of British laws, 17, 26, 27, 29–31 *see also* jurisdiction and amenability of Aboriginal people to British law; 'prior contact' concept
impact of dispersal of settlement *see* containment policy
intimidation of settlers by, 106–9, 127–8
legal status of, 3–13, 15–16, 19–22, 26–7, 34–6, 135, 155–6, 173 *see also* jurisdiction and amenability of Aboriginal people to British law; 'one law for all' policy
proposed assimilation into SA society, 4, 11, 161, 165, 171
relations with Europeans *see* race relations
theft by *see* theft by Aboriginal people
theft from, 12–13
as witnesses *see* admissibility of Aboriginal evidence; weight and credibility attached to Aboriginal evidence
Aboriginal reserves, 4, 172–3
Adams, Jemmy (aka Courkin), 84
Adelaide
   Aboriginal population and visitors, 105–6, 119–20
Adelaide, Bishop of, 87, 92

243

Index

Adelaide Chronicle, 19, 137
Adelaide Examiner, 24, 137
admissibility of Aboriginal evidence, 41–55, 161
   cases (examples), 50–3, 74, 144–5, 149–50
   communication difficulties *see* interpretation and interpreters; language barriers
   corroboration provisos, 45–6, 47, 49, 74
   declaration without oath, 45, 46, 47, 49, 60
   difficulties in obtaining Aboriginal evidence, 53–4, 116
   Eyre's views, 43–4, 46
   Grey's views, 42–3, 46
   implementation of, 46–7
   inability of Aboriginal persons to take the oath, 16, 21, 26, 41, 42, 57, 144–5, 149
   legislative reforms, 44–9
   reliability of Aboriginal evidence, 44, 47, 51, 52–3, 82
   rules of evidence, 41
   unsworn interpreters, 47–9, 50, 57–8, 60
   see also weight and credibility attached to Aboriginal evidence
alcohol
   controls, 161, 202n89
   drunkenness, 84, 115, 214n108
   supply to Aboriginal people, 55, 115, 214n108
amalgamation policy, 4, 11, 161, 165, 171
amenability of Aboriginal people to British law *see* jurisdiction and amenability of Aboriginal people to British law
Andrews (defence counsel), 101, 103
Angas, George Fife, 12
Anstey, George, 168
Armstrong, Thomas, 94, 154
assault and robbery, 67–8, 76, 94, 105–18
   by Aboriginal people upon settlers, 106–14, 178–9, 182–4
   in Adelaide, 105–6
   convictions/conviction rate, 105, 143, 178–9, 182–4
   inter se cases, 86–7, 114–15, 184

   robbery charges against Aboriginal people, 185–6, 189–90
   by settlers against Aboriginal people, 115–18, 143
   sexual assaults, 40, 43, 67–8, 89, 93, 101–2, 113–14
   see also murder; theft
Atkins, Richard, 7

Bagnall, William, 94–5, 111
Bailey (defence counsel), 39, 81
Baird, James, 37, 97–9, 126
Baker, Emma, 114
Bakilti (aka Jem Brown), 65, 93–4, 109–10
Baldanant, 39, 85
Baldock, George, 89
Ballycrack, 80
Bartley (defence counsel), 30, 68, 73, 74, 80, 83, 91, 100, 114, 123, 166
Battara clans, 88
'Beautiful Tommy', 115
Beerdeah, 84–5
Beerea, 39
Beevor, Charles, 51, 65, 93
Bennett, *Mrs*, 108
Berea, 113
Beresford, George, 38
Bergooist, Theodore, 103
Biddeah, Nakundah, 32, 34, 62–3, 73, 90
Biddle (murder victim), 89
Billy, 81
'Billy Goat', 114
Binarambula, 123
Bishop of Adelaide, 87, 92
Bissett (policeman), 59
Boandik language and people, 64, 83
Bobbo (Melaitpa) *see* Melaitpa case
Bonat, Krupkrup, 81
Bonjon, 8, 27, 70, 210n2
Bonney, Charles, 155, 168
Bootha, Bonney, 127
Boothby, *J*, 81, 82–3, 100, 101
Borthwick, Thomas, 117
Bridges (shepherd), 113
Bromley, Walter, 56–7
Brown, Henry, 112
Brown, James, 49, 54, 99, 150–2
Brown, Jem *see* Bakilti
Brown, Peter, 38, 100

Index

Budlaroo, 76
Bullocky, 84
Bummary, George, 194n35
Bungildo, 67–8, 113–14
Butler (Government Resident), 48, 54, 139

Caldecotte, 108
Carney, Richard, 63, 90
Carson, Mary, 120
Carter, William, 147–8
Charley (convicted thief), 127
Charley (defendant), 60
Charley (native constable and interpreter), 62, 63, 73
Christian, Christopher, 58, 118
citizenship for Aboriginal people *see* Aboriginal people: legal status of; jurisdiction and amenability of Aboriginal people to British law
Clark, Grace, 108
Colonial Office
  and Aboriginal land tenure, 4–5, 172–3
  colonial power structure, 9, 23
  and Cooper's objections to trying Aboriginal people, 36
  humanitarian intentions, 2–4, 5, 10–11, 157, 165, 171, 172
  and legal status of Aboriginal people *see* jurisdiction and amenability of Aboriginal people to British law
  and military action against Aboriginal people, 22, 23–4
colonisation, 1–6
  alternative approaches for positive outcomes for Aboriginal people, 171–3
  influence of humanitarian movement, 2–4, 5, 9–11, 92, 157, 160–1, 165–6, 170, 171, 172
  motivations, 2–6, 165–6
  see also European settlement; European settlers; land policy; settlement; South Australia (colony)
Colonization Commission, 3, 9–11, 165, 172
  Resident Commissioner role, 9, 10
communication difficulties *see* interpretation and interpreters; language barriers
containment policy, 2, 5–6, 56, 67, 71

abandonment of, 29, 37, 44, 72, 154, 158–9, 163, 171
convicts
  absence of, in SA colony, 2, 4, 157
  ex-convicts in frontier society, 140, 149
Cooliltie, 95
Cooper, Charles (Chief Justice), 16, 17, 18, 25, 166–8
  and admissibility of Aboriginal evidence, 52, 74
  inter se cases, 73–9, 81
  interpretation of jurisdiction issues, 26–7, 72–5, 78, 167–8
  on language interpretation and interpreters, 48–9, 59–60, 62–4, 67, 90, 167–8
  and Mantyeuldi case, 61
  and Mingalta/Malgalta case, 92
  notion of limited jurisdiction over Aboriginal people, 18–19, 20, 28, 72–3, 167–8
  'prior contact' criterion, 26, 29–38, 167
Coorong massacre and aftermath *see Maria* (brig) survivors, murder of
Courkin (aka Jemmy Adams), 84
Court of Appeals, 6
courts *see* legal system
Crackingyounger, 80
credibility of Aboriginal witnesses *see* weight and credibility attached to Aboriginal evidence
Crocker, Charles, 96, 212n38
Cronk, James, 14, 57, 58
customary law *see* Aboriginal customary law

Dashwood, *Commissioner of Police*, 98
Davenport, Samuel, 168
Davey, *Dr*, 107
Davis, AH, 77, 78
death sentences, 32, 36, 78, 79, 80, 86, 175–80, 182
  appeals for clemency, 32, 37, 38–40, 51–2, 81
  see also executions
deaths in custody, 109
dispersal of settlement *see* containment policy
Donelly, Thomas, 46–7, 149–50
Dowling, *J*, 7

245

Index

Driscoll, John, 13
Driver, Charles, 54, 97, 122, 128–9, 131, 141, 145, 152–3
drunkenness *see* intoxication
Duffield, William, 14, 16–17, 41, 135
Dwyer, Patrick, 152–3

Easton, Ann, 65, 93
Easton, James, 65
Eastwood, 'Yorky', 150–1
education of Aboriginal people, 4, 161, 169
  and amenability to British law, 6, 17, 28–9
  Protector of Aborigines' role, 17, 28–9, 158, 161, 169
Eelulta, 39, 100, 202n67
European settlement, 44
  containment policy, 2, 5–6, 56, 67, 71; failure of, 29, 37, 44, 72, 154, 158–9, 163
European settlers
  assaults *see* assault and robbery
  attitudes to killing of Aboriginal people, 145–50, 155–6
  attitudes to property offences and the law, 122–3, 124, 125, 130, 131–4, 159–60
  brutality, 37, 92, 140
  murders *see* murder and murder charges
  police protection of, 136–9, 154–5, 163–4 *see also* police force
  relations with Aboriginal people *see* race relations
  taking the law into their own hands, 135–56, 159–60, 169–70; factors in, 154–6; incidents, 139–54 *see also* murder and murder charges
executions, 17–18, 22, 25, 39, 40, 51, 65, 102, 135, 150, 155, 175–8 *see also* death sentences
Eyre, Edward John, 43, 145
Eyre Peninsula
  race relations, 37–9, 49, 51–2, 88–94, 95–9, 100–1, 163–4
fairness *see* integrity of government and court officials
Farrell, *Reverend*, 87
Fartch, Adam, 143

Fastings, James, 89
Field, George, 50
Field, W, 22, 23
Finniss, BT (Police Commissioner), 31, 147, 148
Fisher (defence counsel), 39, 52–3, 76, 84, 85, 95, 97, 109, 110, 111, 149, 166
food *see* hunger as motivation for theft
Forbes, *J*, 7
Francis, Anthony, 112
Frost, Frederic, 116–17

Gall, John, 110, 133
Gavan, John, 109
Gawler, George (Governor)
  on admissibility of Aboriginal evidence, 41–2
  affirms official policy concerning Aboriginal people and the law, 15–16
  military response to *Maria* killings, 18, 19–22; public opinion of, 19–20, 21–2
  recall of, 22
  on settler retaliation against Aboriginal people, 136
Gazette and Mining Journal, 78
Geharty, *Sergeant*, 51, 59, 91, 96, 98, 103
Gill (shepherd), 142
Gill, ST (artist), 116
Gilles, Osmond, 168
Glenelg, *Lord*, 3, 26–7
Gonarto, Maria, 67
Gootoognuyerie, 84
government and court officials
  integrity of, 68–9, 103–4, 166–9
  Justices of the Peace conflicts of interest, 168–9
  learning Aboriginal languages, 44, 48, 56, 58–9, 67, 139
Government Gazette, 19
Governor's role and responsibilities, 9, 10, 11
Grant, Charles (Lord Glenelg), 3, 26–7
Grey, George (Governor), 147
  actions against Aboriginal offenders, 23–5
  on admissibility of Aboriginal evidence, 42–3, 46

views on Aboriginal amenability to British law, 27–8, 71–2
Gwynne, *J*, 85, 101

Hack, John Barton, 168
Hailes, Nathaniel, 139, 140
Hallett, John, 15, 148, 168
Halliday, George, 110
Hamp, John, 51, 90–2
Hanson (Advocate General), 18
Hartley (defence counsel), 53, 82
Hawker, George, 146, 147, 168
Hawson, Frank, 88, 136
Heelta, 115
Hinch, Maria, 52
Hindmarsh, John, 1, 6, 11–12, 14, 135
Hobbs, John, 155
House of Commons Select Committee on Aborigines, 26–7
humanitarianism, 2–5, 9–11, 92, 157, 160–1, 165–6, 170, 171, 172
hunger as motivation for theft, 14, 120, 121–4, 127, 130
Hutt, John (Governor), 27

ignorance of British laws, 17, 26, 27, 29–31 *see also* jurisdiction and amenability of Aboriginal people to British law; 'prior contact' concept
Ilgalta, 65
Illamma, 202n67
Impett, Margaret, 101
Inman (Police Inspector), 14–15, 22
integrity of government and court officials, 68–9, 103–4, 166–9
  Justices of the Peace conflicts of interest, 168–9
inter se cases, 7–8, 26, 70–87, 161
  assault and robbery, 86–7, 114–15, 184
  and corroboration provisos, 47, 74
  customary law, 70–2, 74, 75, 77–8, 87
  first conviction, 74
  jurisdiction issues, 26, 39, 70–5, 76, 77–81, 85–7
  jurors' views and customary law, 77–8
  manslaughter, 39, 81, 83–6, 180–2
  murder, 30, 39–40, 63, 72–86, 179–82
  Murrell case, 7–8, 26, 36, 70
  in NSW, 7–8

number and outcomes of cases, 85–7, 179–82, 184
  numbers of offenders discharged, 68–9
  petitions for clemency, 37
  public views on legal action, 73–4, 87
  reliability of Aboriginal evidence questioned, 52–3, 82
  Stevenson's views, 75, 78–9
interpretation and interpreters, 44–5, 46, 47–9, 50
  Aboriginal people as interpreters, 59, 66
  Aboriginal people unable to act as interpreters, 58
  categories of interpreters, 66
  colonists as interpreters, 58, 66
  conflicts of interest, 58, 59
  diversity of Aboriginal languages, 56, 65, 66–7, 171–2
  Kaurna people and language, 56, 57, 58
  lack of competent interpreters, 26, 30, 34, 38, 44–5, 59, 60, 62–4, 66–8, 73, 76, 90, 125, 161
  native constabulary as interpreters, 59
  public perceptions of interpreter bias, 58, 65–6
  unsworn interpreters, 47–9, 60
interpretation of jurisdiction issues *see* jurisdiction and amenability of Aboriginal people to British law
intoxication, 84, 102, 115, 116, 214n108 *see also* alcohol

Jackey, 117
Jeffcott, John (Justice), 6, 13, 166
Jemmy (offender), 106, 108, 114, 128
Jemmy (witness), 47, 149–50
Jenks, George, 95
Jickling, *J*, 166
Jimcrack (interpreter), 50, 58
'Jimmy Brandy', 115
Jolly, Francis, 116
Jones, Harry, 50, 153–4
Jones, John, 100–1
judicial system *see* legal system
juries
  inter se cases and customary law, 77–8
  weight and credibility given to Aboriginal evidence, 45, 50–3, 54–5

247

Index

jurisdiction and amenability of Aboriginal people to British law, 15–16, 20–2, 26–40, 70–2
  application of law in court proceedings, 29–31, 38–9, 72–87
  Cooper's interpretation of, 26–38, 167–8
  failure of British law to protect Aboriginal people, 135–56
  Grey's views, 27–8, 71–2
  inter se jurisdiction *see inter se* cases
  and 'prior contact' concept, 26, 29–38, 62, 167
  reiteration of official policy, 35–6
  settlers' views, 37, 38, 39–40, 139, 155–6 *see also* European settlers
Justices of the Peace, 7, 162, 168–9

Kainmulta, 100–1
Kalamco, 131
Kalinga, 57
Kamalta, 96
Kambalta, 75, 95, 97, 127
Kanadlanna, 202n67
Kaneguiltie, 85
Kangaroo Jack, 147
Kanguworli *see* Worli, Kanga
Karabidne, 101
Katamio, 29–30
Kauadla (aka Peter), 80–1
Kaurna people, 12, 13, 14–15, 44
  as interpreters, 56, 58
  language learned by Europeans, 57
killing of stock *see* stock killing
Kingberrie, 149–50
Kokatha people, 37–8, 97–8, 100
Kokilata, 123
Kokunea, 50
Kondura, 123
Koonko, 110, 133
Koorykownimmi, 89
Kudnaitya, Worta, 42, 144–5
Kudnutya, 62, 65
Kudnutya, Purri, 125
Kulbilti, 97
Kulgulta, 51, 93
Kumbilti, 66
Kumbulta, 111
Kurkrunwilla, 129–30
Kurtainoggaka, 75–6
Kutromee, 76

land policy, 2, 3–5, 9–11, 164–5, 172–3
Langaryngarynga, 83–4
language barriers, 26, 30, 34, 38, 44, 47–9, 56–69
  Kaurna language and interpreters, 56–7
  see also Aboriginal languages; interpretation and interpreters
Larry (defendant), 30, 63, 72–3
Lawson, George, 46, 116, 141
Leandernin, 54, 151–2
Lee, Elias, 111
legal separatism, 11, 161, 171
legal system
  Aboriginal ignorance of laws, 17, 26, 27, 29–31
  admissibility of evidence *see* admissibility of Aboriginal evidence
  conflicts of interest, 168–9
  court system inappropriate to colonial situation, 161–3
  establishment of, 6–7, 11
  failure of British law to protect Aboriginal people, 135–56 *see also* assault and robbery; murder
  integrity of government and court officials, 68–9, 103–4, 166–9
  Justices of the Peace, 7, 162, 168–9
  legal policy and authority, 9–12
  legal status of Aboriginal people, 3–13, 15–16, 19–22, 26–7, 34–6, 135, 155–6, 173
  'one law for all' *see* 'one law for all' policy
  perceived failure of, 68–9, 159–60
  precedence of British law, 12
  settler attitudes *see under* European settlers
  settlers taking the law into their own hands, 135–56, 169–70 *see also* murder and murder charges
  Supreme Court appointments, 6, 166–8
  two systems accepted in practice, 71–2, 161
  Warburton's proposals for circuit magisterial system, 162–3
  see also jurisdiction and amenability of Aboriginal people to British law; land policy; witnesses
Letters Patent, 3, 4, 10–11
Light, William, 96

Index

livestock *see* stock killing by Aboriginal people; stock theft by Aboriginal people
Loorumumpoo, 53, 82

McDuff, Peter, 54
McGrath, George, 89
McKechnie brothers, 38
McKenzie, James, 48, 110
McLean, Jemmy *see* Rallooloolyoo
magistrates *see* legal system
Magulta, 85
Malalta, 76, 77
Maldira, Wira, 89
Malgalta (convicted murderer of Beevor), 51
Malgalta (convicted murderer of Hamp), 51–2, 91–2
Malkeltie, 126
Malpita, 65, 94
Manancowie (aka Robert Mannam), 115
Mandeltie, 85
Mangilti, 101
Mangultu, 95
Manilti, 128, 133
Mann, Charles, 13, 16, 49, 51, 57, 60, 84, 91, 92, 135–6, 205n71
Mannam, Robert (aka Manancowie), 115
manslaughter, 94, 97, 135, 176–7, 180–1
 inter se cases, 39, 81, 83–6, 180–2
Mantamornappa, 112, 127–8, 130
Mantyeuldi, 31, 61–2
Manyelta, 100–1
Mareeku, 109
Maria (brig) survivors, murder of, 18–19
 military action against offenders, 18, 19–20; legal arguments in support of, 21–2; public response to, 19–20
Marielare, 53, 82
Marinna, 58, 114
Markerlembelan, 53
Marnipi, 115
Marrippa, 94–5
martial law, 18–19, 20, 21–2, 28 *see also* police force
Mary (murder victim), 83
Mary (stabbing victim) *see* Kurtainoggaka
Mary (witness), 52
Mason, George, 84
massacres, 18, 24, 25, 137, 155, 169 *see also* murder and murder charges
Mayponin, 77

Meenaltie, 85
Meenbinya, 113
Meendeenya, 113
Meengulta, 103
Meewulta, 130
Melaitpa case, 36, 74–5, 76
Melaitya, Targko, 110
Melaityappa, 50, 153–4
military action *see* martial law; police force
Milmenrura clan, 18–19, 21, 22, 28, 137, 167
Milyalta, 202n67
Minchin, *Sub-Protector of Aborigines*, 67, 134
Mingalta, 51–2, 91–2
Mingulta, 51, 64–5, 93
Minora, 123
Minquilti, 143
Minulta, 85
Mithra, 94
Monaitya, 125
Monaitya, Pritto, 120
Monarto, 58, 118
Monboit, 82
Mongarawata, 18, 22, 41
Moniah, 39
Monichi, 16–17
Monnaitya, 102
Moorcangua, 18, 22, 41
Moorhouse, Matthew (Protector of Aborigines)
 and Aboriginal land reserves, 172–3
 on admissibility of Aboriginal evidence, 46
 on appointment of defence counsel, 166
 argues against reduction in rations for Aboriginal people, 121–2
 concerns about delays in bringing court action, 53, 99–100
 concerns about reliability of Aboriginal evidence, 47, 51
 diligence, 169
 educative efforts, 28–9
 on *inter se* cases, 87
 interpreter, 32, 62, 63
 investigations of murder/assault cases, 98–9, 111, 141–2, 144, 145–6, 147–8, 151–2
 on Kauadla, 80
 and Maltalta case, 79

249

Index

and Mantyeuldi case, 61
and Melaitpa case, 74–5
Rufus River affray, 24, 25, 169
Moorpar, 89, 124
Moorundie government station, 43
Morgan, David, 148
Morris, Henry, 58, 118
Morris, Thomas, 50, 153–4
Mortlock's station poisonings, 49, 152–3
Moullia, 89
Mt Barker affray (1846), 61–2
Mt Bryan case (1844), 47, 146–7
Mt Remarkable incidents (1844), 140
Mowalta, 128, 133
Mukarta, 131
Mulharan, *Corporal*, 61
Mullins, Richard, 113
Mullnullnumelli, 128
Multyilli, 108
Munarabidni, 54, 115
Mungoringa, 127
murder and murder charges, 103, 175–82
   massacres, 18, 24, 25, 137, 155, 169
   murder of Aboriginal people by Aboriginal people *see inter se* cases
   murder of Aboriginal people by Europeans, 42, 46–7, 49–51, 104, 118, 140–54, 178–9
   murder of Europeans by Aboriginal people, 13–19, 32, 34, 37–9, 40, 51–2, 62–3, 67, 88–104, 135–7, 175–8
   outcomes of cases, 68–9, 103–4, 135, 144–54
   reduction of murder charges to manslaughter, 84–6, 94, 97, 176–7, 180–2 *see also* manslaughter
   see also assault and robbery
Murkata, Meiya, 32, 34, 62–3, 90
Murkata, Wodla, 32, 34, 62–3, 90
Murra, 50
Murray, A, 29, 103
Murrell case, 7–8, 26, 36, 70
Murrell, Jack Congo, 194n35
Murtana, Katta, 42, 144–5
Muruss, 129–30

Nacha, Picha Cud, 15, 17
Nadgiltie, 123
Nammoingyu, 52–3, 75–6

Nantariltarra, 50
Nantes, 88
Narritya, 123
native constables, 59, 62, 73, 116, 164
Nelgerie, 103
Neterrie, 53
New South Wales (colony), 7–8, 26–7
Newooman, 81
Ngaiere, 77
Ngalkantyirriorn, 125
Ngallabammu, 39, 81
Ngaloorunger, 124
Ngalta, 112
Ngaltya, Pintia (aka Kangaroo Jack), 147
Ngammin, Ngungu, 116
Nganti, 129
Ngarbi, 32, 89
Ngilmanin, 65
Ngiyeri, 94–5
Ngumbi, 128–9
Ngurkilli, 112, 127–8
Ninchulta, 67
Nintalta, 51, 93
Npungilti, 98
Nucha, Wang, 15, 17, 28
Nulguiltie, 85
Nultia, 89
Nungarinya, 124
Nweka, 131
Nyarrokyppur, 131

oath-taking *see* admissibility of Aboriginal evidence
offences see *inter se* cases; manslaughter; murder and murder cases; property offences; theft by Aboriginal people; theft from Aboriginal people; stock theft by Aboriginal people; stock killing by Aboriginal people
offenders, Aboriginal *see* Aboriginal offenders
O'Halloran, *Police Commissioner*, 18, 22, 23, 24
'one law for all' policy, 12, 135, 170–1
   circumvention of, 25
   failure of, 155–7, 173; contributing factors: 158–72; abandonment of assimilation policy, 161; abandonment of containment policy, 158–9, 171–2; alienation

of Aboriginal land, 164–5, 170, 172; colonists' loss of confidence in the law, 159–60; court system inappropriate to colonial situation, 161–3; erosion of humanitarian values, 160–1; inadequate police force, 163–4
motivations for, 165–6
see also jurisdiction and amenability of Aboriginal people to British law; legal system
overlanding groups, protection of, 22–4

Padlaria, 123
Padneltie, 59, 84
Paliana, 118
Palierie, 124
Palingulta, 39, 100, 202n67
Pandalteroo, 117
Pangkala clan, 38–9, 84, 95, 100
Panmalta, 128, 133
Pannenum, 148
Pantowyn, 89
Parichboorinen, 83
Parker (colonist), 151–2
Parlobooka, 16–17
Parnkalta, 202n67
Parrington (shepherd), 142
Partko, 112, 127–8
pastoral-related offences *see* stock killing; stock theft; theft by Aboriginal people
pastoralists *see* European settlers
Pegler, Enoch, 13–14
Penchungya, 77
Permalooan, 131
Peter (aka Kauadla), 80–1
Piaria, 50, 58, 154
Pilgalta, 58–9, 114
Pinberri, 84
Pinga, 100
Pinkerton (station-owner), 98, 130
Piulta, 39–40
poisonings at Mortlock's station, 49, 152–3
police force
adequacy/inadequacy of, 136–9, 154–5, 163–4
native constables, 59, 62, 73, 116, 164
police and military action against offenders, 18–19, 20, 21–2, 23–5, 46

police force (*cont.*)
role and requirements, 158–9, 163–4
Poolulta, 98
Poowoolupe, 82
Popeltie, 59, 84
Port Lincoln, 88–90, 137–8 *see also* Eyre Peninsula
Potpouch, 80
press and public opinion *see* public opinion
Price, Henry, 143, 147, 152
'prior contact' concept, 26, 29–38, 62, 167
Pritchard, James, 147–8
property offences, 119–34, 185–91
charges and outcomes, 119, 133–4, 185–91
pastoralist attitudes to, 122–3, 124, 125, 130, 131–4, 159–60
see also stock theft; theft
Protector of Aborigines, 3–4, 13, 15
concerns about delays in bringing court action, 53, 99–100
educative role, 17, 28–9, 158, 161, 169
as interpreter of sworn evidence, 58
learning Aboriginal languages, 56–7, 58, 67
local Sub-Protectors, 29, 67
role, 158, 172–3; settler's view of, 146
see also Moorhouse, Matthew
public opinion
on acquittal/discharge of Aboriginal offenders, 68–9
on legal action in *inter se* cases, 73–4, 87
on military action against Aboriginal people, 19–20, 21–2, 24
perceptions of interpreter bias, 58, 65–6
press debate on *inter se* cases, 75, 78–9
press views on status of Aboriginal people, 21–2
on status of Aboriginal people, 16, 21–2, 24
see also European settlers
Puleringa, 130
Pulgulta, 37–8, 65, 98–9
Pullen, *Captain*, 18
Pultirri, 83
Puterpynter, 65, 93–4, 109–10
Puyurin, 120

Index

quasi-military actions *see* martial law; police force

R v Ballycrack et al (1852), 80
R v Biddeah et al (1846) *see* Biddeah, Nakundah
R v Bonjon (1841), 8, 27, 70, 210n2
R v Charley (1845), 60
R v Congo Murrell (1836) *see* Murrell case
R v Donelly (1847) *see* Donelly, Thomas
R v Hinch (1849), 52
R v Kambalta (1852), 75 *see also* Kambalta
R v Langaryngarynga and Eroyngaree (1859), 83
R v Larry (1846), 30, 63, 72–3, 74
R v McDuff (1847), 54
R v Moongeltie and Cooliltie (1860), 53, 206n94
R v Morris and Jones (1849), 58, 118
R v Murrell and Bummary (1836) *see* Murrell case
R v Ninchulta (1855), 67
R v Parkilti et al (1853), 66–7, 210n73
R v Pilgalta (1846), 58–9
R v Roach (1942), 42, 144–5
R v Spratt et al (1844) *see* Mt Bryan case (1844)
R v Wamboureen (1848) *see* Wamboureen, Tatty
R v Wooloobully (1859), 39, 85
R v Yabmanna (1849), 51, 93
race relations, 5–6, 12–20, 22–5, 45–6, 47, 147, 155–6, 159, 163–4, 169–73
 attacker/victim relationships, 14, 110–13, 117–18, 148
 escalation of violence, 140–3, 144
 Eyre Peninsula, 37–9, 49, 51–2, 88–94, 95–9, 100–1
 Flinders Ranges, 99–100
 police protection of settlers, 136–9, 154–5
 Yorke Peninsula, 49–51, 94–5
 see also assault and robbery; murder
Rainbird murders, 40, 101–2
Rallooloolyoo (aka Ronkurri, or 'Jemmy McLean'), 30, 63, 72–3
Rankin, Jemmy, 53
Rankine, Jemmy, 117
rape *see* sexual assaults

Register, 19, 21, 24, 39–40, 44, 51, 71, 79, 81, 140, 154
regulation of settlement *see* European settlement
remand, 53, 59–60, 99–100
Reppindjeri case (1837), 13, 41, 57–8
Resident Commissioner role, 9, 10
Richardson, John, 67
Roach, William, 42, 144–5
Robe, FH (Governor), 33–6, 48–9, 63, 64, 75, 76, 139, 141, 150, 167
Robinson (Magistrate), 67
Rogers (station-owner), 125
Ronkurri *see* Rallooloolyoo
Rose, *Corporal*, 61, 99
Roy, Hugh, 109
Rufus River affray, 22–5, 169

Sanders, Jemima, 116
Saunders, William, 131
Savage, Mary, 114, 128
Sawyer, William, 118
Schurmann, CW, 57, 58, 59, 65, 129, 152
Scott (shepherd/murder victim), 62, 73, 90
Scott, William, 94
separatism (legal separatism), 11, 72, 161, 171 *see also* jurisdiction and amenability of Aboriginal people to British law
settlement *see* European settlement
sexual assaults, 40, 43, 67–8, 89, 93, 101–2, 113–14
sheep stealing *see* stock theft by Aboriginal people
Shepherd, John, 97
Shepherd, Thomas, 68, 113
Smillie (Advocate General), 32–3, 38
 on absconding of the accused in Mortlock's station case, 153
 on interpretation and interpreters, 48, 60
 and Mt Bryan incident, 147–8
 notion of limited jurisdiction over Aboriginal people, 20–2
Smith (defence counsel), 50
Smith, Duncan, 64, 65, 83, 90
South Australia Act 1834, 5, 9, 10, 11
South Australia (colony)

252

Index

amalgamation policy, 4, 11, 161, 165, 171
humanitarian policy, 2–5, 9–11, 92, 157, 160–1, 165–6, 170, 171, 172
land policy, 2, 3–5, 9–11, 164–5, 172–3
law *see* jurisdiction and amenability of Aboriginal people to British law; legal system
Letters Patent, 3, 4, 10–11
planned colony, 1–2
power structure, 9
Southern Australian, 16, 20, 21, 24
Spratt, Charles, 147–8
Stephen (defence counsel), 52, 154
Stevenson, George, 19, 21–2, 56, 75, 78–9
stock killing by Aboriginal people
cases, 130–2
charges and outcomes, 133–4, 191
stock theft by Aboriginal people, 37, 120–6, 187–9
charges and outcomes, 60, 66–7, 123, 124, 133–4, 187–9
from employers, 129–30
hunger motivation, 14, 120, 121–4, 130
large-scale, 94, 97–9, 113, 124–6
pastoralist attitudes to, 122–3, 124, 125, 130, 131–4, 159–60
pastoralist retaliation, 50, 141–3, 147–8, 169–70
Stow (defence counsel), 59, 84, 100–1, 114, 166
Stubbs, Elizabeth, 89
Sturt, Charles, 172
Sturt, Evelyn, 132
Stutely, Sarah, 107–8
summary justice, 18–19, 22, 136, 137 *see also* European settlers: taking the law into their own hands; legal system
Supreme Court
appointments to the Bench, 6, 166–8
establishment of, 6–7

Tainmunda, 80
Tantultara, 112
Tarroti, 77
Taylor, William, 117
Teichelmann, CG, 57, 58
Tennant (station-owner), 130
Tentipurran, 46
theft by Aboriginal people, 120
charges and outcomes, 119, 126, 127–30, 133–4, 185–91
differentiation of cases (lesser/pursued through courts), 127–30, 133–4
hunger motivation, 14, 120, 121–4, 127, 130
instigated by unscrupulous Europeans, 120
from station huts, 65, 95, 126–9, 130, 189–90
stock theft *see* stock killing; stock theft by Aboriginal people
in towns, 119–20
theft from Aboriginal people, 12–13
theory of systematic colonisation, 1, 2
Thompson, Alfred, 109–10
Thompson, James, 15, 17, 41, 135
Tilpardnambi, 109
Tinkanor, 39, 81
Titcherie, 103
Tolmer, A, 22, 24, 67, 93, 152–3
Tommy (witness), 59
Toocherg, 123
Toorapennie, 84
Townsend, Richard, 97–8
traditional Aboriginal law *see* Aboriginal customary law
traditional food sources, destruction of, 14, 121–2, 165
Tukkurm (aka Tukkuru), 76
Tulta, 94
Tunkanayman, 39, 81
Tyerrungi, 96

Utulta, 116

Walkaoinni, 131
Walker, William, 103
Wambarno, 54
Wamboureen, Tatty, 54, 63–4, 90
Wantulta, 116–17
Waranger, Colcola, 109
Warburton, *Police Commissioner*
proposal for circuit courts, 162–3
Warenboorimen, 83
Warraki, 123
Warrapoonen, 65

Index

Warreah, 39
Warretya (aka Goggle-eyed Jemmy), 102
Warretya (aka Kapunda Robert), 102
Warretya (aka Old Man Jack), 102
Warricha, Tippa, 15, 17
Warrinyerrimu, 80
Warrippa, 94–5
Watniltie, 39, 100, 202n67
Watpa, 110, 112, 133
Watte Watte, 80
Watts, John, 149
Weaver (settler), 117–18
Weenpulta, 39, 100, 202n67
Weepin, 77
weight and credibility attached to Aboriginal evidence
  corroboration provisos, 45–6, 47, 49, 74
  at discretion of the court, 45, 49, 52–3
  hypocrisy surrounding, 50–3
  in *inter se* cases, 52–3
  by juries, 45, 50–5
  Moorhouse's concerns, 47, 51
  reliability of Aboriginal evidence, 44, 47, 51, 52–3, 82
  sole uncorroborated testimony, 45, 49
Wekiweki, 89
Western Australia (colony), 27
Whitney (shepherd/murder victim), 62, 73, 90
Widlo, Karkarra, 111
Wikkanin, Nyalta, 76, 78, 79
Wikkanni, Ngalta *see* Wikkanin, Nyalta
Wilcuramalap, 94
Willana, 202n67
Williams (Deputy Storekeeper), 14–15, 57
Williams, John, 113
Williams (stock-owner), 125–6
Williamy, 107

Willis, *J*, 8, 27, 70
Willis, *Mrs*, 108, 127
Willmer, Caroline, 114
Winnulu, 51–2, 91, 128, 133
Wipapi, Yailgalta, 54
witnesses
  absence or suborning of, 53–4, 63, 118, 142, 152
  reluctance to attend court/give evidence, 88, 110–11, 112, 113, 116, 117, 131–3, 134, 145, 148
  see also admissibility of Aboriginal evidence; weight and credibility attached to Aboriginal evidence
Wittoari, 120
Woolocbully, 39, 85
Woringena, 39, 81
Worli, Kanga, 76, 78, 79
Wrochoven, 82
Wyatt, William, 13, 15, 57

Yabmanna, 51, 93, 205n75
Yailgatta, 128–9
Yakaria, 120
Yarkeltia, 123
Yarngalta, 128
Yawaman, 53
Yellarri, 94
Yengki, 113
Yerricha, 16–17, 28
Yertumilkurti, 202n67
Yorke Peninsula
  race relations, 49–51, 94–5
Young, Henry (Governor), 122
Young, James, 53–4
Young, *Mrs*, 127
Youngmonamen, 80
Yurki, 123
Yurnani, 58, 118